JC
596.2
.U5
E28
1986

Eaton, Joseph W.

Card-carrying
  Americans

DATE			

CARD-CARRYING AMERICANS

CARD-CARRYING AMERICANS

Privacy, Security, and
the National ID Card Debate

Joseph W. Eaton

University of Pittsburgh

ROWMAN & LITTLEFIELD
PUBLISHERS

ROWMAN & LITTLEFIELD

Published in the United States of America in 1986
by Rowman & Littlefield Publishers
(a division of Littlefield, Adams & Company)
81 Adams Drive, Totowa, New Jersey 07512

Library of Congress Cataloging-in-Publication Data

Eaton, Joseph W.
  Card-carrying Americans.

  Includes index.
  1. Privacy, Right of—United States.
  2. Identification cards—United States. I. Title.
JC596.2.U5E28 1986 323.44'8'0973 85-24973
ISBN 0-8476-7424-X

86 87 / 10 9 8 7 6 5 4 3 2 1
Printed in the United States of America

In memory of

Stanley R. Ross

Director of the Mexican–U.S. Border Research Program

University of Texas at Austin

A Lifetime of Distinguished Public Service

CONTENTS

ACKNOWLEDGMENTS

Many persons helped me formulate this controversial technological policy analysis. Leonel J. Castillo first showed me the ADIT (Alien Documentation and Telecommunication) card, first in 1977 on an experimental basis. As the commissioner of the Immigration and Naturalization Service (INS) during the early years of the Carter administration, he hoped the use of a machine-readable ID card would make it possible to replace a nearly unmanageable volume of paperwork with computerized data storage and retrieval.

The late Professor Stanley R. Ross, as Director of the Mexico–U.S. Border Research Program, provided a research grant without which this book could not have been typed, nor the data assembled. He and Professor Sidney Weintraub, his collaborator in many studies of U.S. immigration policy and of U.S.–Mexican relations, critically reviewed the entire manuscript. They provided the support and encouragement indispensable to an author as initial ideas mature from the research stage.

V. J. Singh, the Director of the University of Pittsburgh Center for Social and Urban Research, provided an administrative home for this undertaking. Support continued in spite of the fact that this study turned out to be one of the center's minor deficit operations. The administrative details were handled gracefully by the center's business manager, Sadie Weiss. The School of Public and International Affairs at the University of Pittsburgh also provided encouragement.

When I decided to explore the ID card domain, I was a novice among many well-informed experts in a rapidly changing field of technology applications. Many of these experts are employed in government or in business where they become aware of, but cannot address, controversial social policy issues such as the privacy question. They helped to locate sources of data that might otherwise have gone unnoticed. The experts include Eugene Webster, the godfather of the ADIT card of the U.S. Immigration and Naturalization Service (INS), and Frank Kubic, the technical director of the state department unit responsible for the development of the machine-readable passport. Marion Houstoun, who advised two secretaries of labor on policy matters, opened her personal file on this topic for me. George H. Warfel, who wrote the book *Identification Technologies* and who coedits the *Personal Identification News* (PIN) monthly, brought me up to date on advanced computer, optical, and chemical security techniques.

The transition of ideas into a completed manuscript would have been impossible without the friendly sufferance of Ruth Buncher, Cathy Rudd, and Mildred Asbury, who typed its several drafts. Revisions were simplified because it was possible to store the text within the computer system of the University of Pittsburgh. Parts could then be quickly retrieved, changed and then re-stored for subsequent revisions.

The computer world was completely unknown to me when I began this project. I owe much to Elaine and Nicholas Caruso, Lauri Fowler, and George Rogers for helping me to cope with its precision. Clark Rogers and Robert Bates helped in mastering the many technical problems of producing and editing a manuscript by means of word-processing procedures. Mildred Asbury and Anthony De Costa helped to enter various revisions into my data file. My wife, Helen, edited the manuscript, offering invaluable help and support in the process. Spencer Carr, Janet S. Johnston and Mary D. Simmons, my editors at Rowman & Allanheld, were enthusiastic about the manuscript and expedited its publication in record time.

Many officials took time to brief me about relevant concerns of their organizations. They included Barry Baxter of the Associated Credit Bureau, William N. Aitken and Larry Clemente of the Medical Information Bureau; Shoshana Arbeli-Alzmolino, Chairwoman of the Interior Committee, Israeli Knesset; William P. Bock of the Department of the Army, Office of the Adjutant General; William W. Craig of the INS Regional Headquarters at Terminal Island in California; and Professor Wilbur Cohen, a midwife of the Social Security Act and of the Social Security Number (SSN); Roger Conner of Federation of American Immigration and Reform (FAIR); Bonnie Fisher of the Inspector General Office of the U.S. Department of Health and Human Services; Professor Lawrence Fuchs who returned to teaching after directing staff of the Select Commission on Immigration and Refugee Policy; Sarah Garman of the Social Security Administration; Hughes Goisbault of the French Embassy office in New York; Prof. Niles Hansen of the University of Texas; and William Henderson of the International Consumer Credit Association. Each provided data and encouragement.

Discussions with Trudy Hayden, who studied the privacy issue for the American Civil Liberties Union (ACLU) were instructive, as were those with Dr. Manfred Sorg, who directs the population register of the Free

City of Hamburg in West Germany. Data were also provided by Karen Hainer of the Permanent Subcommittee on Investigations of the United States Senate. Judith Huebner, Deputy Director General, Ministry of Interior, Jerusalem; Stefan Gullberg of the ID Kort Corporation of Sweden; Professor Tom Gerety at the University of Pittsburgh School of Law; George Gay of the Division of Vital Statistics of the U.S. government; and Dr. Wilhelm Steinmueller, Professor of Mathematics and Information Sciences of the University of Bremen, were also very helpful.

H. Spencer Nilson, editor of the *Nilson Report*, volunteered to send me a copy of his twice-monthly newsletter for credit card executives. It is considered compulsory reading for anyone involved in research on matters related to the credit and identification card industry. Dean Huxtable stood out as the lone dissenter advocating the adoption of a national ID document, when the remainder of his fellow members of the Federal Advisory Committee on False Identification (FACFI) voted against it.

Others included are Al Lachowsky of the INS office in Brownsville, Texas, and Steve Mertens of the Executive Office of the President. Professor Peter Bull, who took leave of absence from Hamburg University to become the first Data Protection Ombudsman of the Federal Republic of Germany, Hofrat Dr. H. Ambrosi of the Ministry of Interior of Austria, Dr. Joachim Hertel and Ministerialrate Klaus M. Medert of West Germany, and Professor Juergen Simon of the School of Law of the University of Hannover graciously replied to detailed mail inquiries.

Dennis K. Branstad, Chief of the Computer Integrity and Security Technology Project of the National Bureau of Standards in Gaitherburg, Maryland, invited me to participate in and to benefit from their technical Secure Chip workshop, held on July 17, 1985, shortly before this book went to the printer. Researchers, government officials, and representatives of business firms from many parts of the world were brought together to review the accomplishments and the technical problems of the chip card technology. It may be years before the public begins to fully understand how this new industry is in the process of changing the way organization will be administered and how files will be kept.

To all of them, my thanks for making this book an adventure in learning. Privacy and security are in danger, unless those who want to protect our traditional freedoms use this technology to combat those who are now abusing identity documents.

Joseph W. Eaton
University of Pittsburgh

CARD-CARRYING AMERICANS

INTRODUCTION

Will identity cards become a universal phenomenon? To a considerable extent, they already are. In many countries, democracies as well as dictatorships, a national ID card is mandatory for adults. No such requirement exists at the present time in the United States, England, or Canada. In practice, however, most people have one or more ID documents. Many are government issued, like social security cards. Others are provided by department stores, banks, and credit card companies. The *Nilson Report* indicates that 708.6 million cards had been issued in the United States by the end of 1984 by retailers, banks, oil companies, telephone companies and others.[1]

By 1990 more than a billion cards will be in use in the United States, each giving the holder extraordinary fiscal power previously restricted to the U.S. Treasury. Each card can issue the equivalent of real money, up to a limit of its credit. A total of $108 billion in consumer credit had been generated by the end of 1984. In return for each document, the holder provides many details about his life, along with an authorization to cross-check other references. He or she may be asked about prior marriages, a criminal record, or a listing of all unpaid bills. Some of the card-related files, like those kept by Blue Cross and Blue Shield, are somewhat protected against unauthorized access. People can retain a measure of privacy in relation to their neighbors and acquaintances. But credit agencies, private investigators and reporters can access enough of these files to construct a comprehensive profile from records that are public and available through commercial channels, or that are filched clandestinely.

The uncontrolled use of data in these computerized information systems could threaten much of what is still left of our privacy. Some people think that the absence of a formal national identification (ID) system is one of the remaining bastions of our right to be left alone. But on a *de facto* basis, it has already been breached. Other than children, the mentally retarded, and the deceased, how many Americans are without either a social security card, a driver's license, a credit card, or all three of these documents? In return for them, we obligate ourselves to keep one or more of the card issuing agencies informed when we change our address, get married or get divorced. National clearance systems are being maintained about valid drivers' licenses and many types of insurance policies. Nearly all personal records can be accessed by the police and by the FBI with a court ordered subpeona if relevant to a particular law enforcement invest-igation.

PROBLEMS OF BEING A CARD CARRIER

The average American carries more ID cards in his wallet than do people in other countries. But the United States also leads the world in the ease with which forged or stolen documents can be used by others. The fed-eral government has never exercised its power to impose minimum standards of security and accuracy. The most widely used identifier, the social security number (SSN), is particularly prone to being counter-feited. Until recently, it was not even illegal to manufacture a copy.

A growing number of personal files, under public as well as business management, utilize the SSN because it helps prevent confusion among persons having the same name or other similar characteristics. This num-ber facilitates the process of matching and comparing information about any given individual in different files. But even if the SSN is not available, it is relatively easy to match files using such information as a person's name or birthday. Such comparisons are often undertaken by credit bu-reaus, insurance clearing houses, and medical data banks. Dossier as-sembly is also increasingly being mandated by Congress prior to issuing a security clearance for a responsible government position, or to distin-guish between justified and fraudulent applications for a federal loan pro-gram. Computers have woven a net of information about nearly every adult American.

On a *de facto* basis, the United States already has a national ID system. It includes a birth certificate, death certificate, driver's license, and many job related documents in addition to the social security card. Most of them are easily counterfeited and their use is poorly coordinated. The files on which they are based contain much more information than is required for ID purposes. It is difficult for the average person to access his own records to monitor what they contain and to generate corrections of information, when this is indicated.

Beyond the information these files contain about nearly all law-abiding adults and many of America's youths, people voluntarily furnish addi-tional personal details to business, social, medical and other organiza-tions, but yet have little control over how these data are being used.

Prominent persons among us prepare a detailed biographical data sheet to be listed in *Who's Who*. They sport an American Express gold card, in return for current information about their assets. Even the poorest of us are not exempt from sharing our private lives with the file keepers, if we want a job through a government employment security office or to become certified as a food stamp recipient. Administrative actions in the country, at all levels of government and in private business, depend upon the availability of these information systems. Without them, it would be difficult to certify university students for graduation, calculate a social security pension, or send an astronaut into outer space.

A thoughtful minority are concerned about America's transformation into an "instant information" society. They fear that traditions of individual freedom and privacy are in grave danger. They often refer to George Orwell's classic novel, *1984*.[2] Thirty six years ago, Orwell envisioned the people of his "Commonwealth of Oceania" being manipulated to serve the whims of a computerized "Big Brother." The technology of computerized surveillance was not then developed, but it now approaches perfection. Orwell predicted that people would be kept under constant observation even in their bedrooms via a television camera. The once popular *Candid Camera* television program conveyed a serious message behind its practical jokes. In many a public place, people are being watched by a well-concealed camera. In a current sleep research project, volunteer subjects spend the night in such an environment with a computer recording their heart rates and bodily functions; a television camera can be turned on to photograph the entire scene.

Is privacy sacrificed to enjoy the advantages of the computer age? There is considerable supportive evidence, documented in congressional hearings and government reports, as well as in such books as David Burnham's *The Rise of the Computer State*.[3] Or are these fears exaggerated? Are civil libertarians, who vehemently oppose data base matching, tamper-resistant ID cards, and the use of digital reading machines just reborn Luddites? In the nineteenth century they vandalized weaving machines around Nottingham in England in the vain hope of reversing the industrial revolution.

Robert Ellis Smith's *Privacy Journal* circulates up-to-date facts on where the danger lies, in the way government and business keep files about us. An authoritative survey is provided in his book, *Privacy: How To Protect What's Left Of It*.[4] There are, for instance, mailing list vendors who rent the names of 8500 buyers of the *Encyclopedia of Love and Sex*, of buyers of Ronald Reagan's books, or a listing of 52,000 well-to-do Jewish men. Equifax, the nation's largest retail credit company, has at times, used quite superficial techniques to conduct consumer credit investigations. One customer discovered that his record included the observation that he "used his hands in an effeminate manner." A Louisiana oil rig worker started to use his wife's social security number when he discovered he was being rejected from jobs when he used his own. Many of the oil drilling companies would check applicants with a clearinghouse of persons who had filed compensation claims against a previous employer.

At the gut level, many Americans react with suspicion to proposals that the security of U.S. identity documents be improved through federally administered regulations. Many think that there is already too much big government. Yet a flourishing interstate business in illicit documents is out of control due to lack of coordination between federal and state responsibilities for inhibiting it. This law enforcement issue receives a low priority, although more and more of our interactions are with persons not known to us. The rapidity of computer banking, shopping, and information collection must be matched with a higher level of security against misuse of these systems by criminals and terrorists.

THE BIOMETRY GAP

The technology for producing near tamper proof identification documents is, like many other conveniences, a blessing mixed with danger. Few Americans would want to be without a private automobile, although it contributes much to the prevalence of accidents. At the present time, public policy seems to be based on the belief that the average person wants identity documents, but is resistant to immunizing them against fraud and theft. Only a very small proportion of America's many ID cards include biometric indicators, such as retinal eye patterns, fingerprints, handprints, footprints, voiceprints and digitally readable signatures. These unique personal characteristics cannot be stolen and they hardly ever change; most of them are non-stigmatizing. A photograph on a driver's license may be viewed by some as "attractive" or "ugly". It can be touched up by an artist. But the eyeprint of a movie star will look much like anyone's, a random web of capillary blood vessels. They can be digitalized, so that computers can read them and differentiate between them with an error rate of only 7.5 per million for 1 and 1 in a million for both eyes. The false rejection rate is as low as one per 1,000. Recognition time is under two seconds in a file that can include 1,200 different eyeprints.[5]

Fingerprints are equally unique. Even identical twins differ in this regard, as do close relatives. They have a special advantage for crime prevention. Criminals often touch objects with their fingers, leaving a residue that can be copied. Detectives can then use the print to discover the identity of a suspect by matching it with an already known fingerprint or that of someone connected with the offense on the basis of other evidence. Unlike most other biometric indicators, fingerprints can also be taken from recently deceased persons to make a positive ID, even when other features were disfigured as a result of a criminal act or an accident.

Voiceprints have a convenience advantage. Computers can be programmed to read a digitalized sound wave pattern, to open doors that would remain closed to persons not preregistered in the computerized admission roster.

Signature dynamics depends on the fact that every person has a unique handwriting pattern of velocity, acceleration, and pressure which is particularly routinized when signing one's name. These patterns can be captured digitally for direct storage in a computer. A computational as well as a visual comparison can be generated by a device being tested by the Inforite Corporation. Typically, a person signs a document on a template. The signature is then reproduced on a screen, together with the stored sample in the data bank, for visual comparison. A forgery that might match the stored signature in appearance will be rejected since it almost certainly will be written with a different timing sequence. Normal variations of the proper signature will be accepted because the stored characteristics are based on several samples. The values of the mean and standard deviations of its digital algorithms are calculated, stored, and then used in the computational comparison. Whenever another signature is accepted, the program's updating feature modifies these acceptance ranges, thereby allowing for normal variations in the person's handwriting.

Not even the person writing his name would know the digital pattern by which he produces it. The human brain cannot measure the milliseconds of velocity and acceleration that differentiate the letter formation of one person from that of another.

An added security feature could be a digitalized photograph, imprinted on paper by laser. It could not be removed without destroying the document. Up to 800 pages of medical history data can be imprinted on the projected laser printed *Life Card* that is being readied for nationwide adoption if a test program by Blue Cross/Blue Shield in Maryland lives up to the expectations of its utility. Chemical and optical safety features could also be added to the controlled paper stock, much like the way money is printed. Many other innovations are appearing on the market. Even the most thorough surveys of the ID card technology are somewhat out-of-date by the time they appear in print.[6] Generations of basic patents replace each other quickly.

Digital codes of a signature or fingerprint look like what they are—a set of code numbers. They are bias proof since they will not reveal the race or the religion of the individual. These techniques therefore do not threaten privacy. On the contrary, they provide protection against the misuse of our ID documents by an unauthorized person.

This sophisticated technology for using biological recognition features to produce near tamper-proof ID documents could be a source of danger when used by a repressive regime as part of an overall surveillance network. This is likely to happen within a decade. But it can also be used effectively in a free society to counteract the criminal underworld, terrorism, and to protect a reasonable state of privacy in the information society that computers are helping to create.

Biometric indexes are not necessary for routine transactions. They are of little use without a digital reader, and they are very much underutilized. Where a high degree of certainty is desired, biometric recognition features can verify, almost without error, that the person who presents a document is in reality the individual to whom it was issued. Type I errors, rejection of a person whose ID card should have been verified by the machine, can be reduced to less than two per thousand. Type II errors, acceptance of a false ID document, is even less likely. Such standards of reliability are important when a passport is obtained, when a marriage is consummated, when a physician is licensed, or when an individual is entitled to be admitted to a restricted work area. Hospitals can use such screening devices to limit access to the storage area for prohibited drugs.

ID documents also have come to play a growing role in the administration of U.S. immigration policy. Aliens and citizens who regularly cross the border are eligible to receive a free, federally monitored, and machine-readable I.D. card. It validates their right to be in the United States, and when pertinent, to accept employment. This document facilitates border crossings by reducing red tape. Persons who entered the country without proper ID are, of course, without this convenience. They provide a ready market for the sale of false documents. The American policy of facilitating legal border crossings contrasts sharply with the practices of many nations that restrict population movements. Some countries even regulate domestic travel, e.g., the Soviet Union, China, Tanzania, and the Republic of South Africa.

Identification documents are the key to most population movements. The absence of such a document can spell tragedy. This was recently demonstrated in Nigeria. While hundreds of millions all over the world watched on television, more than 1.2 million Africans were expelled on short notice. They had come to Nigeria when that country experienced a development boom. But when the price of oil, Nigeria's principal export, declined, jobs grew scarce. Unskilled aliens were among the first to be fired. Nigeria acted within its sovereign right to reserve jobs for its citizens. But if all other countries were to adopt the same policy, tens of millions of migrant workers would become dislocated.

For a few of the victims of this sudden reversal of Nigeria's immigration policy there was a ray of hope. They could obtain a false document, from friends or through a bribe, enabling them to remain in their homes. They did not have to abandon their few treasures and trust their very lives to a leaky, overcrowded fishing boat, or trek to the border by foot.

ID inefficiency provided a saving grace for the victims of many a tyrannical regime. Some of the Jews who emerged from hiding in Nazi-dominated Europe escaped from gas chambers by posing as Aryans. No one will ever know how many Russians and East Europeans were able to escape from a Stalinist grave at the end of World War II with false documents. Trainloads of Greeks were repatriated through Czechoslovakia into the U.S. occupation zone. They were survivors of concentration camps who knew not a single word of Greek. They were on their way to Palestine. Those who made it were quickly issued false ID documents by Jewish authorities in rebellion against the British colonial rulers.

No member of a generation who is aware of the life saving utility of false ID documents can approach this topic only from the viewpoint of law enforcement. But the decision to mask one's identity has become more complicated in the computer age. Forged passports are still in use, but the technology to detect them when they are machine readable is well advanced. Spies and terrorists who travel with false documents will no longer be able to travel as freely as they can today.

The cost and benefit question of false ID cards needs review in the light of these developments. Are the claimed benefits of administrative laxity in the issuance of ID cards commensurate with the abuses to which people would be subjected when such documents are used to commit criminal fraud, engage in misrepresentation, or commit an act of terrorism? Is it necessary to accept the existing levels of tax evasion, unauthorized use of entitlement programs, and illegal immigration? They are, to a considerable extent, facilitated by America's technologically outdated procedures for issuing identity documents.

A BACKDOOR TO NATIONAL IDENTIFICATION

Congress has repeatedly considered a nationwide ID system. Controversy has been avoided by authorizing a number of specialized ID documents to reduce the ease of filing false claims on entitlement programs, like federally subsidized student loans, disaster relief, or food stamps. The principal feature of current immigration reform legislation is to limit the right to work to citizens and to aliens with a federal work permit. In order to enforce these limits, all U.S. residents, who want a paid job from corporation executive to onion picker, would have to obtain a federally monitored document similar to the identity card now issued to aliens. This Alien Documentation, Identification and Telecommunication card (ADIT), represented the cutting edge of technology for producing and using a trustworthy ID document. It is still more tamper-resistant than most other federally issued ID cards but it has already been outdated by the invention of interactive credit-card size computers with a memory, the micro-chip ("smart") card, and the Drexon Laser or optical memory card. All of them are more counterfeit-proof than the credit cards now in common use. Some of them can generate thousands of dollars worth of credit. Burglars no longer need to invade private homes to enrich themselves. It can be done with finesse by computer criminals.

It is illegal to enter the United States without proper documents, but it is not illegal to hire someone who did. Eleven states have their own antialien employment laws, but only one case of enforcement was reported by 1980. The employer was fined a nominal $250, a minute proportion of the savings that probably accrued to him by paying wages below market level. Employers have been known to rely on the legal immunity of the "Texas Proviso" to cheat some of their workers. Some unscrupulous firms have tipped off the Immigration and Naturalization Service (INS) about an illegal resident just before the next payday, in the hope than an INS agent will arrest and deport him before he has to be compensated.

The Simpson-Mazzoli-Rodino Immigration Reform and Control Act versions of the last four years would shift the law enforcement bite from the often underpaid illegal alien to the employer who benefits economically from exploiting him. The key to this new approach to illegal border crossing would be the requirement that employers hire no new workers without a good faith effort in checking the latter's work entitlement. The prospect that a plastic card could seal U.S. borders more effectively than a massive increase in armed guards and naval and air patrols, intrigues budget-minded administrators. But the proper use of this technology comes with a "price."

The United States would have to adopt administrative procedures for identifying almost everybody. The easily counterfeited Social Security cards, birth certificates, baptismal records, and drivers licenses which are generally used as ID documents, would have to be validated against the more thoroughly verified basic employment entitlement document or procedure. Illegal aliens, lacking such a document, could then no longer be hired legally, unless they were already settled and would be permitted to remain under the amnesty provision included in the proposed reform legislation.

When Congress adjourned in December 1982 without enacting immigration reform legislation, *Newsweek* columnist George Will chided the lawmakers.[7] He noted that the number of unemployed Americans was roughly equal to the estimated numbers of illegal immigrants. Nothing had changed since 1980, when the U.S. comptroller general issued a report, *Prospects are Dim for Effectively Enforcing Immigration Laws.*[8] Milton D. Morris came to the same conclusion in a comprehensive study published almost five years later.[9] The overwhelming majority of the senators and congressmen seemed ready to take a big step in support of a *de facto* national ID card. But opponents thought that the prospects of achieving a higher degree of control over illegal immigration was not worth adopting a compulsory work entitlement program under which each person would have to keep the government informed about changes of address.

For four years this question has been discussed with passion by specialists with only marginal involvement of the public at large. But if immigration reform legislation were to be passed in 1985, the president would probably be required to propose one of several alternative procedures to enforce it. The question will have to be addressed: Should the U.S. adopt the most trustworthy of these enforcement options—a tamper resistant document that could turn into a *de facto* national identity document? If the answer is to be "yes," the next question would be: should such a document be made mandatory or elective; also, should it include one or more biometric indicators, which would restrict its use to the person to whom it was issued?

In this book the policy issue of a national ID card or of an even more general international document will be dissected into its logical components. "Don't leave home without it," *Career Insight* advertised to recruit new American Express Card applicants from among graduates of America's Ivy League colleges.[10] For some people credit cards are the only identity they can prove whenever they are among strangers. Along with their drivers' license, it is with them most of the time. Advocates of the use of this technology need to respond to the concerns of civil libertarians:[11] Won't America shift excessively to having a 'snoopy' government? How much privacy will have to be sacrificed to become part of the computer era?

By 1988, the president will be expected to make recommendations to Congress for the enactment of comprehensive legislation on federal identification systems. This provision was part of the *Comprehensive Crime Control Act of 1984* (H.J.648 and P.L.# 98–473). It provided for a number of what Congress regarded as overdue administrative reforms:

1. Personal descriptors or identifyers utilized in ID documents should employ common descriptive terms and formats. Their aim is to "reduce the redundancy and duplication of identification systems," so that information could be utilized "by the maximum number of authorities."
2. Facilitate the positive ID of bona fide holders of documents.
3. Give due consideration to protecting the privacy of persons whose personal data are stored in an ID system.
4. Recommend appropriate civil and criminal sanctions for misuse or unauthorized disclosure of personal ID information.
5. Make recommendations providing for the exchange of personal ID information as mandated by federal and state law or executive order of the president or the chief executive officers of any of the several states.

Anonymity, privacy and security have to be redefined as a result of the impact of computers on the storage and use of personal records. Technology will influence the range of choices, but the fundamental decision about policy—what Americans want to see happen—will depend on the wisdom and ideological assumptions of those elected to act on behalf of the public interest.

This book discusses these important adjustments to life in the twentieth century and to computer technology, which will do much to shape it.

REFERENCES

1. Nilson, H. Spencer, *The Nilson Report*, Los Angeles, California, no. 342, October 1984:3.
2. Orwell, George, *1984*, New York, American Library, 1949.
3. Burnham, David, *The Rise of the Computer State*, 1983:59; 102–103.
4. Smith, Robert Ellis, *Privacy: How To Protect What's Left Of It*, New York, Anchor Press: 1980; also "You Know My Name: Look Up The Number", *Datamation*, May 15, 1985: 111.
5. *The Nilsen Report*, no. 349, February 1985:2.
6. Fisher, Bonnie, *False Identification: The Problem and Technological Options*. Washington, D.C., Office of the Inspector General, Department of Health and Human Services, 1983; Warfel, George, *Identification Technologies*, Springfield: Charles C. Thomas, Publisher, 1979.
7. Will, George, *Newsweek*, January 3, 1983.
8. Comptroller General of the United States, *Prospects are Dim For Effectively Enforcing Immigration Laws*, Washington, D.C., November 5, 1980:10.
9. Morris, Milton D., *Immigration: The Beleagured Bureaucracy*, (Washington, D.C., The Brookings Institution, 1985).
10. Eaton, Jonathan A., Editor, *Career Insight*, Providence, Rhode Island, Vol. 1, No. 1, 1983.
11. Smith, Robert Ellis, *Privacy: How To Protect What's Left Of It*, New York: Anchor Press, 1980.

CHAPTER ONE

THE CARD THAT COULD CHANGE AMERICA

A POLITICAL TIME BOMB

The quality of identification documents (ID) is not yet a major issue in the heartland of America. But along the Mexican border and in many urban centers, tamper-resistant ID cards are being issued. This policy was the adopted in spite of concerns that the Alien Documentation and Telecommunication (ADIT) card might be just a first step toward the adoption of a universal population register. The idea had been considered quietly by a number of technical committees during the administration of both Presidents Ford, Carter, and Reagan. Each of them had apprehensions about endorsing such an innovation. It was perceived to be very controversial. Conservatives and liberals have come down on both sides: Should every American become a card carrier, at birth, in adolescence, or when he starts to work? Would Americans end up with more or with less freedom and privacy?

Concern that unreasonable invasion of privacy is just around the corner is an understandable reaction to the fact that we moderns record much more about our personal lives than the pharaohs of Egypt would ever let their scribes commit to papyrus. In fact, many organizations keep track of what we do. For the ordinary citizen, a dossier can also be assembled whenever someone is willing to invest the necessary time and money. Through match-codes, even without a uniform index number like the Social Security Number (SSN), multiple files can be combined into a comprehensive profile.

As a result, will the United States slide down the same totalitarian groove as roughly two-thirds of the United Nations membership? This is a most unlikely outcome. Tamper-resistant documents, like all technology, have an impact, but there is nothing inevitable about how they will be used. Jet planes can be instruments of war, but they can also unite the world into a global neighborhood, take people on vacation, and speed aid to earthquake victims. The interest in identity document improvement surfaced in response to evidence that identity fraud and misrepresentation are widespread.

The Federal Advisory Committee on False Identification (FACFI) documented in a 780 page research report in 1976 that taxpayer losses exceeded $16 billions. Adjusted for inflation, the estimated cost in 1985 would be over $25 billions. CBS *News* estimated that the losses from fraudulent use of credit cards would reach $1 billion in 1982.[1] However, advocates of the status quo in ID documentation regard this level of victimization as preferable to risking what they fear would be a continued decline of our already limited rights to privacy.

The *Wall Street Journal* warned in an editorial that more widespread use of the tamper-resistant ID technology would subject Americans to abuses similar to those now commonplace in dictatorships: "It conjures images of Soviet and Nazi tyranny, of South African pass laws, or, on a more benign level, of French bureaucrats imagining they are some kind of Napoleon everytime they ask to see your papers."[2] The U.S. Supreme Court ruled in 1985 that police officers could stop any person without a warrant if they had reason to suspect that he might be in violation of the law. Such a measure is welcomed by many who are worried that not enough is being done to combat crime, especially in metropolitan areas. The easy availability of forged identity documents facilitates much otherwise preventable fraud, misrepresentation, burglary, and terrorism.

The honest majority rarely use a false document. Most Americans are proud of their identity. They value a drivers license with their photograph, a passport, or an American Express Gold card. Each is a status symbol. Confiscation or invalidation of one of these documents is viewed as a severe punishment, to be imposed only after a fair hearing, such as the loss of one's license for driving while drunk or cancellation of a credit card for failure to pay one's debts.

Will the need to protect the creditability of these documents bring about a Europeanization of the United States? In most of Europe a permanent identity dossier is cumulatively maintained for every resident. Such a development has been forecast by the editor of the *Nilsen Report*.[3] Within a decade, he predicts, all wallet cards will be based on a tamper-resistant and carefully monitored basic ID document. A worldwide network for verifying personal identity is seen on the horizon. People will need a basic document to work, travel, buy food, own property, get married, receive an education, be admitted to a hospital, and to collect their social welfare entitlements.

Bank cards or access to a time shared computer are now policed by a numerical code, allegedly known only to the card holder and to a few officials in the organization which issues the code. The security of this mechanism leaves much to be desired. A secretary and a computer consultant know the number which monitored access to the manuscript of this book, as it was being composed on a word processor. High school students playing computer games have been able to circumvent the access protection system of some of the country's most secret data storage installations.

Digitally readable retina prints, fingerprints, handprints, signatures or voiceprints could provide much more secure control mechanisms. Computers could be programmed to accept only those belonging to authorized persons, while differentiating among them. Confidential personal files could be protected from anonymous snoopers. Authorized users would have to leave a permanent digital record of their identity. The serial number of the digital reading machines used to access them could also be recorded. Would this be an invasion of privacy or an added guarantee against those who might violate privacy by subjecting people to *Comprehensive Information Analysis* ("CIA") without their knowledge and consent, by collating information from many different files about a given person?

In America's early history, notary publics were commissioned to witness people's signatures. This practice continues to this day, although as a security device it is totally worthless. Much of the time, the notary does not know the person whose signature is to be verified. Anyone willing to swear falsely can thus purchase a measure of legal credibility for $1.50. How many more years or decades will need to pass before it is recognized that in the computer age, there are more valid ways of verifying personal identity?

THE SILICON REVOLUTION

The capacity of micro silicon chips to store multi-billion items of information, "the silicon revolution," is pregnant with many changes in how individuals relate to each other and to their society. For instance: 1. Strangers can be identified quickly and with a high degree of validity. It is technically feasible to reduce the risk of fraudulent identity to near zero in situations where this is deemed important such as accessing defense related computerized data banks or initiating a large monetary transaction. 2. Computer-computer "talking," can go on day and night, seven days a week. Unauthorized *Comprehensive Information Analysis* ("CIA") is technically feasible. Strangers can accumulate more information about ourselves than we are likely to remember. Abuses of privacy, blackmail and theft can occur which will be difficult to trace. 3. Freedom of information is guaranteed by the U.S. Constitution through prohibition of censorship, and through support of freedom of the press. These rights will increasingly conflict with the right to be protected against unauthorized disclosure of personal data by the media. Many disclosures of private facts are designed to expose someone to ridicule.

Americans are prone to choose order over anarchy when they feel their safety is seriously threatened. They already pay extra money to live in a condominium with safety features. No one can enter without first being screened by a guard. Millions already carry a visible ID card while working. They take their children to a police station to get them fingerprinted; if kidnapped or killed, this would facilitate identification.

It is impossible to prevent the planting of a bomb in an airport luggage compartment or in a government building. But do we have to make it quite so easy for almost anyone to purchase explosives anonymously or under a false identity? There is likely to be a good deal of public support for the idea that the marketing of dangerous substances be subjected to tighter control. A Valid Identification Program (VIP) would give the country the power to choose between most transactions which should continue to remain unregulated, and those which need to be monitored in the public interest.

The whole world recoiled when some still anonymous demon laced Tylenol pills with cyanide. The over-the-counter medicine industry lost hundreds of millions of dollars. Several copycat sabotage incidents followed including the insertion of pins into processed food. Similar acts of personal malevolence will continue as long as poisons, explosives, and other instruments of sabotage and terror are freely available. Water supply systems have been poisoned by anonymous truckers dumping waste products to make a few extra dollars. Terrorists in Europe injected mercury into oranges to harm one of Israel's main export industries. The campaign stopped only when it became counterproductive to the Palestinian cause and to Arab orange exporting countries.

No absolute counter-strategy exists against sabotage, terror, or simple malevolence. Safety switches can be turned off and sand can be put into the gas tank of a disliked neighbor. But the risk of detection can be enhanced by controlled access to certain substances. The issue at the threshold of public controversy is what measures are worth taking to improve ID document validity.

FREEDOM TO MISREPRESENT

The honest majority leaves a detailed trail whenever credit cards are used, checks are written or interactive cable TV is turned on. Are these transactions protected from unreasonable invasions of privacy or from commercial exploitation? Is it worth knowing who signs a lease for an apartment, takes out a marriage license, or presents a document entitling them to cross our borders? Should it be made easy to use forged papers in such important transactions? These questions deserve to be weighed on the basis of evidence rather than on oratory and prejudgment.

An accurate date of birth is crucial when taking out life insurance or when documenting one's entitlement to a retirement pension. Forms distributed to the public indicate that the Social Security Administration (SSA) will accept one of fifteen basic documents. Two or more are generally demanded because all of these "breeder" (basic) documents can be forged, some easily and others with a certain amount of technical skill.

TEXT OF LISTING OF PROOFS OF AGE ACCEPTABLE TO THE SOCIAL SECURITY ADMINISTRATION

"(a) The best evidence, if you have or can obtain it is either:

A birth certificate or hospital birth record established during the first few years of life and certified by the custodian of the record, or

A church baptismal record which shows date of birth and was established during the first few years of life."

"If you do not have one of these records in your possession, try to obtain one. Churches usually do not destroy their records and if there was a record of your date of birth made when you were an infant or a child it is probably still on file at the church."

"We have a complete list of addresses and fees for public birth records in the U.S. and in many foreign countries. Call us to find out where to write and how much to send to obtain your birth record."

"If you cannot get one of the documents listed under (a), furnish whatever proof you can. Try to obtain a record established early in life; old records are generally the best records. Additional evidence of age may be requested if the document which you submit is not sufficient. We will help you if you are having difficulty finding the proof you need. Records which might be available are:

- A school record.
- A school record showing date of birth or age.
- A State or Federal census record.
- A statement signed by the physician or midwife who was in attendance at the birth, as to the date of birth shown on his records.
- A Bible or other family record. (Do not remove the page; we must examine the publication.)
- An insurance policy which shows age or date of birth.
- A marriage record showing age or date of birth.
- A passport.
- An employment record showing age or date of birth.
- A military record.

- A delayed birth certificate.
- A child's birth certificate which shows age of parent.
- Some other record which shows age or date of birth, for example, hospital treatment record, labor union or fraternal record, permits, licenses, voting or registration records, or poll tax receipts."

"Records which might be available to those born in foreign countries are those listed above plus the following:"
- A foreign passport.
- An immigration record established upon arrival in the U.S. (We can provide information and application form which will help you in obtaining this record.)
  - A naturalization record (citizenship paper.)
  - An alien registration card."

The diversity of this listing of acceptable basic documents highlights the fact that there is a lack of confidence in the trustworthiness of all of them. They can be altered or false copies can be produced. In the southwestern states, money can buy a certificate from a midwife that she attended the birth of an infant in a rural area who actually was born in Mexico. Blank baptismal certificates can be purchased in many stores carrying religious specialty merchandise.

One in ten executive job applicants was found to have lied about his academic degree.[4] Only one third of a surveyed sample of employers checked on the acclaimed credentials. The misuse of documents is against the law. But in most jurisdictions, the mere possession of a document will not lead to prosecution.

There also is considerable tolerance of innocent or idealistic deceptions. There are circumstances under which white lies are widely approved. Sissela Bok, in a searching book, *Lying: Moral Choice in Public and Private Life*[5] calls attention to the fact that lying is often condoned, if not preferred to the truth. Lying is acceptable to protect one's family or clients, for the public good, to comfort the sick and dying. Many a couple can tell stories above having travelled as "married folk" before wedding banns had been exchanged. Young people want to be able to flash a false document to purchase a drink. Some of their elders want to shave a few years off their age in a mature courtship or when applying for a job.

Diplomats are persons well paid and often overfed to lie for their country. This is only a slight exaggeration of the moral code of *legitimate dishonesty* that governs the conduct among nations. The FBI provides selected informants, hunted by the Mafia or by the KGB, with a new identity. Reporters sometimes resort to deception to get a story.

No society could function without white lies that reflect the desire to protect people from needless emotional discomfort, to be diplomatic and polite. Less often posed is the question of how important this freedom is to misrepresent our identity or any fact about our private affairs, when it also provides cover for criminals?

Some civil libertarians clearly favor the retention of the right to misrepresent, under circumstances where no one is injured or no law is violated. In a nationally syndicated column entitled "A Computer Tattoo for Every Citizen,"[6] William Safire admitted that "most Americans even like the idea of a piece of plastic that tells the world, and themselves, who they are." But he warned his readers of what will be designated in this book as a "CIA" type Comprehensive Information Analysis:

> Once the down staircase is set in place, the temptations to take each next step will be irresistible. Certainly every business would want to ask customers to insert their identity card into the whizbang credit checker. Banks, phone companies, schools, and hotels would all take advantage of the obvious utility of the document that could not be counterfeited. Law enforcement and tax collection would surely be easier, because the federal government would know at all times exactly where everybody was and what they are spending.

On a voluntary basis, many Americans have already made themselves part of just such a computer operated information system. They have greatly reduced their freedom to misrepresent themselves or to take on a fictitious identity. The average credit user has several cards. One specialist estimates that the Federal Government alone maintains an average of eighteen files per person.[7] Many more are operated by state and local governments; and by business, educational, medical and social organizations. Public or private investigators can quickly assemble a dossier on most Americans, by matching data files, usually with full authorization of the person who furnished the information.

THE IMPORTANCE OF BEING SOMEBODY

Identity is what makes everybody a *very important person*, a "VIP" to himself and those who know him. People lacking this sense of self-worth are regarded as sick and abnormal. In severe cases this will lead to treatment for a clinical depression in a mental hospital. Parents watch gleefully as their newborn baby shows evidence of being able to differentiate himself from the environment through smiles and recognizable sounds. Children want to be known by others by name. They wait impatiently for the sixteenth birthday, if this is the minimum age of being allowed to drive. Parents do not want their children to marry "just anybody." Politicians practice identifying people they have no reason to remember. Some of the people become warm supporters because they feel recognized as individuals. An individual deeply resents being dealt with as if he has no identity, something approximated in impersonal bureaucracies or during army boot training.

There are times when it is to the advantage of a person to withhold essential aspects of his identity. Few X-rated magazines are purchased with credit cards; most buyers prefer the anonymity of paying with cash. This freedom of choice need not necessarily victimize anyone or result in criminal misrepresentation.

A German-American research firm proposed to undertake a worldwide study to combat the growing misuse of automated teller machines (ATMs), credit cards and check fraud. Its brochure, (already outdated by new developments), noted:[8]

> Conventional identification techniques like signature comparison and magnetic strip cards are becoming outmoded in this world of electronic systems and sophisticated criminals. . . . Computer advances have made fingerprint identification faster and more economical. Electronic signature analysis and even retina scanning may soon be practical for many applications.

Security-sensitive installations, some banks and universities increasingly rely on the available ID technology. University of Pittsburgh dormitories experimented with a double security screen for admission to its rooms. Access is monitored from a manned duty desk. But should the guard be too involved in doing homework while allegedly checking each visitor, a digital reader would also monitor the ID card of persons seeking entry. Strangers would have to be vouched for by a resident. There were some objections to his innovation, in spite of the fact that crime on campus is a worrisome problem. A student was strangled by an unauthorized visitor several years ago. Resistance to such security precautions is rooted in understandable distrust of those hired to watch us in order to protect us.

Such reservations not withstanding, the race is on, worldwide, to develop a more sophisticated tamper-proof ID card, some with a built-in memory. High technology firms in the United States, West Germany, Sweden, Japan, England, France, Israel and Norway are trying to outdo each other in research and development efforts. They are getting ready for what could be a big international market for ID cards that can never be cancelled, except by death.

ROBOT SECURITY

Should residential guards have the power to ask who is visiting whom? Might a record be kept of the comings and goings of people? Who should have access to these records? Every plush condominium with security guards now has the capability of such surveillance of the social life of its owners. Many large businesses maintain similarly comprehensive surveillance procedures of the staff in the office or while traveling.

A code of fair information practices to contain the dangers to privacy of the new technology was proposed about a decade ago by the Department of Health and Welfare[9]:

1. No file should be kept whose existence is secret.
2. Individuals should have the right to look at files that contain personal information about them and have access to a simple procedure for correcting outdated, erroneous, or incomplete information.
3. Agencies that use personal information should not collect and keep more than they need for their purpose. The information should be accurate, reasonably current, and complete.
4. Information should be used only for the purposes for which it was gathered, unless the data subject gives consent to some other use.
5. Personal data should be safeguarded against unauthorized access and improper use.

Several of these principles cannot be implemented without VIP type secure ID documents. Before someone can be allowed to see his own record, the organization must be able to make sure that the request comes from the data provider. Mixups will be minimal when it is possible to clearly identify each individual concerned. The FBI no longer records negative data without a fingerprint to verify that it is added to the proper dossier. The keepers of personal data files also must be identified, so that they can be held responsible in the event of violation of their trust occurs. Existing ID documents fail to provide such guarantees. Most of them are easily counterfeited.

Privacy cannot be absolute without a negative cost, like the secrecy provisions of the Swiss banking system. It protects billions of dollars of stolen money and wealth diverted by the Mafia or by dictators to their personal use. Privacy becomes anti-social when a claim to secrecy is used to defraud an entire nation or to permit criminals to live from the loot taken from their victims. Privacy involves a sensitive balance between the right to be left alone, as Samuel D. Warren and Louis D. Brandeis defined it[10] and each person's right to know important facts affecting his life.

Few civil libertarians would prefer to be cheated by persons presenting a false drivers license, someone else's birth certificate, or a stolen credit card. But there is no foolproof control system without occasional violations, like those so widely tolerated during the McCarthy era. The Privacy Act of 1974 and the Fair Credit Reporting Act of 1970 were enacted to restrain the intimidating capacity of computers to store, retrieve and use personal information. Vigilance has always been necessary to protect our privacy.

THE RIGHT TO DOCUMENTATION

In much of the world, people still live in small communities where they and their kin are known by most of the people with whom they interact. But in the United States, even the White House staff has become too diversified to make it practical for guards to recognize them. Special ID cards are issued.

A new form of social-fiscal stratification is emerging among the "in-people" with $5,000–$8,000 level credit, liberal check cashing privileges, access to the TWA Ambassador Lounge of a busy airport, or a diplomatic passport. The non-privileged get a lower credit card borrowing limit. Cards are also being issued to persons in large cities entitled to receive food stamps. The Department of Defense is trying out several different techniques for improving its ID cards which are issued to military personnel and to their dependents. The objective is the reduction of an estimated $50 million annual loss in fraudulently obtained medical services and commissary privileges.

At the bottom of the heap are the undocumented. They are without credit or a basis for expecting trust. Many are unemployed, poorly educated and alone. Others are illegal immigrants, without proper documentation. They are "just nobody" when dealing with strangers. An unfortunate motorist on a transcontinental trip will quickly discover this, if his car breaks down. "No money, no fixing" he will be told by the only mechanic for miles around. Without a credit card, the traveler has to get money wired to him at much expense. Motels are not likely to offer him credit. An undocumented person suspected of being an illegal immigrant can spend days, weeks, and longer in detention, until his status can be clarified.

There is another identity-related class system: those who choose to live with two or more false sets of identity records. Their number is large but not documented. Some are illegal immigrants; others are professional criminals. Ordinary ID cards are therefore often suspect. More than one document is demanded in situations where trust is an important feature of the interaction. The technology to issue a highly reliable identity card is very advanced and is growing by quantum leaps. They can be made secure with little personal data. A name or number, and a biometric index like a fingerprint and/or a signature are the only facts needed to make a card both visually and digitally verifiable. Validity would be enhanced if breeder documents used to verify each person's name and/or identity number are checked with the agency which issued them. Other personal facts may be added, but no ID card needs to contain information that would normally be viewed as private by the average person. It would not require the storage of intimate photographic poses and career details which actors, singers, models and other entertainment industry job seekers pay to have stored by the "International Computer Casting Company" for distribution to anyone willing to pay the access fee.

Those who favor a VIP program see in the adoption of more trustworthy ID documents a means for nonviolent and nonintrusive reduction in burglaries, terror, fraud, and illegal border crossings. They want to put an end to the unreliable rituals, by which Americans can now acquire any number of identity records, so well described in a letter to David Muchow, then chairman of the Federal Advisory Committee on False Identification (FACFI):[11]

Dear Mr. Muchow:

I was very interested in your work on false identification. Here at the . . . Department of Motor Vehicles we issue drivers licenses and I.D. cards all day. You have no idea what goes on.

Birth certificates are accepted without anything to connect them with the bearer. If he says it is his, that is final. Uncertified photostats are accepted as conclusive, and you know what can be done with any document in a photostat machine. In the case of a female, only the first name need match, if she says she is married.

We see the same faces getting licenses and I.D. cards in different names all the time; for the purposes of welfare fraud, and illegal alien fraud.

Why do we do nothing? Because all employees are terrified of courtesy complaints. The attitude of supervision is, "Don't rock the boat; your job is to issue." Employees who expose fraud in identity face real, and I mean *real* trouble. Avoiding courtesy complaints is the foremost aim of the Department, and always was.

We are keeping our fingers crossed for you and your group. We have no interest but seeing this farce corrected.

If it were known who wrote this to you, the Department would try to bring dismissal charges against me, civil service notwithstanding; and therefore I cannot sign this letter. Please believe we are almost all fed up with what is happening.

Sincerely and best wishes,

Could a VIP remedy these abuses? This policy controversy will be dissected in considerable detail in the remaining chapters of the book. How and to whom should such tamper-resistant documents be issued? What risks are inherent in such proposals to fully utilize the technology for monitoring the accuracy of identity documents? Can freedom and privacy survive in the computer age?

Both privacy and effective controls over the unauthorized use of data files are an issue. The awesome speed and efficiency of information storage and retrieval must be matched by electronic security measures to safeguard personal data from malevolent politicians, from bureaucrats, or from persons inclined to use them unlawfully for their commercial benefit.

REFERENCES

1. CBS News, December 13, 1982.
2. *Wall Street Journal*, September 2, 1982.
3. H. Spencer Nilsen, *Nilsen Report*, Los Angeles, Nov. 1982.
4. *Wall Street Journal*, July 3, 1985, 15.
5. Bok, Sissela. *Lying: Moral Choice in Public and Private Life*. New York: New Pantheon Books, 1978.
6. *Pittsburgh Post Gazette*. September 10, 1982; reprinted from the *New York Times*.
7. Barry Reid *The Paper Trip II, For A New You Through New ID*, Fountain Valley: California, 1981.
8. Batelle Corporation; Columbus, Ohio *Personal Identification Technologies A Proposal*, 1982.
9. Grant S. McClellan *The Right to Privacy*, New York: H. W. Wilson, 1976: 209.
10. Samuel D. Warren and Louis D. Brandeis, "The Right to Privacy," *Harvard Law Review*, (1980):195–96.
11. Federal Advisory Committee on False Identification, *The Criminal Use of False Identification*, Washington, D.C.: U.S. Government Printing Office, July 25, 1976, Appendix F 15, Nov. 1976.

CHAPTER TWO

NATIONAL ID CARD OPTIONS

THE POPULATION REGISTER OPTION

Identification documents are more than neutral technical instruments. They impact the administration of the larger social system in which they are being used.

In France, every resident, except small children, is issued an identity card bearing his signature, place of birth, and age. It includes a photograph. When one ear is showing, visual inspection permits a comparison of the photo with the actual ear of the person, even when the document owner went to a hairdresser, grew a beard, or otherwise changed his appearance. Until recently, a fingerprint was included. It could be verified against the card-holders fingertip to be matched if it becomes important to further validate his identity.

Several other nationwide identity records are issued. A *livrette de famille* (family booklet) provides personal details about each family member and an *extrait de cassier judiciare* can be provided by the national police to certify to an employer the absence of a recent criminal record. No one can make a permanent move in France or most of Western Europe without notifying the police and presenting an identity document. It is often used when picking up registered mail at the post office, when cashing a check, or when getting a marriage license. Identity documents are also helpful in the investigation of criminal cases or in locating amnesia and accident victims.

In Denmark, everybody is registered at birth and is assigned a CPR (Central Personal Register) number for life. It will not change, as the name might when a woman gets married. Technically, no national identity document is mandatory. Residents cannot be stopped by the police merely to have their credentials checked. But in daily life few persons leave home without a driver's license or with a national health insurance card, which includes their CPR number. Both are widely used as a general identifier. They are issued after verification against each person's file in their hometown where the basic family data are stored and updated. These rosters have been maintained for generations and in Sweden for over 300 years. The files are only partly computerized, but they could be used to conduct a quick and inexpensive population census in place of a house-to-house survey.

In Hong Kong, an identity card is required of every individual over the age of 11. It has a dual purpose: identification, and entitlement to hold a job. The card is printed on controlled paper stock and laminated. Additional security features are scheduled to be added, including a machine readable capacity and storage of all data in a computerized record system.

Would there be a practical purpose for the United States to adopt some such national roster system? Americans probably carry more identity documents than nationals of any other country—an average of 7.2 credit cards for each of the 98.9 million card holders, plus social security cards, drivers licenses, and others.[1] Enough of them are counterfeit or stolen to undermine their creditability in situations where identification is essential.

A central population registry might add an element of efficiency to the way personal data files can be used by saving time and storage costs. People sometimes need to fill out dozens of forms each year most of which contain some of the same data. Each is kept in a separate location and maintained at considerable cost: birth registers, marriage registers, tax rolls, draft registers, passport records, food stamp lists, rosters of beneficiaries of agricultural subsidies, plus the many files we allow banks, insurance companies, and health centers to maintain for their and our convenience.

A person applying for a federal job could insert his ID card into a computer and within a minute or less receive a pre-coded printout of the basic ID data in his file. He could then check the information, fill in additional details and in short order the employment application would be completed. Savings in citizen-time would be significant. The document could be printed out in one of several lettering styles of the person's choice. Storage space for maintaining multiple files could be reduced since the ID data could be kept in one location, accessible via a unique personal number, to all linked data banks.

The task of protecting just a single central file against unauthorized access would be easier than under present circumstances when the same data are also stored in thousands of local, state, and federal government data banks. Updating all of them would now be a time consuming task. Access to the information in the central file could be electronically restricted to any given agency on the basis of a need-to-know determination. Each citizen would be able to periodically update his basic ID file. Local, state and federal governments could use them to make an instant and fairly up-to-date census, in spite of population movements.

Computer-generated and categorized information from such a population register can be used in planning new schools, hospitals, roads, and other facilities, without publicly disclosing anyone's personal circumstances.

The central file could also be used to check on the consistency of federal, state, and local income taxes—something that is already being done under a congressional authorization. No new data matching powers would be conferred on public officials, but many of those who now operate clandestinely under several identities would be restrained. They would be more likely to pay their fair share of the tax burden.

A basic ID file could be operated with very limited data. It need not replace the many specialized records kept by government, business, educational, health and other agencies. The Internal Revenue Service would continue to store detailed accounts about income and expenses. The roster of military personnel would contain career data on the education, military, and work experience of persons eligible for service benefits. Food stamp recipients or defense contractors would continue to be registered in a specialized and restricted computer file, with information documenting their entitlement for specific benefits. Hospitals would continue to keep their own files on medical services rendered and the billing of costs that were incurred. A high-level and carefully monitored computer program could prevent the organization of a "super roster," based on combinations of functionally separate information systems. This prohibition could be enforced more effectively than is possible when data files are kept manually. The latter can be invaded clandestinely, with minimal risk of discovery of who was responsible.

A central ID file would offer another convenience. Travel to and from the United States could be facilitated without long waiting lines. Upon entering a transatlantic plane, the identity document of each traveler could confirm his citizenship, entry visa, or other travel entitlements by the time the plane reached its destination.

Multiple uses of central population registers are well developed in Europe. The Registration Statute enacted by the city of Hamburg[2] specifies the following purposes in addition to the collection of demographic census type data:

1. Preparation of lists of eligible voters.
2. Preparation of lists for the collection of taxes.
3. Basis for issuing identity cards to eligible persons.
4. Administration of the draft for military or for noncombatant civilian service.
5. Administraton of laws affecting landlords and tenants.
6. Providing information about local residents in response to inquiries from other localities and their officials.

7. Assistance in locating missing persons.
8. Administration of youth protection laws, including school attendance laws.
9. Administration of public health services.
10. Administration of welfare and entitlement services (not specifically mentioned in the statute).

Computers utilized in a free society with well enforced safety features to protect people's privacy, even from the government, are programmed for quite different purposes in oppressive regimes where they can be used to harass dissidents and unpopular minorities. They facilitate the enforcement of influx control regulations and exit permission in the Soviet Union, South Africa, Tanzania, and Mainland China. Citizens in these nations are not free to change their permanent address—permission is required to relocate. Such restrictions are designed in part to prevent an excessive population concentration in big cities, as is occurring in Calcutta, Mexico City, Cairo, and Buenos Aires. But they have also been used punitively to exile dissidents to isolated regions of the Soviet Union and South Africa. Further computerization of population registers will increase the repressive efficiency of these regimes. Given the still decentralized administration of personal documents in most totalitarian countries, the authorities seem to experience no serious problem maintaining themselves in power by the use of fear and terror. False identity records are uncommon. Penalties for forgery and other unauthorized uses of ID cards are draconic: heavy fines, prison, forced, labor or exile. In Nigeria, ruled for a time by a popularly elected regime, few foreign workers appear to have been able to avoid obeying the sudden order issued in 1983 to leave the country. Most of them obeyed out of fear of arrest or of mob violence.

What protects the United States from such a fate is our constitutional system, including the well enforced Bill of Rights. This fact has been generally underestimated in the policy controversy about replacing our unreliable ID documents with more secure versions. The Constitution is not, however, self-enforcing. Existing laws and administrative procedures will need to be updated periodically to keep up with the technical changes of how computers enable people to *use and to abuse* their capabilities for handling large volumes of data.

IMMIGRATION POLICY ENFORCEMENT AND ITS LIMITS

Documents cannot stop panic migration. But no asylum is secure without a temporary residency permit. There is a growing number of countries in the world where living conditions for the ordinary citizen are economically hopeless and politically oppressive. Some of their citizens flee at the risk of their lives. More would leave, if this could be done with agreement of their government.

Throughout our history, some of these persons reached our shores, legally or otherwise. They and their descendants helped build a great nation. Between 1820 and 1980, just short of 50 million persons were admitted as legal immigrants. Most of the country's population are among their descendants. Special provisions have been implemented which give preference to immigrants who are relatives of United States residents. There are also laws to facilitate the entry of some categories of immigrants, e.g. Amerasian children fathered by U.S. servicemen in Japan, Korea, Vietnam, and the Philippines who would be subject to severe discrimination in Southeast Asia, and in other ethnocentric cultures. Senator Jeremiah Denton of Alabama led the campaign for this moral gesture, which encountered no opposition in Congress.

The United States leads the world in the number of immigrants and refugees admitted each year; for instance, those who fled from Hungary's courageous but unsuccessful revolution in 1956. Cuban and Soviet dissidents, Poles, and Vietnamese who are victimized because of their association with the United States can enter outside normal quotas. They are also eligible for financial aid during the early period of adjustment. But they represent only a small fraction of those who are homeless and persecuted. Even larger numbers are ready to leave home for economic reasons, especially from the Carribean Islands, Central and South America, Asia and Africa.

Within the framework of extending hospitality to refugees, approximately 915,000 Cubans had entered the United States by 1980, about 10 percent of the island's population when Fidel Castro took power. Most of them have legal status as immigrants or refugees, and with a U.S. issued document, entitlement to work. Some arrived without proper documentation. Unless they make the effort to legalize their status as refugees, they have reason to live in fear of being arrested.

The world community is almost powerless to regulate the timing and composition of panic population movements once a government decides to adopt repressive policies. This was dramatically demonstrated by the Mariel Affair: on April 4, 1980 Cuban authorities removed their police guard at the Peruvian Embassy after a policeman was killed by a dissident who had rammed through the gate to apply for an emigration visa. Within a few days 10,000 additional Cubans had crowded into the embassy garden. They were camping under intolerable heat and other privation, while the world watched them on television. All were seeking asylum and asked for permission to emigrate. President Carter, responding to pitiful photographs of these desperate people, arranged to transport them to the United States and to a few Latin American countries.

President Castro responded on April 20 with an unexpected decision: Cubans would be allowed to depart freely from the port of Mariel. This temporary liberalization of Cuba's emigration practices triggered a massive reunification effort by Cuban-Americans. Even some of those who had recently arrived in the United States and could not yet request a family-reunion entry visa for their relatives, seized the opportunity to bring them into the country at once. Boats were chartered to pick them up at Mariel, usually without first obtaining a United States entry visa.

Boat owners saw an opportunity for profit and sailed back and forth between Cuba and Florida, offering passage at high rates to Cubans without friends or relatives able to pick them up. But the Cuban government had a hidden agenda in its seemingly liberal policy. Most boat captains were forced to take a number of persons not scheduled to be picked up. Many turned out to be convicts and mental patients. Cuba had decided to unload some of its social problems for care in the United States. Officials from the president down, were slow to realize that they were innocent witnesses to a new weapon in international conflict: *panic migration*.

This policy was extensively used in Czarist Russia before World War I. Nazi Germany applied awesome standards of efficiency to *its* implementation. Most of the people they regarded as subhuman were exterminated *en masse*; sometimes their bones were collected to be turned into glue, their hair into cushioning material, and their gold fillings into foreign exchange. Some of the healthy were allowed to live for a while as slaves, as unwilling prostitutes, or as hostages held for exchange against valued German prisoners, captured by the Allied forces. In some instances, the Germans offered to spare people in return for money, trucks, or other supplies. An awesome choice was placed before the civilized world: rescue people we do not want under conditions set by us or you will be responsible for their fate including maltreatment, imprisonment, exile and death.

While the Mariel refugee program was being reviewed in Washington, some boat owners on the East Coast thought of another get rich quick scheme. Near Cuba is the impoverished island Republic of Haiti. It has been misruled for many generations. In 1957, power was seized by one of the most cruel and ruthless of modern day dictators, "Papa Doc" Duvalier. While there have been slight improvements since his death, about half the country's income still goes to about one percent of the population, including Papa Doc's family, members of the ruling clique, and the notorious Tonton Macoute police. Corruption is traditional at all levels of society. Per capita income is under $300 a year. Between 1938 and 1980, erosion and neglect have reduced the amount of arable land by 52 percent while the population is growing rapidly, in spite of a life expectancy of only 51 years.

Those who could raise the money for a passage left everything behind to escape the hopelessness of their circumstances. Some captains crowded people into boats without enough food or water for the voyage. En route, some demanded additional money. There were cases of passengers being dumped into the sea to make more room, to punish them for not having more money, or for being unwilling to part with a watch or wedding ring. Some of the boats capsized; bloated bodies of their unfortunate passengers washed up on South Florida's gold coast of luxury hotels were visible evidence of these tragedies. The gruesome details were shown on television screens in many American homes.

By June 20, 1980, a total of 114,000 Cuban refugees had arrived in the United States, along with about 15,000 Haitians. Most of those who contacted the Immigration and Naturalization Service were given a parole document, while their status was to be legally adjudicated. A large proportion simply failed to show up for the hearings set to make a determination of their legal status. Federal relief expenditures, mostly for those with official refugee status, reached $532,000,000 by February 4, 1981, plus added costs defrayed by local government units and private voluntary agencies.

The new media in Florida began to highlight spectacular crimes committed by former Cuban prisoners. There also were charges that the newcomers were competing for jobs at a time when unemployment in many parts of the United States was escalating.

President Carter found himself widely criticized for lack of decisiveness in failing to counteract the Cuban strategy of exploiting the American commitment to aid refugees while ridding his nation of an unwanted and economically marginal population segment. He became the first United States president whose vacillation in immigration policy became a regional election issue. Enough Floridians resented the growing influence of Cubans in their state to probably have contributed to his defeat in Florida in 1980.

After President Reagan entered the White House, more decisive steps were initiated to discourage illegal entry. The sea lanes to the United States were patrolled intensively. Boats used to smuggle people were confiscated. Refugees who made it to American shores were asked to leave at once on a voluntary basis or to face indefinite detention. Thousands of Haitians preferred being placed behind barbed wire to returning home. They had risked life itself for a chance to live under better conditions in the United States. They were not prepared to give up this dream easily. They asked to be given refugee status. Supporters in the United States and a sympathetic public provided free legal services.

After a period of detention, sometimes in excess of a year, most of the aliens were given a parole status or acquired false ID documents. Years will pass before all the pending parole cases can be judicially reviewed to determine who is deportable and who is entitled to permanent asylum as a political refugee. In December 1984, however, Cuba agreed to take back 2,746 criminals and mental cases whom the United States found to be unacceptable as immigrants in the first major diplomatic accord between the two countries in seven years. Early indications are that the returnees are able to live normal lives, unless they were convicted of a crime in the United States. Most of them will be expected to complete their sentence in a Cuban prison. The government of Cuba appears to be desirous of signalling that it no longer favors a policy of forced migration as an instrument of national policy.

Panic and forced migration continue, however, to engulf tens of millions around the world. The United States leads all other nations of the world in providing a permanent home to refugees, but for each of these lucky individuals there probably are more than twenty who languish in a refugee camp. Few can even entertain the hope for a better future for themselves and for their children. No one will offer them an ID document so that they will be able to live in a society with full human rights entitlements.

The millions who live in the United States without proper documents are relatively fortunate. They enjoy most constitutional guarantees, their children can attend public schools, and they are entitled to emergency medical care. But if found travelling alone, they may be detained, as about 2,000 children have, because of a 1948 INS policy that prohibits the release of children on bond to anyone but parents and legal guardians. The latter are unwilling to come forth because, after claiming their child, they and their whole family will become subject to deportation. Other illegal immigrants become parents of children who are citizens by birth. Some have been in the United States for many years, even decades. Their large-scale apprehension and deportation, while authorized by law, would create legal, human rights, and political complications which no one in a responsible post has been willing to precipitate.

There are no easy answers to the controversies regarding the chronic underenforcement of immigration laws. A generous amnesty has been proposed, if associated with evidence of more effective immigration law enforcement in the future. This plan would put an end to the marginal status under which millions of illegals are now living and working.

Tamper-resistant ID documents would have to be issued to them, replacing those now used, most of which are false, counterfeit or stolen.

THE DETERRENCE STRATEGY

No individual can normally claim to have been injured when someone crosses America's borders without proper authorization. Such infractions are widely regarded as technical rather than moral. Border patrol agents are issued guns, and use helicopters and police dogs. They may be required to use force against those trying to enter the United States. Such man hunting is an aspect of the nation's current strategy to enforce immigration laws. But is is not popular, least among the border patrol of the INS, who risk being ambushed by smugglers whenever they go on patrol.

Deterrence by reducing incentives to enter the United States without proper documents would be a preferable strategy. Such an approach would be good for the morale of the INS enforcement staff. No one enjoys hunting people who are objects of sympathy. Reducing incentives for illegal border crossing would also be better for America's diplomatic relationships with the nations from which these people have emigrated. No pressure would have to be exerted to get their governments to agree to receiving the deportees.

In 1980, the United States legally admitted 880,000 immigrants and refugees. An even larger number regularly enter via illegal routes. Between 1971 and 1980, 8.3 million were apprehended. The INS estimates that 10 percent of all tourists who enter the country legally remain in the United States and enter the work force. Only about 3 out of 10 tourists come from Mexico. In fiscal year 1979 alone, over 1,076,000 persons were apprehended and identified as deportable under United States immigration laws. Ninety-three percent of them were Mexican nationals[3] whose illegal border crossing is not necessarily an indication of an intent to settle permanently in the Uniteed States. But a significant, though unknown proportion, do remain. Some illegals were found to be working in the cafeteria of the Washington headquarters of the INS.

This inexhaustible reservoir of people in need of "territorial" therapy — an environment where they have new opportunities[4] — generates the incentives that bring illegal immigrants, not only into the United States, but into all the Western democracies. It is a criminal offense to cross an international border without proper identification. It is punishable by fine and imprisonment. But none of the democracies keep their jails filled with such technical offenders, who have violated no moral norm. They are largely impoverished people willing to take risks to assure a better life for themselves and for their family.

In the United States, Congress as well as the policy makers at the executive level have always found it difficult to draw a balance between the readiness of most Americans to keep an open door to immigrants and the desire of most of these same persons to keep the number down to a reasonable annual total. Illegal immigration is obviously against the law but is also encouraged by it.

The Immigration and Nationality Act of 1952 (the McCarran-Walters Act), while limiting legal immigration in many ways, exempted employers of illegal immigrants from prosecution. This so called "Texas Proviso" has been effectively defended by ranching interests and employer groups. F. Ray Marshall, the secretary of labor in the Carter administration thought these lobbies favored the employment of illegals because they are inclined to work "hard and scared." They are an almost union proof source of labor.

This policy ambivalence is also mirrored by the cleavage of views between those who regard illegal border crossers as a threat, and those who believe that they serve an important economic function. Enforcement of immigration laws is therefore spasmodic.

Aliens in domestic service or others in low-paying jobs, are rarely pursued by INS inspectors. Some employers are able to hire contractors who will have illegal immigrants delivered to their farm or plant whenever they are needed. Congress simply does not allocate enough resources to immigration law enforcement to arrest, confine, prosecute, and then deport all violators. In a nation where law enforcement lacks the resources to investigate many murders, rapes, and burglaries, illegal immigrants are not viewed as a high law enforcement priority.

The adoption of employment barriers is advocated as the most promising of available deterrence policies to discourage illegal immigrants. How many future illegal entrants would risk arrest, detention and even their lives to be smuggled into the United States if there were no prospects of finding a job? Tamper-resistant identity documents are essential to any such strategy to reserve employment to citizens and to legally admitted aliens.

But if this deterrence approach is to work, *all* American workers would need tamper resistant ID documents, backed by a readily accessible verification service. Employment entitlement could be verified within seconds by inserting the ID card of the prospective worker into a digital reader connected by telephone or teletype to a central identification roster. The employer would receive a printout of the necessary and verified information as his receipt of having complied with the provisions of the proposed Immigration Reform and Control Act. It would not include some of the stored data, such as the prospective employee's family composition or prior residences. The printout would simply confirm that there is a Roberto Alvarez, who is a resident alien, with a given social security account number, and an entitlement to accept employment in the United States. The central identification roster might, however, contain additional information useful for confirming a birth certificate or marriage license. It could be released only after the individual would verify his consent by his retina pattern, fingerprint, or signature, whose digital characteristics might also be stored in the file. It would be almost impossible for anyone else to impersonate him in order to get unauthorized access to his file.

IS ILLEGAL IMMIGRATION EXAGGERATED?

Opponents of a national identification card strategy doubt that illegal immigration is a cause of such centrality as to justify reversing America's current hands off policy. This preference is implicitly endorsed by the reports of scholars who cite evidence from small sample populations indicating that the economy as a whole does not suffer from their presence. Michael L. Wachter suggests that illegals have an adverse distributional effect for the domestic low-income workers, but if they would not be available, the United States would have to develop a guest worker program. He forecasts that in the decade of the 1980s, "the number of young workers in the labor force should be declining."[5] Government analysts confirm this estimate. They predict that if present demographic trends continue, 25 million jobs will be added to the economy, with only 13.4 million Americans added to the labor pool.[6] Vegetable growers in California are lobbying hard to retain their current supply of migrant workers from Mexico should an immigration reform and control act be enacted in 1985.

Sidney Weintraub and Gilberto Cardenas reported in a study commissioned by the governor's Budget and Planning Office of Texas that illegal immigrants contribute "far more to the state's coffers in taxes than they take out in health, welfare and other publicly financed services."[7] The Social Security Administration estimates that it nets about eighty billion dollars in payments that will never be collected. Even if not all of this sum is contributed by illegal immigrants, this figure provides a rough index to their economic impact on the U.S. economy.

The liberal journal of opinion, the *New Republic*, calls for an "opening of the floodgates" as the "only honest solution to the immigration mess." They would admit Mexicans as guest workers to pick perishable crops but also to adopt generous quotas for permanent immigrants and refugees.[8]

An even more pro open door policy has been advocated by the *Wall Street Journal*:

> If Washington still wants to "do something" about immigration, we propose a five word constitutional amendment: there shall be open borders. Perhaps this policy is overly ambitious in today's world, but the U.S. became the world's envy by precisely this kind of heresy. Our greatest heresy is that we believe in people as *the* great resource of our land . . . . Trembling no-growthers cry that we'll never "feed," "house" or "clothe" all the immigrants, the immigrants want to feed, house and clothe themselves . . . .
>
> America, after all, is a nation founded on optimism. The Republic will prosper so long as it does not disavow this taproot. The issue is not what we offer to the teeming masses, but what they offer to us: their hands, their minds, their spirit, and above all the chance to be true to our own past and our own future."[9]

Most labor union leaders take quite a different viewpoint. They prefer strict immigration law enforcement. They ascribe some of the high rates of unemployment, especially among minority youths, to competition from undocumented aliens willing to work for low wages. A Congressional Budget Bureau estimate in 1981 indicates that the average unemployed person would need $7,000 per year in unemployment insurance and other benefits. The Environment Fund suggests that over $8.4 billion a year is needed to pay the unemployment benefits to persons whose jobs were allegedly taken by illegal aliens. This estimate is predicated on a conservative estimate that there are only four million illegals, and with only a third of them having a position that would be held by an already resident person looking for work.[10]

Stanley R. Ross, in reviewing the status of illegal immigration noted that there is a good deal of polarization in the United States about immigration policy.[11] Strong domestic political forces favor a hands off policy. They are countered by others who stress its national problem component: "a severe national crisis" says former United States Attorney General William Saxbe. Immigration made the cover of *Time Magazine* showing America being swamped by an endless flood of foreigners.[12]

Occasionally even more alarming claims surface: there are people who assert that the United States is being bilked of many billions a year in fraudulent claims for governmental benefits, mostly by illegal immigrants using falsified ID cards. Such extensive losses have never been documented. In fact, studies indicate the opposite. Most illegal aliens are afraid to become involved with the system, even when they need hospital care. The use of free schools, medical, and other public services is restricted largely to those who were able to bring their families.

Illegal immigrants do account for a sizable proportion of the country's population increase. Between 1970 and 1979, 4,336,003 immigrants were admitted to the United States. In addition, 217,552 refugees were allowed to remain. Most of them will be given the option to acquire U.S. citizenship. In 1979, 158,000 were naturalized.

While immigration issues are often discussed in the media, it remained a secondary issue even during the depression atmosphere of 1982–83. It was not mentioned in any of President Reagan's State of the Union Addresses. The Immigration Reform and Control Act of 1982 became a temporary election issue during the 1984 Democratic primary campaign. The three major candidates, Walter Mondale, Gary Hart, and Jesse Jackson spoke up against the passage of the bill then pending in Congress. As vice president, Walter Mondale had worried aloud that "the United States is overrun by illegal aliens,"[13] but as a presidential candidate he thought he needed to court spokespersons for Mexican-American groups.

SECURE ID DOCUMENTS WITH LIMITED USAGE

The Immigration Reform and Control Act of 1982 proposed to bypass the alleged privacy threat by linking its call for a valid nationwide ID procedure with severe restrictions on its use. The 1985 revision of this bill deletes the requirement of any federal pre-employment verification. Employers would have to keep records of two ID documents presented to them, but the issue of how to increase the trustworthiness of the already issued ID cards was avoided as being too controversial to be included in this third attempt to get the legislation approved by a majority of Congress.

Earlier versions included provisions that law enforcement agencies could not tap the proposed employment entitlement roster, not even in pursuit of tax fraud or other criminal investigations. *The Washington Post* commented in an editorial that there are risks of abuse if a nationwide roster were to be maintained, but added that "opponents grossly exaggerate it":[14]

> Why the fuss, then, about a more systematic identifier designed solely to deal with illegal immigration: The rights of illegals (including their privacy) would probably be strengthened through a national identity card system. The federal government would find it possible not only to identify probable abuses by employers or local authorities but also to extend legal protection and social services to workers whose presence in the United States had been legitimized by the new cards.

Congress, while devising a national identity card system, should provide elaborate safeguards, possibly through amendments to the 1974 Privacy Act. Whether the identifier should be a forgery-proof identity card or some other proposed mechanism remains to be determined. Only through adopting such a system, however, can America reassert the primacy of *lawful* entry into this country. Endless and inappropriate evocations of George Orwell will not make the problem go away.

The 1985 revision of the immigration reform legislation was introduced in the Senate without any requirement for Federal pre-employment verification. Employers would have to keep records of the documents presented to them by prospective employees. They would become subject to investigation only when other sources of information would place them under suspicion of having knowingly hired illegal aliens.

The secure ID proposal is neither inherently pro- nor anti-immigration. It is not a liberal nor a conservative issue. Without a trustworthy ID card, both the privacy and accuracy of files kept about individuals are in jeopardy. Malevolent persons can easily feed informatin to a file of a person whom they wish to harm. They can also get access to his file by impersonating him. Such violations could be minimized if the technology to issue and to verify tamper-resistant ID documents were more fully utilized. But there are equally public spirited officials who fear that such innovations would soon lead to enactment of legislation for a compulsory national ID card. Leaders are quite polarized about what might best be done. The high points are summarized as follows:

PRO

Father Theodore M. Hesburgh, Chairman, Select Commission on Immigration and Policy—Without a simple means to identify who is qualified to be in this country and who is not, sanctions against employers hiring illegal aliens cannot be enforced. Illegal aliens cannot be deported. Illegal immigration will continue unabated.

Ray Marshall, U.S. Secretary of Labor in the Carter Administration—There must be some form of worker identification, not necessarily a card or a number. The standard that ought to apply is this: any test of worker eligibility ought to be simple and fair. It should lend itself to discrimination against foreign workers; and it should be trustworthy.

Dean L. Huxtable, Member, Federal Advisory Committee on False Identification (FACFI)—To establish a system to identify our citizens in a democratic society may cost us a minor degree of personal freedom. Not to do so may cost us all of it.

CON

John H. F. Shattuck, National Legislative Director American Civil Liberties Union—To establish a population registry and an identity document, either of them alone, could prove an irreversible last step in the loss of personal privacy that all Americans have felt so acutely.

John Huerta, Mexican American Legal Defense and Education Fund—Will the employers ask all job applicants for work eligibility cards, or only those who look "foreign"? Most likely employers will only scrutinize Hispanics, blacks, and Asians, and will hire Anglos. Because the burden which employer sanctions place on the employees, they may try to reduce their risks by cutting down on hiring minority members of the work force.

Arthur Flemming, Chairman, U.S. Commission for Civil Rights—The availability of a compulsory identity card, work permit, or other standard universal identifier would provide the means for a serious invasion of privacy.

The Select Commission on Immigration and Refugee Policy proposed a number of special legal powers for reducing illegal immigration.[15] In spite of objections by some civil liberty maximalists, the majority of the commission favored border patrol officials having a wide range of law enforcement powers to screen persons suspected of having entered the country without proper identification:

Temporary Detention for Interrogation Inspectors should be authorized to temporarily detain a person for interrogation or a brief investigation upon reasonable cause to believe (based on articulable facts) that the person is unlawfully present in the United States.

The Commission did not recommend overturning by legislation a Supreme Court ruling allowing immigration officers to stop vehicles for a brief time and to question their occupants in reasonable proximity to the border, even without suspicion of impropriety. In 1985, the Supreme Court broadened police power to stop and question people anywhere without a warrant if they had reason to suspect that a crime had been committed.

Arrests With or Without Warrant The Commission favored arrest with or without warrant, when supported by probable cause that the arrested person might be in the United States illegally.

The law provides explicit authority for immigration inspectors to search vehicles for persons and evidence related to illegal immigration, with or without warrant.

Evidence Illegally Obtained By a majority of 10 to 3 the Commission favored that evidence obtained illegally should not be excluded from consideration in deportation cases, but that enforcement officials who used illegal means be punished.

Right to Counsel The Commission favored, by a split decision, that the right to counsel be mandated only for persons involved in an exclusion or deportation hearing. Such counsel should be provided at U.S. Government expense only for persons who were legal resident aliens. They represent just over one percent of those affected in 1978, when 70,410 aliens were formally deported or required to depart.

At the present time, persons accused of residing illegally in the United States do not enjoy all of the due process rights of permanent residents and citizens. One of the obstacles to this policy change is quite pragmatic. Extension of all U.S. constitutional due process rights would require an expensive expansion of INS detention facilities and legal services. Even under present policies, contested deportation cases, like those involving about 2,000 Haitians in 1981–82, hearings can be dragged out by legal technicalities for many years. The federal legal system could not handle the additional volume of litigation, without a sizeable expansion in the number of immigration judges, appeals panels, and legal staff. Funds would also have to be appropriated to pay for the legal defense of the many illegal aliens who are indigent. Requests for the hundreds of millions of dollars necessary would be in competition with funds needed for road construction, the reduction of crowded prisons, and welfare services.

THE "FALSE IDENTITY CRIME" PHENOMENON

U.S. Law and the administrative practices of both government and business organizations now leave a great deal of choice to individuals to decide if and when they wish to act under their own identity. FACFI,[15] after a review of much evidence concluded:

> A growing army of criminals and fugitives is using a screen of false credentials in welfare fraud, illegal immigration, drug trafficking, passing bad checks and phony credit cards, and in hundreds of other crimes. They have one thing in common: The taxpayer picks up the tab.
> False identification is the criminal's best friend. They can appear and disappear at will by creating fictitious paper people. Often victims are not even aware that their rights have been violated.

The FACFI was a volunteer task force, convened by former attorney general William B. Saxbe on October 14, 1974. It included representatives of government agencies at the federal, state and local levels, law enforcement groups and business organizations, such as the American Bankers Association, the American Banknote Company, and the Polaroid Corporation. The committee considered arguments in favor of a national ID card, including the following: 1. Such a document could be more easily recognized, controlled, and protected against abuse. 2. Document systems that include everybody would thereby be foolproof. 3. Government has an obligation to provide a reliable means of personal identification for public and private transactions among its citizens.

The case against a national ID system was viewed to be self-evident. But other than the cost and the administrative complexity of developing it, no hard evidence was provided to substantiate the assertion that "documentation is in opposition to American traditions and represents an invasion of personal privacy. . . . Criminals could reap benefits far greater than they obtain under the current system."[15]

There was a minority of one, Deane Huxtable, registrar of vital statistics of the State of Virginia. Since then, evidence has been accumulating that the issue should be reopened. Could it be that the lone voice among eighty other experts who in 1974 reviewed policy merits of a tamper-re sistant ID card was more realistic than the overwhelming majority?

The FACFI was convened under the shadow cast by the Watergate scandal. President Richard Nixon and his attorney general, the two highest law enforcement officials of the nation, were found to have conspired to violate the privacy rights of some persons whom they regarded as politically antagonistic. They compounded their offense by lying, in a vain effort to cover their tracks. Attorney General John Mitchell was imprisoned and President Nixon might have shared this fate but for a general pardon granted by his successor for any crimes that he might have committed while holding the nation's highest office.

The FACFI study, after a flurry of media reports soon after publication, disappeared from public concern. Not even a policy study was commissioned of the social-political cost-benefits of available antifraud strategies. Neither of the major political parties, nor Presidents Ford, Carter, and Reagan placed the prestige of their office behind efforts to fully utilize available technological means to inhibit the use of false documents.

Congress has also avoided action on legislation to tighten federal laws against the manufacture, transfer, possession, and use of false ID documents which they issue. But it is difficult, and often impractical, to prosecute persons who use a false document in one state that was produced in another. It is perfectly legal to manufacture and to own most false documents, as long as they do not contain a restricted seal placed such as those issued by the federal or state governments.

It is not against the law for a middle-man to furnish personal particulars regarding a dead man in California to a person born in Minnesota. Both states permit unrestricted applications for birth and death certificates. A criminal in Miami can then apply to Minnesota for a copy of the decedent's birth certificate and use it as his own. The middle-man committed no crime. The criminal, even if arrested with such a false document, could usually not be prosecuted. He would have to be caught in the act of committing a crime.

The absence of state and federal standards for ID card security generates pressure to close this legal loophole. Efforts were made once more in

1982 to plug it with a consolidated statute, the False Identification Crime Control Act of 1981. The Senate passed it but the House of Representatives shelved the bill in its rush for adjournment in December 1982. The Act would have increased the penalties for producing of the false IDs.

THE LOSS OF PRIVACY QUESTION

How warranted are the fears of loss of liberty that have paralyzed past efforts to attack the false ID problem with full vigor? Middle-class people, with a well defined social status in their community, know how to defend themselves against misrepresentation. This is less true of the poor and members of unpopular minority groups; they are quite vulnerable, as Terry Dean Rogan discovered.[16] He was arrested for allegedly committing two burglaries and two murders in Los Angeles after the police investigated a noisy fight with his girlfriend in Saginaw, Michigan. The prime suspect in California, whose fingerprints had been left at the scene of one or more of these crimes, had used Rogan's driver's license and other identity documents that disappeared when Rogan's wallet was lost more than a year earlier in Detroit. This is why the FBI's National Crime Communication Center had an alert out for Rogan, even though he lived thousands of miles from the scene of the crimes. The Saginaw police thought they had made quite a catch when they handcuffed the shocked, unemployed, black part-time college student and carted him off to jail.

After being notified, the Los Angeles Police Department issued a warrant for his arrest and extradition. What saved Rogan from being destroyed by a long trial and a possible conviction for crimes committed by someone else? His fingerprints did not match those the suspect had left at the scene of his crimes.

Rogan's misfortune did not end there. The Los Angeles Police Department failed to notify the FBI to remove his name from the list of suspects, though they had dropped all charges. Rogan found himself arrested four more times during a period of fourteen months, after being stopped for routine traffic checks. At each stop, they radioed for an identity check through the National Crime Information Center. Each time, Rogan was targeted as a hot suspect and found himself confronted by officers who kept him in custody until the FBI verified the stolen ID card.

Mistaken identity is not a commonplace event; Rogan's case is fortunately unusual. But its occurrence highlights the importance of the public debate about the pros and cons of America's anarchic system of personal identification.

ID ROSTER AS A SOCIAL POLICY TOOL

A national ID roster is inherently neutral. It could provide up-to-date statistical information about the country's population between the decennial censuses; it could reduce the incidence of misrepresentation; it could reduce the influx of unauthorized border crossers. But Valid Identity Programs (VIPs), as passbooks, ID cards or as computerized central files, can also be used to keep residents under surveillance.

The growing interest in tamper-resistant ID documents in the western world is generated by the rapid growth of automatic teller machines, interactive television, and the growing volume of computer crime. The unreliability and lack of validity of a significant proportion of ID documents exposes a sizable number of persons to exploitation by the criminal sector of the society.

Modern life cannot function without trust. When people are born, they acquire an identity which is the legal basis of many entitlements, including the right to attend a public school free of charge, to inherit property, to get a federally guaranteed loan, and to be elected to a public office. The validity of a claim to identity is therefore a matter of vital public interest. This fact, by itself, would justify a review of current standards for issuing ID documents. The credit industry is working on this problem in order to reduce its losses from fraud and misrepresentation. Government agencies are also being pushed to counteract the ease with which most of their identity documents can be altered and forged.

There will be many significant changes in our social system should the ID technology become more widely utilized. The ID card controversy has therefore come to the forefront of public debate, but for more narrow reasons than crime control, containment of terrorism, and the battle against the underground (untaxed) economy. Identity documents are believed to be more effective in discouraging illegal entries than increasing the border guard. The decision of the INS to issue an Alien Documentation, Identification, and Telecommunicaton (ADIT) card, and its policy implications, therefore needs to be examined.

REFERENCES

1. Nilsen H. Spencer, *The Nilsen Report*, No. 347, Jan. 1985.
2. City of Hamburg, *Hamburgische Gesetz und Verordnungsplatz*, no. 25, May 27, 1982.
3. Vialet, Joyce, *Illegal Undocumented Aliens*, Washington, D.C., Congressional Research Service, Issue Brief no. I B 74137, November 6, 1981:1.
4. Joseph W. Eaton, *Migration and Social Welfare*, New York: National Association of Social Welfare, 1971: IX–XVI.

5. Wachter, Michael L., "The Labor Market and Illegal Immigration: The Outlook For The 1980s." *Industrial and Labor Relations Review,* vol. 33, no. 3, April 1980, 342–354.

6. *Newsweek,* June 25, 1984, 23.

7. *New York Times,* November 15, 1984 p. 9, April 1980, p. 342–354.

8. *The New Republic,* April 1, 1985.

9. *The Wall Street Journal,* ca June 3, 1984.

10. Immigration Reports, FAIR, vol. IV, no. 7, 1983:2.

11. Ross, Stanley R., "Mexican-American Problems Loom Larger Than Ever," *Foundation News,* January/February 1977:19.

12. *Time Magazine,* February 22, 1982:10–17.

13. *Ibid.*

14. *The Washington Post,* March 17, 1981.

15. Federal Advisory Committee on False Identification. *The Criminal Use of False Identification.* (Washington, D.C.: Government Printing Office, November, 1976).

16. Burnham, David, *The New York Times,* February 12, 1985.

CHAPTER THREE

THE DETERRENCE TECHNOLOGY

CONVENIENCE AND TRUST

Anyone stopped by a traffic policeman will recall his unhappiness if the driver's license had been left at home; the law requires that it be carried by anyone operating a motor vehicle. But people are rarely *arrested* if they are without it. They are given a chance to drive home and report to the police at a later date.

In April 1982, 107 aliens were picked up by the Immigration and Naturalization Service for suspicion of being in the country illegally. They were arrested on the spot. Two thirds were released after proving they were legal residents but the other 36 were subject to deportation.

Most Americans prove their identity by flashing a card, often with a photograph. But there is much justified skepticism in the trustworthiness of these documents. When cashing a check, merchants often require two ID cards. Mexicans or Canadians who enter the United States with proper authorization, are offered an alternative to a passport—an Alien Documentation, Identification, and Telecommunication (ADIT) card, a hard-to-forge identity document. It includes a biometric indicator. The Simpson-Mazzoli Immigration Reform and Control Act would require a comparable means of identification for all American workers. If it were to be enacted, it would not be long before nonemployed Americans would clamor for a similar document. Investors, retired persons, and homemakers would be handicapped without an optimally trustworthy ID record. Many states already issue licenses to nondrivers, for use as a personal identifyer.

Passports, drivers' licenses, Automatic Teller Machines (ATMs) and even many sensitive computer data banks are lacking in biometric indicators. They rely on a rather primitive protective device: a personal ID or PIN number. Since many people (seventy percent in one study) carry their PIN number at all times, a pickpocket could use their credit. High school students playing computer games were able to guess the access number to sensitive medical and military data banks, and then survey them "just for fun." Another source of insecurity is the fact that PIN numbers are known to some bank employees and other organization insiders.

For each of the identity documents, people must furnish information about themselves. The average American has surrendered much of his privacy to obtain credit, an education, good medical care, and many other services. Equifax, the largest of America's many consumer credit agencies, is reported to have computerized dossiers on 48 million persons.

During an election for mayor, an incumbent was accused of viewing a "soft-porn" channel offered by Warner Annex Qube Corporation. Employees were first suspected of having been the source of this information. It had actually been volunteered by the mayor himself, who contended that his viewing "was out of civic duty, not moral terpitude. As mayor," he said, "I should know what's on the Cable TV System franchised by my city."[1]

THE ADIT CARD

The national ID card controversy was raised to the level of a national debate after the INS began to explore options in the early 1970s for issuing tamper-resistant cards to immigrants and border-crossers free of charge. The then existing documents were almost useless as are most of those issued now. They are still being forged with impunity. To make border inspection both quicker and more reliable, the ADIT card was devised. Early models with various technical features, laminations and plastic covers, as well as alternate photographic and fingerprint equipment were first tried out in the El Paso area. The object was to develop a durable plastic card that would identify people by a combination of three types of indicators:[2] something *known* by the individual; something *possessed* by the individual—biometric measures; something *about* the individual. Two types of verification were to be made possible: visual verification with reasonable accuracy, unless the inspector is bored, tired or drugged; digital verification with close to perfect accuracy.

Before any information is accepted for use on an ADIT card, it is checked by trained INS employees. Each alien is required to appear in person to be interviewed and to have his credentials examined. An ADIT card cannot be ordered by mail or anonymously. Breeder documents are checked to minimize the use of false birth certificates and passports.

All ADIT cards are manufactured at a special INS card facility in Arlington, Texas and the production process is carefully monitored. Each

ADIT card includes encoded information about the owner's background, for instance, his parents' name and his place of birth, information not likely to be generally known except within the immediate family or by close friends. There also is a witnessed signature and a fingerprint of the person to be identified. A color photograph is fused onto factory controlled paper, sold only to one customer. It may include special engraving constructed to glow under ultraviolet light. Salmon colored lines emanating from the INS Service insignia flow into the photo area without impairing photo recognition. A rolled, straight pressed-on fingerprint is obtained for digital coding and for electronic matching with a copy in the INS central file.

In important cases, the actual fingertip of the card holder could be compared to that reproduced on his card. Once Congress authorizes the purchase of the necessary card readers and computer terminals, it will be possible to determine whether the person presenting a card is, in fact, its lawful holder.

From a privacy viewpoint, ADIT cards use data less stigmatizing than the details recorded in most of the other personal information systems. The ADIT card, which is also called the most trustworthy "green" card of the INS, includes no political data, no casework information about any social problem, health, or income information. Nor is religion included, something quite common in Europe, where some nations collect church taxes and pay state salaries to priests, ministers and rabbis.

FRONT

1. Date of birth
2. A profile photograph of the card holder showing the shape of one ear which can be compared visually to the features of the person who presents the card.

3. Non-machine readable signature, which must be verified by an INS employee. For persons holding a security position the signature could be digitally coded for machine readability.

4. Sex is not included. It can be inferred from the name and the facial photograph.

5. Alien Registration number (not the Social Security number).

6. Location of the first port of entry and date of card issue.

7. Administrative classification for admission to the United States.

8. Personal Biographical Data Index, which is a short numerical code known to immigration inspectors for interviewing card holders about their family composition.

9. Admission or adjustment date if there was an immigration status reclassification of the lawful card holder by the INS.

10. A code which must be consistent with the name on the card, one of several devices to reject forged versions when a digital reader is used to verify the card.

11. Fingerprint. Its inclusion permits quick visual authentification against the actual finger of the person offering the ADIT card. Even more conclusive verification against the original print could be made, if the INS uses digital readers at each border station.

12. Selected parts of the ADIT card glow under ultraviolet light.

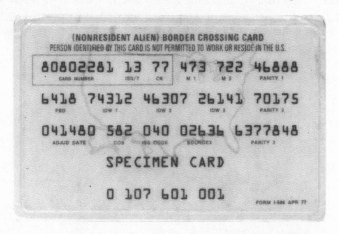

BACK

1. Alien Registration number (same as on the front of the card).

2. A numerical code of type of ADIT card issued.

3. A computer-generated code number based on all of the information on the card. Should the card become lost and replaced, the new card will be issued but with a different code. The old number will automatically appear on a list of invalidated documents to discourage any use of stolen cards.

4. A code describing the holder's fingerprint characteristics were on early versions of the card. It will be deleted as long as the INS does not have digital readers at its entry stations.

5. Several different encryption algorithms. If any part of a line on the card is changed, a digital reader will note the discrepancy between these algorithms and what the number should be in view of the alterations. The altered card would be invalidated and confiscated.

Many additional security devices are being developed by researchers in the United States and overseas. Some, such as a patterned or ribbed plastic cover bonded to the document; a magnetic stripe; microdots; a digitally-readable signature or a voiceprint could be added to the ADIT card, if an even higher degree of security is needed. Micro-chip or "smart" cards with a built-in memory are also available. The Drexon Lasercard technology offers more than two megabytes of storage. These interactive products could be read every time they are presented at a border, providing evidence of when, how often, and where the holder is entering or leaving the country. This capacity would handicap smugglers and terrorists who want to hide their travel patterns so as not to call attention to themselves. An increment of security would be added, although the system would be far from foolproof.

The current ADIT card version conforms to the twelve standards regarded as essential for a secure ID document by the International Civil Aviation Organization (ICAO) in 1974.[3] The card must:

1. uniquely identify the bearer in a simple and visual way
2. be difficult to alter, in order to deter or prevent unauthorized modification
3. be difficult to counterfeit
4. be easy to use and understand by means of reliance on standardized features
5. be durable, for at least 3–5 years
6. be designed for machine readability
7. be convenient to carry, in terms of size, weight and flexibility
8. contain a unique ID number, useful for ease in issuing and handling the document in a secure and organized manner
9. be cost-competitive with other similar cards
10. be capable of being produced under government control, to ensure a secure production environment
11. be nationally acceptable as a standard card configuration
12. allow for a statement indicating special status of the bearer, such as "resident alien," "regular border crosser" or others.

Through February 1985, 5.3 million ADIT cards have been issued. Manpower shortages limit the number of border-crossers and aliens already in the country who can be credentialized. Each applicant must be interviewed, fingerprinted, photographed, and observed while signing his name. Completion of the program will depend on the readiness of Congress to add funds for the INS to hire more immigration inspectors. At the present rate of production, the INS is *just* able to keep up with issuing ADIT cards to all new immigrants and border crossers. Millions still need to rely on less trustworthy documents, including 72–hour passes which are written on a simple piece of paper. They are not even serially numbered, so that forgers can reproduce them with impunity. While this technicality will be corrected in the near future, the INS continues to honor the older border crossing documents that are easily compromised.

The fiscal year 1987 INS budget requests funds to recall all these older documents and to replace them with ADIT cards. Those failing to respond within a given deadline will find that their documents will no longer be accepted. Millions of forged green cards will lose their value. In previous years, Congress repeatedly rejected the allocation of funds to pay for this updating process. It would expose illegal immigrants, some of whom have used false domestic documents for many years. Also, the legislation is viewed as controversial by a significant proportion of legislators. Nevertheless, the debate will occur annually. Ignoring a problem does not make it go away.

As the ADIT program expands, the profitability of worldwide criminal enterprises which produce and sell false U.S. documents will for a time only be marginally affected. About nine out of ten illegals enter the country without being checked by anyone and acquire false documents after they are here. This is the "market" that would ultimately be hurt by a general reform of standards for issuing all U.S. identifying documents.

SMUGGLERS PREFER THE STATUS QUO

Several legislative hearings on the ADIT cards have been held which posit that a fateful choice between freedom and tyranny is being proposed. The real alternatives involve less dramatic options. Should the United States continue to maintain the status quo, with borders which can be crossed easily with false documents or without any inspection at all? The INS has never been given anywhere near the necessary personnel or funds to enforce the laws for which it holds primary jurisdiction. Prosecution of offenders who are apprehended is not an effective deterrent because our judicial system cannot handle any additional volume. Offenders now number well in excess of one million each year.

Since 1978, when a counteroffensive was instituted by the INS, against smugglers of illegal aliens, 61,000 offenders were apprehended. But of those arrested in 1979, only 12 percent were prosecuted. In subsequent years, the INS concentrated its enforcement efforts on major smugglers and was able to prosecute 50 percent of them, with an 83 percent conviction rate. But few smugglers serve long prison sentences. The financial rewards of those engaged in this business are well worth the modest risk, although Congress recently strengthened the enforcement powers of the INS. Vehicles used in smuggling aliens can now be confiscated and sold for the benefit of the treasury. A 1983 report indicated that a total of 5,145 autos, trucks, airplanes, and boats had been seized, at an appraised value of $12.6 million. But prospects of quick profit continue to keep the people-smuggling business flourishing.

The first Haitian illegal immigrant, arrested in 1981 and freed more than a year later by a court order, spent more time in a detention facility "than almost all persons arrested on smuggling charges in Florida over the last four years," claimed one anonymous defense attorney who regularly represents illegal aliens. He wanted to prove that Haitians were being subjected to discrimination in comparison to entrepreneurs who profit handsomely from a career of immigration law violations. Smugglers continue to have more to say about who can enter and work in the United States than the INS and the Department of State – the agencies responsible for implementing U.S. immigration policies. But the ADIT card program has the potential of reversing this situation.

REDUCING PAPERWORK

Plasticized cards can provide an instant and machine-readable contact between a person and his record. Entries to update or change information can be made quickly. A phone call to a master card business office will result in the instant retrieval of one's personal file, once the operator is given the code number. Questions can be answered, new information can be recorded, and problems can often be resolved right then and there. These efficiencies are not possible within the manual record-keeping system of the INS. A file in the Brownsville, Texas office has to be physically transfered if someone needs it to help an alien who has moved to Chicago. Records often are misplaced in this process. The magnitude of the problem is illustrated by the inability of the INS to handle even the most basic requirement of a record-keeping system – an up-to-date file of addresses.

On December 29, 1981, President Reagan signed an amendment to the Immigration and Nationality Act of 1940 removing the requirement that aliens register their current address every January. It was replaced by the more practical requirement that aliens notify the INS within ten days after they change their address. For years, the INS had lacked the staff to check these annual post card reports. There were not enough clerks available to match the address reports with each person's original immigration and naturalization record. The INS could not even check who had failed to report and when this *was* known, few could be contacted or picked up for investigation.

In 1980, the INS printed 18 million postcards to be distributed to post offices all over the country and in INS regional offices. Some 5.3 million aliens dutifully reported their address, but an unknown and very large number did not conform to the law.

The INS had spent an estimated $1.2 million for the annual registration ritual. During the 1979 hostage crisis, the attorney general ordered a review of the status of Iranians in the United States so that those who had violated the terms of their admission could be expelled. But, it did not give the agency the capacity to locate Iranians in the country. The INS shifted about 1,200 employees from their usual tasks to that of verifying the status of an estimated 73,600 students.

Almost a year and $3.3 million later, the agency was still unable to determine the size of this student population or the whereabouts of many of its members.[4] The INS lacks the simple computer capability for routine follow-up used by a growing number of businesses and service agencies to send out monthly bills and to differentiate those which are paid promptly and those which are past due.

The new address updating procedure—when needed rather than annually—will save money. Without machine-readable entry documents and a computerized central data bank, the INS has to file the address changes manually. This routine is being overlooked due to other priorities. The INS is almost drowning in an information flood, and is "a bureaucratic basket case," as *U.S. News and World Report* (April 12, 1982) called it. Many routine statistics have not been published since fiscal year 1978, such as those on the admission of aliens permitted to enter as nonimmigrant workers. The INS information system cannot cope with the massive flow of data. The agency hopes to remedy this gap during fiscal year 1985. At present, there are not enough employees to man the telephones for persons seeking information. There are in excess of 57 million files, many of which are misplaced and lost while they are being used.

The record keeping process at U.S. borders has outgrown the manual procedures that are still in use. Among those who now move into and out of the country, tourists, most of them American citizens, vastly outnumber immigrants. There also are many millions of regular but temporary border crossers from both Mexico and Canada. They come to shop in the United States and then return home at night. There are border points where tens of thousands of such shoppers must be checked every day. Only a tiny proportion, less than one third of one percent, are entering with immigrant visas.

At over two hundred and fifty official stations, border-crossing officials check the documents of all arrivals, with little or no prior notice. The rate of clearance depends in part on the physical adequacy of the entry facilities. Many were built before the mushrooming volume of border traffic. At major international airports, planes would have to be turned back if customs and immigration officials were to check entering persons with anything but perfunction during the rush hours. Waiting room, luggage room, and bathroom facilities become overcrowded during peak traffic periods. Congestion heats up tempers at popular border posts and bridges, where thousands of cars may seek to cross within an hour. In southwestern entry points, rows of waiting cars, emitting carbon monoxide and other pollutants, periodically extend for miles into Mexico. Diplomatic protests are then generated about alleged American insensitivity to the comfort of Mexican visitors.

The Custom Service and Department of State have started to computerize some of their control data. The Treasury Department has developed the Treasury Department Enforcement Control System, TECS, to alert custom inspectors or drug enforcement agents to individuals who are suspected of violations. The Department of State has the Travel Department Insurance System, TDIS, to automate its passport production system. It also has begun to establish the Visa Applicant Control System (VACS), a prototype of which has been organized in Mexico City and in London. Once the software program has been perfected, and the funds for computers are allocated, border stations would be able to verify a visa electronically by contacting the VACS data bank.

At a few airports, the INS staff have access to the Custom Service Computer base, TECS. It cross-references the names of inadmissable or suspected persons. However, when the computer malfunctions, both the Custom Service and INS fall back on printed lookout books which are still being issued. Otherwise, the screening process of aliens would have to stop or border crossers would have to be admitted without screening.

The urgency for developing a more managable information system is highlighted by the fact that in 1977, almost 300 million people and 80 million vehicles crossed our borders. There were 160,000 ships, with about three million crew members and passengers. Over $7 billion in custom duties were collected on more than $250 billion in imports and exports. Twenty million persons and huge volumes of air cargo arrived on 350,000 commercial, military and private flights. And yet the border crossing traffic continues to grow.

Sixty-five percent of all drug arrests appear to be based on leads generated by the INS and its staff. But there is no way of estimating how many are missed, while bringing contraband across the borders. Without better technical means of verification, the spotting of professional smugglers, drug pushers, and illegal immigrants with false papers is a hit and miss process. They are interspersed with a large number of welcome shoppers, tourists, and business travelers. There is neither the manpower nor the space at most border points to screen more than a minute portion of these border crossers with any degree of thoroughness.

A machine-read ADIT card would reduce a great deal of paperwork. It would permit most border crossers to check themselves into the country. A digital reader could compare the tip of the entrant's index finger with the fingerprint on his ID card, record his entry, and issue him a printed receipt of his immigration status. Those arriving by automobile would simply have to insert their identity card into a portable digital reader.

IMPROVED SURVEILLANCE EFFICIENCY

People involved in legitimate travel and trade will carry a valid passport. But the criminal community takes advantage of the fact that American citizens can still travel to Canada and the Bahamas with a driver's license, a voting registration, or a birth certificate, each of which can be forged with ease. A tamper-resistant and digitally readable federal identity card would complicate the smuggling of people, merchandise, and drugs. Fewer could arrive as alleged tourists and then remain indefinitely, as about 10 percent do, without coming to the attention of the authorities. After frequent crossings, even at different border points, the computers would target them for special attention. The roughly $80 billion narcotic drug business in the United States and its foreign suppliers would face an enhanced risk of being traced through money laundering activities. Billions of dollars in small denominations must be transferred in large units to foreign banks where they can be withdrawn under bank secrecy guarantees and then reentered as investments into the legitimate sector of the economy. If persons depositing or changing large sums of money had to use a biometrically verifyable Automatic Teller Machine card, those who transact business at many different banks would call attention to themselves. Persons without an explanation for making large and multiple cash transactions in many different locations, could be subjected to investigation.

None of these law enforcement aids are now being used. Information has to be processed too quickly to differentiate between more than 20 administrative categories of persons who are eligible for admission to the United States, in addition to those who are citizens. In 1977, the most recent date for which detailed information was available, the Department of State issued about 3,750,000 nonimmigrant visas in locations all over the world. This number has been increasing, in spite of several new bilateral treaties with foreign nations in which most visa requirements have been mutually waived. There also were 300,000 applications that were denied. Computers are needed to handle such a volume of records efficiently. A good ID document would make it easy to administer such a work load and to locate the files of persons in need of service without delay.

A machine-readable document may be even more important for handling a constantly growing volume of domestic paperwork. The INS knows that many students, tourists, and other aliens overstay the authorized period. In 1979, a test survey was made of 3,734 persons at random, who were suspected of having overstayed, with the results shown on the accompanying table.

Status Report on a Random Sample of Aliens
Who Overstayed in the United States in 1979
(N = 3734)

Unable to locate alien because of illegible data	6.7 percent
Unable to locate alien or verify departure	58.4 percent
Verified that alien had departed	33.7 percent
Aliens located in the United States and found to be in legal status	1.1 percent
Aliens located and found to be deportable	0.1 percent

Source: Report by the Comptroller General of the United States, *Controls over Non-immigrant Aliens Remain Ineffective*, Washington, D.C., U.S. General Accounting Office, GGD-80-87, September 11, 1980:28.

A total of 8,700 staff hours were needed to obtain the data. This expensive effort yielded only four deportable aliens because sixty-five percent of the border-crossers could not be located.

There are no prospects at present for enhanced efficiency in the administration of our borders and of aliens in the United States without developing a computerized data base. It could be made comparable in speed and accuracy to those now in use by the airline or the credit card industry. Once such a data base becomes operative, illegal immigrants crossing the border with false documents would become vulnerable to detection. Many others would be discouraged from entering the country without inspection because of greatly reduced prospects of finding paid employment.

The magnitude of the current open border leakage is suggested by the recent exposure of just one alien smuggling ring. The INS estimates that it brought 24,000 illegal immigrants into the country during each of four years of its existence. Mexicans would pay $650. Central and South Americans, who usually had more money, paid $1,600 to $1,700. The customers would be assembled in a small hotel in Ciudad Juarez, appropriately called "Villasana" or "Safe House." Teams of drivers would take them from there across the bridge as shoppers or tourists to El Paso during the daily rush hour traffic. From there they were moved by teams of drivers into a network of U.S. safe houses and motels in New Mexico. Most of them would then go on by train to various midwestern cities, especially Chicago.

New Mexico is a popular area for smugglers. Most of the INS staff is concentrated in Texas and California. There also is a big Mexican-American population in the area. Local people may suspect that something illegal is happening, but they usually prefer not to get involved. The ticket agent at a small hamlet, where the illegal aliens often boarded a train to Chicago, explained: "I just sell tickets. They got money, I'll give them a ticket." A local contractor noted that the whole town has been aware of shady dealings, but "people mind their own business."[5]

Illegal entries have been rationalized by some otherwise law-abiding people by noting that it simply takes too long to legally qualify for admission. A petition by a U.S. resident to enable a foreign-born spouse to become a legal resident will take at least a year to be reviewed. Some applications are lost in the process, along with all their hard-to-replace birth certificates, marriage licenses, and other documents.

Legal immigrants from Mexico, who complied with the law and completed all the necessary paperwork to be reunited with their families in Mexico, had to be told in the summer of 1981 that applications filed in 1968, thirteen years before, were just being acted upon.[6]

OTHER IMMIGRATION CONTROL TECHNIQUES

Opponents of the tamper-resistant ID document proposal often suggest a less controversial alternative: enforce minimum wage and labor standards legislation aggressively. This would increase the risk of being fined for employers, some of whom hire illegal aliens because they are more likely to accept substandard working conditions than U.S. workers.

This policy recommendation can be flawed on two counts. Most illegal immigrants are employed at or above the minimum wage, mostly in dead-end jobs, low in prestige, and high in discomfort. Many Americans will take such positions only as a last resort. But illegal immigrants evaluate such marginal employment more positively. It is better than any job they could have found in their country of origin. Labor and safety standards, even if marginal in the United States, are often absent or not enforced in their country of origin.

During the Carter administration, the enforcement of minimum wage and hour legislation was strengthened, especially in states near the Mexican border. The labor department also has a policy against blowing the whistle on an illegal alien who cooperates with them in the enforcement of labor standards. They may help secure his proper wages and may also inspect the work site to pressure the employer, if needed, to provide adequate safety precautions and other minimum standards. Their enforcement staff would have to be increased many times, not just doubled or tripled, in order to significantly reduce the violation of labor standards in marginal businesses and on some farms. What actually took place under the Reagan administration is just the opposite. Local enforcement personnel was cut all over the nation by as much as fifty percent.

Illegal immigration might also be discouraged, if the enforcement of immigration laws was less specialized. It is now a monopoly of INS. Other federal, state, and local law enforcement officers lack the authority to investigate a person's citizenship or immigration status, unless this fact is directly relevant to another violation of laws under their jurisdiction. INS officers must be contacted, if a person is to be detained for violating an immigration law.[7]

THE NEARLY OPEN BORDERS

Americans can move within and between states without anyone's permission. They can freely leave or enter their country. Freedom of mobility for aliens is more restricted. Admission to the United States, on a temporary or permanent basis, is subject to conditions legislated by Congress.

The United States has the world's record in illegal immigration, although precise data are hard to obtain. Illegal residents were undercounted by the 1980 census. Sidney Weintraub and Stanley R. Ross's thorough analysis of the available data concludes: "It is not that we don't know anything, but we don't know very much."[8] Estimates of illegal aliens range from under a million to fourteen million persons. Scholars using Mexican census data came up with much lower estimates, "no more than four million and with the probable total number being even less."[9]

A nation which cannot patrol the streets of its capital against rampant crime is understandably reluctant to employ hundreds of thousands of agents along its borders. The U.S. borders extend for 3,897.1 miles along Canada and 1,933.4 miles along Mexico. When the coasts and islands are added, roughly 96,000 miles have to be patrolled, more than twelve times the distance from the North to the South Pole.

The INS work force of 2,890 border patrol agents authorized for employment in 1982 is totally incapable of more than partial surveillance of these extensive borders. There usually are not more than 450 agents in the field during the average eight hour shift. This coverage means that only a few locations can be monitored. At the bridges across the Rio Grande River, one study showed that during rush hour only eight seconds could be devoted to screen the credentials of aliens entering by car. At airports, the time is generally less than one minute per person.

Other border related functions are exercised with equal or less intensity by eight other federal border management services. They include the Customs Office (Treasury Department), the Drug Enforcement Administration (Department of Justice), the Public Health Service (Department of Health and Welfare), the Plant Protection and Quarantine Program (Department of Agriculture), the Fish and Wildlife Service (Department of Interior), the Travel Service (Department of Commerce), the Federal Aviation Administration (Department of Transportation), and the Coast Guard (Department of Transportation).

The border crossing surveillance functions of these nine agencies are poorly coordinated. Proposals for a unified Border Management Service never went beyond the blueprint stage (*President's Reorganization Project*, 1977 and *Office of Drug Abuse Policy*, 1977). Even if their manpower and equipment could be combined, they would miss many details about who or how many persons enter the United States illegally.

The vast majority of illegal immigrants arrived undocumented. Among the 766,600 deportable aliens identified during fiscal year 1975, 87.1 percent had come to the United States without inspection. Few of them owned even a false ID document, most of which are acquired after people settle down in the United States. Of the 1.1 million illegal immigrants captured near one of the borders, only 8,700 were found to have a false ID card in their possession. They represent less than 1 in a 100 border-crossers. Others with high quality false documents evade being detected by immigration inspectors. The remainder tend to purchase such documents once they reach our shores. There also are legally admitted visitors, students, crewmen of boats, and agricultural workers who remain beyond the date which has been authorized. This large population provides a profitable market for counterfeit documents.

Modest improvements in border control have been achieved at selected border crossing points and at airports where immigration and customs inspectors began to cooperate by having a one point inspection procedure. One official of either agency checks documents, baggage, plants, animals, and exposure to infectious diseases. But each of the various services maintains its own local supervisory structure, plus regional and national offices. Vested interests in each government department, reenforced by opposition from civil service labor unions, conspire against a more comprehensive and unified border management approach.

A national machine-readable identity card would facilitate instant data exchanges among these services. Digital readers could also check identity documents with greater reliability than human inspection, to accomplish such tasks as the following:

1. Quick and gracious admission of citizens, legal immigrants and alien visitors, sailors, and other transient persons
2. Administrative adjudication and changes in immigration status within and outside of the United States
3. Exclusions of illegal or inadmissable border crossers
4. Identification of known terrorists and criminals on the basis of their biometric characteristics
5. Quarantine of persons, animals, and plants with certain diseases
6. Collection of U.S. Customs duties
7. Reduction of frequent border crossings by persons engaged in smuggling
8. Reduction of importation of illegal drugs, explosives, and other regulated substances
9. Efficient collection of statistics about immigration and the importation of goods for policy analysis and future-oriented planning

Shortfalls in the achievement of these goals is often blamed on anonymous bureaucrats. But much of the responsibility for underperformance can be traced to evasion of controversial policy options by Congress. Federal agencies, like the INS or the Social Security Administration (SSA) have been starved for funds to quickly digitalize their record keeping system. They are still expected to manage very large data files with outdated manual equipment.

REDUCING BORDER-RELATED TENSIONS

The power to review and decide on who is to be admitted is largely delegated to the Visa Section of the Department of State and the INS. Under present nonautomated procedures, their personnel rarely can respond with reasonable promptness to requests for legal admission to the United States. It is therefore tempting to try the illegal route, especially since smugglers are readily available. Some operate on a large scale; others are interested only in helping their own family.

Whenever the INS launches an enforcement campaign, protests mount quickly from religious groups, civil liberty advocates, ethnic spokespersons, and local politicians. And why not? The illegal immigrant is not a criminal. He merely is a poor person, unable to live decently back home. He is willing to work hard for low wages to support himself, often under difficult circumstances. When apprehended because he lacks proper identification, he easily becomes an object of public sympathy.

The reaction of Federal District Judge William Matthew Byrne, Jr. was typical when he ordered the INS to desist from deporting 150 of 425 Mexicans arrested there. A busload about to leave Los Angeles for Mexico was halted with an order that all those who had been apprehended be asked first if they wanted a lawyer. Lawyers for four civil rights groups told the judge that these persons were being denied access to counsel, questioned unfairly, and then pressured into signing voluntary deportation orders.[10] INS officials became instant media villains for enforcing the will of Congress.

Improved surveillance can, at best, reduce the incidence of border crossings and of organized smuggling. But it will do little to deter well financed border-crossers who want to enter the country without proper documentation. They can reach the United States comfortably in a rented pleasure boat, landing at the thousands of wharves that are not being monitored or at one of the many unchecked airstrips throughout the land. They can arrive as tourists who simply don't use their return ticket. They can obtain a temporary 72 hour pass and disappear. They can also resort to other techniques, from entering into a fictitious marriage to overstaying their leave as seamen or students. Students enrolled in the University of Pittsburgh "Semester at Sea" Program reported offers of marriage from total strangers to enable them to come to the United States as an alleged spouse from various Asian ports. Wealthy aliens can receive a visa as certified investors. They only need to bring $50,000 and invest it in a business that will employ Americans. This sum may soon be increased to $250,000 under a proposed law.

Control over U.S. immigration by means of border surveillance is a no-win situation. Congress has never been willing to allocate funds for anything close to the required manpower and equipment. What would be needed, the publisher of *U.S. News and World Report* commented editorially, "is a Berlin Wall, 18,000 miles long, turned around to keep people out."[11] Congress is understandably seeking better means to limit the admission of aliens without proper documentation.

Machine-readable entry documents, with biometric security features, would hamper this illegal traffic by making it more risky to use false or altered documents. Since digital readers could check for the in-built electronic security features, the central visa data bank would not confirm that a visa was issued.

Fewer prospective immigrants would therefore risk taking the illegal route, as did thirteen middle-class refugees from El Salvador. They had responded to an advertisement for a $1,000 bus tour to Phoenix. From there, they were to be flown to Los Angeles. The unsuspecting people who had traveled in their best clothes, including women with high heels, were walked across the border at a time when the desert heat reached as much as 160 degrees Fahrenheit. Some died from dehydration after trying to stave off death by drinking aftershave lotion, perfume and their own urine. All would have perished, but for rescue efforts of the INS Border Patrol after it discovered their presence.

In 1979, the last year for which details were available, 172,688 aliens were apprehended while being brought into the country by 15,280 smugglers. Most of them were small time operators, trying to bring in a friend or relative. 329 vehicles were seized. There are also occasional cases of actual peonage. Labor contractors have been known to purchase groups of workers, smuggled into the country, for the cost of their transportation. Like the indentured servants of earlier centuries, the group was expected to harvest crops for only a subsistence income until their debt was paid. The debt was increased by unscrupulous employers through the impositions of exorbitant fees for transportation, food, and medical care. Disputes were usually resolved in favor of the employer. Recalcitrant workers might be beaten or returned to the INS to be arrested and deported.

America is not alone in facing immigration pressures from less favored countries. Mexico imposed visa restrictions and strengthened its border control in 1983 to stem the influx of Salvadorans and Guatemalans. The minister of the interior explained that they had taken jobs away from Mexicans and caused social pressures because of the excess demand on all services. Mexico plans to issue ID cards to all its citizens to differentiate them from tens of thousands of illegal immigrants streaming into its southern border from Central American states. But such a nationwide ID program is administratively complex; it may even be beyond the nation's capabilities.

Mexican citizens are officially charged about $35 for a passport, but the actual cost can easily reach $700. People often have to give a *morbida* ("bribe") to get the required breeder documents such as a birth certificate. For males, an army discharge paper is also required. This may be difficult to secure, especially by young people who avoided doing their tour of mandatory national service. Passports are not issued without a completed file of relevant documents. Mexican officials are apt to invite a payment for expediting the process. This may be their only way to supplement their meager salaries and it is widely tolerated. The ADIT card issued by the American government is free, but it can serve the same purpose as a Mexican passport—facilitation of legal entry into the United States.

Most countries welcome tourists, international trade, and intellectual exchange when there is prosperity and a labor shortage. Well-to-do and gifted people moving across international borders are sought after. The receiving country benefits from the importation of capital and talent. Saudi Arabia and the Gulf states could not function without imported manpower necessary to their rapid modernization.

Democratic nations are even more attractive targets of opportunity for people who are poor and persecuted. Switzerland, Austria, West Germany, the Scandinavian countries, England, France, Israel, Hong Kong, Australia and some others have experienced a significant change in the cultural and ethnic composition of their population through immigration. But they have also addressed issues of how to regulate this population movement to conform to their national interest, while maintaining open borders to genuine political refugees.

TERRITORIAL THERAPY

A report of the *Economic Policy Council* of the United Nations Association of the United States[12] notes that normal population growth in the world will—at present rates—add 600 to 700 million job seekers between the year 1980 and 2000. ADIT cards, even when backed up by an effective work entitlement procedure, will not resolve controversial issues, such as: who should be admitted to the United States temporarily, as a tourist, investor or worker? And who should be entitled to permanent residence as an immigrant or refugee?

Until World War II, Europe was the main source of immigration. Among those now admitted legally, Vietnamese, Philippinos, Chinese, Indians, Mexicans, Caribbean Islanders and other non-Europeans predominate.

No major American political or social group is in favor of totally open borders. No one advocates that they be entirely closed. But on one issue there is little debate: Who should decide who comes to the United States: the government or those who are in the immigrant smuggling business? The validity of entry documents has a bearing on this question.

Illegal immigrants are not constrained by the requirement of acquiring proper documents. A few, most of them with money, purchase false documents. Most of the remainder enter the country without being inspected at the border. They purchase false ID documents after their arrival. Most of the remainder are young and single, from neighboring Mexico or the Caribbean Islands. Quite a few return home several times a year. Mexican government researchers in 1978 found that the average deportee, whom they were able to interview, admitted an average of 1.89 illegal border crossings during the prior year.[13]

Why do people want to migrate in such large numbers? Few aliens are casual about leaving the community where they are born; few wish to part forever from where their families are rooted without compelling reasons. Many more seek *territorial therapy* to escape a hopeless environment in exchange for a country with more opportunity. Others fear for their lives. Lofty human rights statements embodied in United Nations resolutions have not diminished the prevalence of misery which generates migration pressure in so many parts of the world, both within and between nations.

The right to asylum for persons who are persecuted on political, racial, religious or other grounds is enshrined in U.S. law. Before World War II, this right was interpreted very restrictively. While ID card technology was not well developed and false documents could be produced easily, few refugees were able to stay in the country illegally for lack of employment opportunities. The frightful human rights violations that took place around the world were played down and sometimes censored. Relatively few permanent reporters were stationed in the various trouble spots. David Wyman has distilled the inescapable conclusion from U.S. diplomatic archives that:[14]

> The American State Department and the British Foreign Office had no intention of rescuing large numbers of European Jews. On the contrary, they continually feared that Germany or other Axis nations might release tens of thousands of Jews into allied hands. Any such exodus would have placed intense pressure on Britain to open Palestine and on the U.S. to take in more Jewish refugees, a situation the two great powers did not want to face. Consequently, their policies aimed at obstructing rescue possibilities and dampening public pressure for Government action.

At present, the American government takes leadership in mobilizing world interest in human rights. It contributes more than other nations to rescuing some of the victims from nations where human rights violations are widespread. Official policy comes close to the sentiments expressed by Rev. James R. Nelson, before the Subcommittee on Immigration and Refugee Policy of the U.S. Senate:[15]

> As long as there are refugees in the world we need to do our part in providing for them. For the Cubans, the Indochinese and others of most recent as well as the distant past, we still offer a sanctuary of opportunity. It was the force that brought the first pilgrims to these shores. We simply need to understand that the pilgrims have been coming here since 1610, and no doubt will continue to do so as long as we seek to stay the 'land of the free.'

The doors are kept open to refugees, but their number is limited. As a result, there are many who arrive illegally. If caught, they are likely to apply for legalized status by documenting their refugee condition.

A Chicago based Religious Task Force on Central America coordinates information for these illegal refugees. It includes about four hundred and fifty religious congregations willing to support the idea that these people be offered sanctuary, even if they are not accorded such a status by the INS. The congregations include American Baptist, Community Bible, Brethren, Episcopalian, Lutheran, Mennonite, Presbyterian, Quaker, Roman Catholic and other churches, plus some Jewish congregations. Some of the religious leaders were arrested in 1985, but they defended their illegal activities on the basis of a higher moral law. The issue will have to be decided in the federal court. Church leaders can point to tragic cases, like a young El Salvadorian, who was deported, arrested at the airport upon arrival, and never heard from again.

GENOCIDE PREVENTION

A refugee has been defined by the UN as:

> A person who owing to well-founded fear of being persecuted for fear of race, religion, nationality, membership in a particular social group or political opinion is outside the country of his original nationality and is unable, or owing to such fear, is unwilling to avail himself of the protection of such country.

The United States went beyond the spirit of this definition in the *Refugee Act of 1980* (Public Law 96–212), also including "any person who is within the country of such person's nationality . . . who is persecuted or has a well founded fear of persecution." In all other respects, refugees are like migrants: *ordinary people in extraordinary circumstances.*[16] The United Nations Convention on the Status of Refugees asserts that refugees are entitled to the same basic human rights as nationals of the asylum country.

No country lives up to this principle in full. For some of those who enter the United States without inspection from the Caribbean Islands and from Central America, the distinction between a genuine refugee and illegal immigrant is blurred. They want to escape the deadly combination of poverty, dictatorship, and hopelessness in the land of their birth. The 1985 survey from Freedom House showed that 42 percent of the human race is living in oppressive countries; another 23 percent live in nations which are only partly free. These ratings are based on the analysis of existing political rights, civil liberties, and on the treatment of political dissidents. Refugees are primarily generated in the 53 "not free" countries. There are relatively few refugees from the 59 partly free nations like Kenya, Jordan, Egypt and Senegal. Thirty-five percent of the world's population, in 53 countries, live in the free world, where they can expect full protection of their right to privacy and dignity.[17]

In a number of countries, much military and state administrative power is exerted to prevent emigration. East Germany has collected ransoms for people regarded unfavorably or who are in prison for political offenses. West Germany pays it quietly on a per capita basis. For a time, Rumania required that emigrants pay a tax equal to the alleged cost of their education. Professional persons had to be ransomed by friends from the outside or had to raise funds several times their annual earnings. The Soviet Union, Ethiopia, and Syria are using people who want to emigrate as a bargaining chip in international negotiations. As mentioned previously, Castro's Cuba has offered to allow dissidents to leave if the United States would accept them. Foreign Minister Nguyen Xo Thach of Vietnam offered to free all labor camp inmates if the United States would accept them.

The United States and other free countries are thus targeted with blame for the fate of these unfortunates. Asylum privileges are actually available for only a token number of those who would like to emigrate. If the free countries would open their gates to welcome them all, the volume of asylum seekers would quickly exceed current immigration quotas. It is not likely that such a massive population movement would receive domestic support in the receiving countries.

Human beings continue to be used as weapons of political and ideological warfare in many parts of the world. There have been many instances of genocide since World War II—in Bangladesh, the Sudan, Cambodia, Uganda, Ruanda, and elsewhere. The 1981 U.S. State Department *Country Report on the World Refugee Situation* notes that it is impossible to get an agreed estimate because of differing definitional perspectives and insufficient information about refugees. But about 7.5 million from over 45 countries were receiving assistance from the international community in first asylum nations. Some may ultimately be able to return home. A few will be able to migrate. Many will have no place to go, condemned to a life of never ending temporary asylum. The numbers have grown since then.

Severe immigration restrictions are now in place in all Western countries. No one knows how many Vietnamese boat people drowned for lack of concern for their rescue. Hunger and fear stalk many of the developing countries of the world. In the Sahel region, in Somalia, and in Ethiopia, food often cannot reach the starving people who manage to reach a camp. Millions have become victims of deliberate murder for holding unpopular views or for belonging to a minority ethnic or racial group.

The *Dishonor List* of countries is long—very long, from Afghanistan to Lebanon, from India and Pakistan to Burundi, from Uganda to Indonesia, not to mention the mass exterminations by Cambodia's Pot Pol of its own people. Only a small proportion of these victims have a territorial therapy option, the opportunity to migrate to a free nation, where human rights tend to be honored. Both West Germany and Sweden have reversed their welcome mat for foreign workers. Policy makers want to radically reduce competition between foreign workers and the growing number of domestic unemployed. Some are also alarmed over forecasts that foreigners who are already in these countries will be the parents of 10 percent of the school population in the year 2000. For the first time in their history, Sweden and West Germany have sizable ethnic minorities.

The British government reversed its immigration policy even more drastically. It enacted the Nationality Act of 1982, which deprived most residents of former colonies and Commonwealth territories of their former right to come to England and to settle there. Persons born in Hong Kong or Bermuda now need special permits to come to England. A seven century old tradition of *ius soli* was abandoned; children born in Great Britain would no longer acquire British citizenship automatically. Each application would have to be made individually to the Home Office in London.

The new law repealed an act passed 35 years earlier when some 950 milion people in the more than 47 mostly non-White members of the British Commonwealth were offered citizenship by their former rulers. Great Britain is a heavily populated and small island nation of 57 million inhabitants. Public opinion has turned against this open door to Commonwealth citizens. Some of the opposition is generated by concerns about job competition. Others fear that Great Britain would experience increased tensions that would be racially or ethnically based.

The lack of control over illegal immigration into the United States provides fuel to the expression of similar antiforeign sentiments in the U.S. But they are balanced by forces favorable to a more open door policy. Since 1950, the United States admitted more than half of the homeless accepted anywhere for permanent settlement.

ID CARD UTILITY

Congress and the executive want to exercise their responsibility to decide who among the multitudes of persecuted persons are to be given asylum. Staff and budget shortages and the inability to efficiently store and retrieve information also limits the capacity of the INS to exercise these delegated powers. Under the law, this agency is expected to promptly facilitate the enjoyment of certain rights of resident aliens:

1. The right of certain nonimmigrants and temporary residents to adjust their status to that of a permanent resident or a United States citizen.

2. The right to family unification, under quota preferences for aliens who have been admitted to permanent residency in America or as refugees.
3. Work permits for temporary resident aliens. Some may be stranded, while their sources of income from abroad are cut by unrest of revolution at home. Others are here as students.
4. The right to travel outside the United States or visit their country of origin, with a guarantee of being allowed to return.
5. The right to apply for U.S. citizenship. 158,276 persons were naturalized in fiscal year 1979.

The processing of papers to facilitate these rights can be subject to delay for months and even years. The INS is often unable to find a person's file or lacks the staff to deal with cases promptly. Delays in serving the needs of immigrants leads to reliance on expensive immigration experts just to process paper work which should be done free of charge by the staff of this agency employed to serve the public.

The INS pays a heavy price in administrative efficiency for lacking the staff and the budget to manufacture and distribute ADIT cards more rapidly. This also slows down its capability to computerize its sizable record system. The "too costly" argument, even when made by such prestigious Federal agencies as the Comptroller General of the Unites States, is contradicted by the experience of private industry. But as long as the INS has to continue to operate with a precomputer record storage and retrieval system, the entitlements of aliens will continue to be dealt with slowly and often outside the law. As the *New York Times* commented editorially:[18]

> Undocumented farm workers from Mexico, for instance, may be brave and industrious. But each takes a place that, if society were choosing fairly, might be assigned instead to a refugee from Somalia, a sister from Korea or a more deserving Mexican (legal) applicant. The country is not now making the choice.

BEYOND THE IMMIGRATION ISSUE

Curbing illegal immigration is too narrow a policy base on which the issue of a national ID card should be debated. Valid Identification Program (VIP) documents are needed because security and privacy in general in the United States are in jeopardy without them. The probability for being victimized is mushrooming in a nation where people can easily masquerade under multiple identities.

As noted, the United States can claim the world record in reliance on false identity documents. There are no federal, state, or local standards that govern the many public, private, or business enterprises which issue the ID cards we carry in our wallets. This freedom comes at a price. It can be calculated in terms of distrust, in the purchase of guns to protect our homes, and in the growing frequency of burglar alarm installations.

Technology is constantly changing how Americans live. Automobile and airplane travel expose more and more people to an environment where nothing is known about them. Home computers provide instant access to information sources all over the world. Computerized shopping, computer dating, and electronic employment brokerage services are already here. The accuracy of personal identification in such transactions will have to be geared to fit the crime prevention requirements of electronic mail, checkless banking, and computerized record keeping.[19] The first case of "computer terror" reached the Los Angeles County courts in April 1985. Two teenagers calling themselves "Modem Maniacs" left extortion messages and death threats on the home computers of people in their area.

BACKDOOR TO A FORMAL NATIONAL ID SYSTEM

If politicians were the guardians of conventional wisdom, the question of a national ID card would still be in the closet. No major national figure is in favor of the wide loophole through which it is easy to acquire and use multiple identities. But not even top FBI officials wish to be quoted that they favor combating crimes by resorting to a national identity card. What is denied in theory, however, is already on the process of becoming an accomplished reality. More and more government and business agencies are relying on improved identifiers, issued under somewhat controlled conditions to minimize fraud.

There are taboos in every culture, ideas regarded by "conventional wisdom" as inherently evil and unacceptable. The national ID roster represents such a taboo in the U.S.A., Canada, and Great Britain. Its underlying axioms are therefore not subjected to critical analysis by specialists, who know that American vital statistics records are an open invitation to the fraudulent acquisition of false identity records. But many of them fear to express views favorable to comprehensive ID card reform that are apt to be labeled reactionary or insensitive to the risk of preparing the groundwork for totalitarianism.

It is within this context that the legislative strategy of the pending immigration reform and control legislation must be understood. Its sponsors hope to avoid getting entangled in the emotional controversy about the pros annd cons of a nationwide ID card system. Precise details for a work entitlement document are not spelled out. Implementation would be worked out during a three year study under the direction of the president. Six options were mentioned in staff meetings and in congressional hearings:

1. *Status Quo Maintenance.* Employees would present any of the existing ID documents to support their entitlement to accept a job in the United States. The employer would be asked to keep a record of these documents, to be available for spot-checks made either by the Department of Labor or the INS.

   Counterfeit documents could still be used. An employer would not be expected to evaluate the validity of each document presented to him. He only would need to keep a new set of records about what documents had been shown to him.

2. *Spot Check System.* Each potential employee would complete a form providing information and documentation about his or her work entitlement. The employer would transmit the records periodically to the INS. Its staff could spot check them for discrepancies against their own data base. Short term employment of illegals might go undetected, since the INS would not be able to check its records within twenty four hours.

   Employees suspected of being in the country illegally could be asked by the INS to present additional documentation about their work entitlement. This option would require a good deal of paperwork, spot-checking and detention of persons found to be working. There would be no improvement in technical standards of quality of the commonly used American ID documents.

3. *Telephone Data Bank System.* A government agency, possibly the Department of Labor, would develop a nationwide file of persons eligible to accept employment in the United States. Persons entering the job market for the first time or changing jobs would be among the first to be enumerated. After a few years, the annual rate of registration would decline to about twelve million persons per annum.

   Each individual would be given a number, corresponding to his central file. It would contain non-stigmatizing identity facts, such as the person's first and last name, mother's first name, and citizenship.

   As part of the hiring process, an employer would check by phone that the applicant was registered. The employer would then be given a code number to document that he had checked the credentials. He would not need keep a new set of files. But there would be no thorough check to identify false documents or persons who laid claim to several identities.

4. *Improved Social Security Card.* All Americans who receive wages, pay taxes or earn interests must have a Social Security Number (SSN). Provisions are on the drawing board to make the cards more tamper-

resistant by producing them on controlled paper, similar to that used to print money.

This would make it less urgent to adopt a new document, but the projected new Social Security card revision would fall very much short of being tamper-resistant. Professional criminals who counterfeit twenty dollar bills could also duplicate the new Social Security card or steal blanks from its headquarters. Other safety features and a biometric indicator would need to be added.

5. *National but Locally Administered Standards for ID Card Security and Privacy.* The Federal Government could adopt national standards governing technical security features to be incorporated in the future issue of identity documents. The standards could be enforced by law or by inducing voluntary compliance by offering a federal subsidy to State Bureaus of Vital Statistics to pay for the extra cost necessary to verify information before it is used on breeder ID documents, like birth certificates.

Under this procedure, the incidence of counterfeit prone ID documents would be reduced gradually, without adding a new administrative function at the federal level that would have to deal directly with every American. But the standardized cards would function much like *de facto* national ID documents, comparable to a drivers license or a Social Security card. It would be technically simple to make the different state systems compatible to facilitate quick verification of documents under circumstances when Congress would authorize it. This procedure would preserve existing state functions in the maintenance of birth and death records.

6. *A National ID Card, Federally Administered.* Issue of a national identification card, that could be used for many different purposes. It would use technically advanced features to attain a high level of resistance to be being stolen, altered or counterfeited. The card could include imprinting space for additional information that could be stored at the initiative of the holder. Such modifications would be made at his expense and thus would provide a source of income for the government.

Micro-chip cards and laser-print cards can accommodate such additional information. Access to it could be restricted by security features and codes under the control of the holder. Individuals could thus reduce the number of cards they need to carry. Congress could review the details of any such proposal and monitor its implementation.

Some legislators would prefer the elimination of any document verification feature from the pending immigration reform legislation. But the majority of Congress appears to regard this feature as crucial if a preventive emphasis is to replace the current palliative strategy to control America's borders. Without replacing America's easily compromised identification procedures, they see no likelihood of being able to enforce any immigration policy.

The immigration control issue is thus acting as a catalyst bringing a much broader and quite different issue into the forefront of public policy: should the United States change the way identity documents are issued, monitored, used, and protected against fraud and misrepresentation? How would this added federal responsibility impact on administration of public and private programs that offer services in return for personal information? Arguments for and against a national ID system will be reviewed in the next two chapters.

REFERENCES

1. Westin, Alan F., "Home Information Systems: The Privacy Debate," *Datamation* July 1982:113.

2. Davis, Ruth M., Institute for Computer Sciences and Technology, United States Bureau of Standards, United States Department of Commerce. Springfield, VA: FIPS Pub. 48, April 1, 1977:8.

3. International Civil Aviation Organization. (ICAO), *Working Paper on Passport Travel Documents*, Montreal, Canada: April, 1974.

4. General Accounting Office, *Controls Over Non-Immigrant Aliens Remain Ineffective*, Washington, D.C., GAO 1980: 4–6.

5. *The New York Times*, July 12, 1982.

6. *Pittsburgh Press*, August 16, 1981.

7. Comptroller General of the United States, *Administrative Changes Needed to Reduce Employment of Illegal Aliens*. Washington, D.C.: General Accounting Office, HRD 81–15., January 30, 1981.

8. Weintraub, Sidney and Stanley Ross, *The Illegal Alien From Mexico: Policy Choices for an Intractable Issue*, Austin, Texas: The University of Texas, Mexico–United States Border Research Program, 1980.

9. Warren, Robert and Jeffrey S. Passel, "Estimate of Illegal Aliens From Mexico Counted in the 1980 United States Census," Population Division, U.S. Bureau of the Census, Washington, D.C., 20233. A paper presented at the annual meeting of the Population Association of America, Pittsburgh, Pennsylvania, April 14–16, 1983.

10. *The New York Times*, April 30, 1982:p.A10.

11. *U.S. News and World Report*, April 12, 1982.

12. Economic Policy Council of the United Nations Association, New York, 300 East 42 Street, New York 10017, 1981.

13. Cross, Harry E. and James A. Sandor, *Across the Border*, University of California at Berkeley, Institute of Governmental Studies, 1981.

14. Wyman, David S., *The Abandonment of the Jews: America and the Holocaust, 1941–1945*, N.Y., Pantheon Books, 1984.

15. Nelson, James R., Remarks before the Subcommittee on Immigration and Refugee Policy of the U.S. Senate. October 8, 1981, Serial No. J–97–68.

16. U.S. State Department. *Country Report on the World Refugee Situation*, Office of the United States Coordinator For Refugee Affairs, Washington, D.C., September 1981.

17. Gastil, Raymond D., "The Comparative Survey of Freedom, 1985," *Freedom At Issue*, January–February 1985, number 82:3–16.

18. *The New York Times*, March 1, 1981.

19. Little, Arthur P., Inc. *The Consequences of Electronic Fund Transfer*, Washington, D.C.: United States Government Printing Office, 1975.

CHAPTER FOUR

THE CASE FOR A VIP CARD

NEWISM: IS INNOVATION ALWAYS AN IMPROVEMENT?

In much of the world, tradition dominates. Social and technological changes face an uphill fight. Cows are left to roam in India while many people are malnourished. In the United States, traditionalism is on the defensive. The theory of "Newism" is in the ascendancy: "If it is new, it's better."[1]

Last year's model car is allegedly outdated. Yesterday's best seller is displaced by a new one. The media bombard the public with an unending succession of new and improved products. People buy them, generally at higher cost, and sometimes without a proven utility.

Are tamper-proof ID programs such a faddish innovation? Or are they part of a permanent shift in how Americans want to interact with one another? In 1982, losses through credit card fraud were nearly three times the losses from bank robbery, $128 million compared to only $46.8 million. Inadequate security precautions in the manufacture, distribution, and use of most ordinary credit cards invite such abuses.

"Smart Cards" which include a microchip have been invented, as have laser printed cards. Both types have the capacity to store information about access restrictions, and have readability only to persons authorized by code, a PIN number, or specific biometric features. Each card can store the code number of all persons using it and of digital reader machines used to decipher its content. These features provide a high level of protection against fraud and misuse, much above that of any of the existing ID documents. They also can give each holder information about any and all uses made of his document, in case he suspects that his privacy may have been compromised. No paper file provides such a high degree of protection against anonymous snooping. These interactive cards are being increasingly considered, by both government and business organizations and cost about $1.50. They can keep track of banking and retail transactions eliminating many clerical handling costs and errors.[2]

At the University of Pittsburgh, many of the coin operated photocopy machines are now controlled by a plastic card. Its microcomputers can be set to reflect a fee paid by each user. After 60 pages have been copied, the tiny memory in the plastic card will cease to authorize its further use. An additional fee must be paid to get it recharged. The university can thus reduce its costs for money changing machines in the library and funds for the photocopying machines can be collected at one location. Employees formerly needed to empty the machines can be given other tasks. The check-out desk is less busy since it no longer has to provide change to operate the photocopy equipment. The price of each card is $ .45. It can be validated repeatedly for any amount upon payment of the fee. But it does not include in-built ID characteristics. Like money, the card can be used by anyone who has possession of it.

Among information specialists in government and industry, there is growing interest in adopting this technology. Biometric indicators are generally avoided, although they provide a high level of security against misuse. Even the more commonly used safety features, such as watermarks and coded high-energy magnetic stripes, provide a much higher level of security than most of the existing credit cards. They can be made impervious to being changed by a magnetic field. The cards can also be enclosed in a tamper-resistant laminate.

COMMERCIAL UTILITY

Automatic Teller Machines (ATM Cards) enable the public to do their banking at any time of the day or night, including Sundays. Gone are the banker's hours that forced people to do their business at times that often were inconvenient. Banks are also beginning to push electronic check cards. When used, they authorize instantaneous transfer of funds from the account of the purchaser to the account of the seller. Before the buyer walks out with the merchandise, the merchant knows he has been paid. The savings in the reduction of bad checks and reduced labor costs more than cover the cost of installing "Point of Sale Terminals," at least in the larger retail stores.

Army trainees at Fort Benjamin Harrison in Indiana will soon get a computer paycheck. Those with a bank account will get their pay deposited directly. An estimated 3,000 trainees without bank accounts will collect their own pay from a cardless automatic teller machine. They simply have to place their hand over a fingermatrix reading device. The digital dimensions of each soldier's fingerprints will release an amount of cash equal to his or her pay for the month. The convenience of such cashless transactions also explains their use when banks transfer money between themselves or across continents by electronic means. There are fewer expensive transfers of gold and of banknotes to tempt crime syndicates to plan robberies.

The use of uniquely programmed cards to replace hotel room keys is just one of many other uses to which identity cards are being put. A previous occupant of the room will not be able to enter it, as he might, if he had kept the key that was issued to him.

Secret documents to be read by only a limited number of persons can be imprinted on a laser card. Even if they were to fall into unauthorized hands, they could not be deciphered except by the individuals whose biometric measures and/or code numbers are imprinted in the cards. When they are reproduced on a terminal, the code number, the time the material was deciphered, and other information can be programmed to be recorded permanently on each card. A hostile mob, invading a U.S. embassy, as occurred in Teheran, could have captured such cards and a digital reading machine, without being able to access the encoded information. Bulky documents could be reproduced on one plastic card, up to about 800 pages of text. This would greatly facilitate the transportation and storage of restricted documents and their quick destruction under conditions of emergency.

PEONAGE REDUCTION

There were no passports or identity cards when the biblical patriarch Jacob took his flock of seventy Hebrews to Egypt to escape a famine in the Holy Land. For generations, his descendants continued to be identified as foreigners. Later they were exploited as slaves until a mass exodus led them to liberation.

Exploitation of immigrants is a worldwide phenomenon. When their very presence is illegal, they are apt to be a most accommodating source of labor and avoid legal appeals. Even when they are victimized, illegal residents have reason to be afraid to protest to the police. The Department of Justice was reported to be investigating 25 forced labor cases in 11 states in 1981. Employees were paid low wages and charged for their expenses so they were continually in debt. Force was sometimes threatened or used to keep them on the job until they paid off their contrived indebtedness.[3]

The proposed employer sanctions backed up by a trustworthy ID system would take the profit out of peonage. No amount of exploitation through the payment of substandard wages could compensate an employer for the risk of being fined or imprisoned for knowingly hiring an undocumented worker. The extreme economic abuse of illegal aliens would become rare, as would the employment of that much larger majority who are hired at or above the minimum wage.

A more promigrant alternative to reduce economic exploitation was proposed by economist Mark Perlman. He proposes that entrepreneurs could be discouraged from hiring illegals by providing the workers with an entitlement to receive a terminal pay bonus and then have the employer pay for the cost of their homebound journey. The INS would pay out the money and then collect it from the employer. Illegal aliens, if hired after they earned some badly needed cash, would acquire an economic incentive to leave the country voluntarily.

It will be quite controversial for the INS to take employers to court on a criminal charge of knowingly harboring an illegal alien. Criminal offenses are apt to be fought hard by resorting to legal technicalities and time consuming jury trials. It would be easier for the government to enforce civil laws for payment of legislatively authorized benefits on behalf of an illegal immigrant.

COMBATTING THE FORGERY INDUSTRY

The false document industry in the United States is able to function well in part because biometric indicators are not widely used. Without fingerprints, retinal eye patterns, a digitally readable signature, or other unique personal characteristics, it is easy to use multiple identity documents. They can be acquired with little risk. There also is no link between birth and death registration. The Vital Statistics offices of fifty-seven states and territories where these data are collected are independent of each other and no clearinghouse exists for the detection of falsified vital statistics.

There is *some* procedural coordination through the National Center for Health Statistics, first instituted in 1977. It maintains a close working relationship with the Association of State and Territorial Health Officials and the American Association for Vital Records and Public Health Statistics. But these professional bodies have avoided confronting the politically controversial question: can more be done to enforce standards of accuracy and validity in the roughly eight thousand villages, cities, and counties, each of which can issue birth and death certificates? And can these records be coordinated to reduce the prevalence of false ID documents throughout the nation?

A birth certificate is now mandatory in all states. But these documents are poorly protected against misuse. For a fee, an enterprising white collar criminal will locate a dead person with characteristics that roughly match the race, age, and sex of a person who wants a new identity. Each death certificate shows the place of birth. A certified copy of the birth certificate can then be procured, often by doing nothing more than writing a letter, accompanied by a check for a nominal fee. In Pennsylvania, for instance, only a simple application form needs to be filled out. No reason needs to be provided for wishing to obtain a copy.

H105.102   REV. 11-81   PENNSYLVANIA DEPARTMENT OF HEALTH   If Veteran (✓)
VITAL RECORDS   See Other Side

APPLICATION FOR CERTIFIED COPY OF BIRTH OR DEATH RECORD

PLEASE PRINT OR TYPE   To avoid delay please complete all items.

DO NOT WRITE IN THIS SPACE

INDICATE NUMBER OF COPIES	BIRTH $4.00 DEATH $3.00	
Date of Birth/ Or Date of Death	Place of Birth Or Place of Death County Twp. or Borough	
		File No.
Name at Birth Or Name at Death	SEX	Index By Search By
Father's Name First Middle Last		Certified No.
Mother's Maiden Name First Middle Last		Refund Ck. No.
Hospital Funeral Director		Date — Amount
Reason for Request (Check One): ☐ School ☐ Marriage ☐ Passport ☐ Other (Specify)		
How Are You Related to This Person?		Postage: $
Applicant's Signature		
Applicant's No. Street		
Address City State Zip Code		
Applicant's Phone No. Area Code Number		

Prices for Certified Copies Are: Births: $4.00 each — Deaths: $3.00 each
PLEASE DO NOT SEND CASH.
Check or Money Order should be made payable to VITAL RECORDS
Please enclose self-addressed stamped envelope for return of copies.
Records available are from 1906 to the present

☐ Prev. Amend ☐ Adopt ☐ Affidavit
☐ Usage ☐ Court Order ☐ Issue Affidavit

PENNSYLVANIA DEPARTMENT OF HEALTH
APPLICATION FOR CERTIFIED COPY OF BIRTH OR DEATH RECORD

With a genuine birth certificate, a forgery-bent person can then procure a U.S. passport. He can travel abroad and make financial transactions under several names. If he is an alien, he can begin to enjoy the entitlements of American citizenship, including the right to vote. No one will know, for instance, how many foreign criminals were able to escape detection in the United States in such a disguise, secure from discovery because they had assumed the identity of a dead person.

The procedures are explained in detail in an Eden Press publication, *The New Paper Trip.*[4] Over 100,000 copies are claimed to have been sold by the publisher. For $14.95, the mail delivers 160 pages of instructions on how to circumvent data protection procedures. The book promises to disclose "everything you ever wanted to know about disappearing, leaving your past behind, and becoming someone else." An additional $2.00 will bring a supplementary pamphlet on *100 Ways to Disappear and Live Free.*[5] Advocates of guerilla war in the United States also included instruction on "Change of Identification" in their revolutionary manual, *The Road Back.*[6]

The false document industry has international connections. Forged papers are produced and distributed both in the United States and abroad, especially in Mexico, Columbia, the Philippine Islands, Hong Kong, the Arab countries, Iran, and Canada. One 20 year old man, when arrested with a suitcase filled with counterfeit documents, confessed that it had earned him $45,000 during the prior six month period. False Social Security cards were going for thirty dollars each in the Dallas Flea Market. Fraudulent birth certificates would bring more, as much as $1,000. John Edwards, a self-styled immigration consultant, was convicted and jailed for furnishing false documents to persons who wanted to use them. More than 1,500 bogus Social Security cards, birth certificates, and federal immigration registration cards were found in his possession.

For five to ten dollars, a more primitive ID card can be purchased through the mail. The cards are used mostly by juveniles to purchase liquor. No effort is made by the seller to verify the information provided by the applicant. These cards can even be purchased in some department stores. Mail-order business is solicited through advertisements in college newspapers and other general magazines.

The cards are well designed to look like an official document. One version has as its heading: "State of New York," with an official seal of the "Bureau of Identification." There is no such bureau and the business is headquartered in Berkeley, California. The cards can be shipped anywhere in America, except to Colorado and Kansas, where it is prohibited by state law.

Counterfeit documents are so commonplace that only the more flagrant offenders can be investigated. Less than half of all smuggling of alien cases are prosecuted. Many violations are reduced to a misdemeanor for reasons of administrative expediency, mostly to save expensive court trials. Witnesses often disappear; some are deported; others escape from detention centers. One U.S. assistant attorney was quoted, "They (INS investigators) have the information. They simply don't have the resources to put the big case together. . . . If you get caught bringing drugs in, you get 10 years. If you are caught bringing in aliens, you get nothing."[7] Some cases are closed because prosecutors take too much time to reach trial. Punishments are generally minimal. Prosecution is not now a significant deterrent to what is a highly profitable international underworld industry.

Identity misrepresentation is often an essential part of more dangerous law violations. Mafia mobsters, spies, and assassins can freely move in and out of the United States. The growth of international terrorism raises the prospects that hostile elements will take advantage of America's chaotic approach to personal identification to transport more dangerous substances than heroin and other narcotics: nuclear weapons, potent poisons, or plague-producing bacteria.

Tamper-resistant ID documents will only marginally deter terrorists who are often agents of hostile governments and travel on a diplomatic passport. Terrorists also have a compulsive political motivation and will take heavy risks. But professional hit men could no longer move freely if diplomatic passports were to include fingerprint or other biometric indicators. Their identity, once known, could not be camouflaged. They would have to be retired, to be replaced by less experienced and often more vulnerable operators.

Good ID documents can certainly significantly reduce the incidence of white collar crimes; acts committed by nonphysical means, by concealment of guile; to obtain money or property; to avoid payment or loss of money or property; or to obtain personal advantage.[8] Many white-collar crimes are based on rational cost-benefit calculation. Offenders will have to worry about the added risk of becoming entrapped by computerized verification procedures, which cannot be held up with a gun, bribed, or blackmailed like people can.

A more effective system would not be a panacea. It will take years to transform America's existing identification procedures. Not even the most sophisticated tamper-resistant ID is immune to abuse, but only highly skilled, well financed persons with insider contacts can even attempt the complex process of compromising a security focused ID system. The average white-collar criminal will be put out of business. Even the well staffed and financed secret services of various nations will rarely, if ever, be able to circumvent the growing variety of safety precautions for very long, without being detected.

SOCIAL SECURITY AS A NATIONAL IDENTIFIER

The unreliable ID documents now so widely used generate a great deal of administrative waste. Nothing illustrates this better than the Social Security Number (SSN). It is issued on the basis of the following information supplied by the applicant:

- Real name
- Name used at work or in business, if it is different
- Date and place of birth
- Present age

- Mother's maiden name
- Father's name
- Sex
- Color or race
- Mailing address
- Telephone number

The Social Security card is printed on simple paper stock. And why not on more tamper-resistant paper? It was originally designed for just one use—to track earnings that determine the level of Social Security taxes credited to each account. The use of two cards or numbers could only hurt the individual concerned by reducing the record of earnings that determines his benefits upon retirement. However, if he could succeed in collecting double benefits, he would gain financially, although collecting such payments is illegal. There also was no apparent need to keep the original information up to date, except for official name changes. Current addresses and telephone numbers are not needed until an individual wants a service from the Social Security Administration (SSA), such as a disability or retirement pension.

The first step of turning the SSN from a specific program into a general numerical identifier was taken in 1943. Executive Order 9379 authorized all Federal agencies to use this same number. In 1961, the Civil Service Commission adopted it as the identification number for all federal employees. The Internal Revenue Service requires its use for filing tax returns. In 1967 the Department of Defense dropped its own numbering system for military personnel and replaced it with the SSN. States were subsequently authorized to use it for tax purposes, drivers licenses, motor vehicle registration, and entitlement benefits. Although in 1976 a law was passed by Congress prohibiting additional pressure on people to give their SSN without their consent, such refusals are rare.

More and more private businesses, educational institutions, and medical facilities use the SSN as an index to their personal files. In spite of its unreliability as a unique personal identifier, this number is now used widely on drivers' licenses and on other state and local documents. A false Social Security card can thus become a breeder document for a whole set of legally issued identity records. Each is technically genuine. It allows a criminal to operate under an identity other than his own.

Before 1978, anyone was able to secure a valid SSN and card by mail. Nothing was done to verify the information given. It was not a crime to counterfeit, alter, lend, sell, or reproduce a Social Security Card until the passage of Public Law 97–123 in December 1981, provided the background seal of the Department of Health and Human Services was excluded in the false document. A publicity conscious entrepreneur obtained a Social Security Card for *Waterhole Ike,* a syndicated beer guz-zling pig.

After 1972, applicants who were age 18 or over or were foreign born were required to submit evidence of age, identity, citizenship or alien sta-tus. But it was not until 1978 that *all* applicants had to submit such evi-dence. The thoroughness of the inspection of the validity of these docu-ments varies with the sophistication of the individual SSN employee. Only quite recently has the SSA begun to provide staff training in how to spot forgeries.

Close to 300 million legal cards have been officially issued since the start of the program. Over 1,300 SSA offices take applications for about 13 million requests for new and duplicate cards every year. Errors or acci-dental use of previously assigned numbers are unlikely because the ac-tual card is issued centrally from SSA headquarters. Sometimes, few persons acquire more than one number when they marry, change their name, or because they forgot their previous number.

In 1938 the Woolworth chain sold a plastic wallet with a John Doe sample Social Security card. Over 25,000 people have since then used this number. 1943 was the record year, with 5,755 wage earners reporting their income on it. Even in the 1980s, about ten earnings a year were still being reported under this number although it was never assigned to any-one. There are twenty additional "pocketbook" numbers. Advertisers are now urged to use impossible numbers which will be rejected by the elec-tronic system. But there is no law forbidding businesses to use fictitious SSN numbers for advertising purposes.

Legislative reforms can and probably will reduce these misuses. But the Social Security card will continue to remain a less than trustworthy per-sonal identifier until all outstanding cards are reissued and after careful verification of the true identity of each card holder. Forgeries or other misuses of Social Security cards are now a felony, punishable up to one year in prison and/or a fine of up to $5,000. As a further deterrent, plans have been adopted to issue future cards on banknote paper. For budget-ary reasons, this change had been postponed for years, although the esti-mated cost of replacing half of the existing cards with the new and more secure version is only 1.3 million dollars.

We only have occasional clues to the number of persons with more than one SSN for fraudulent purposes. For instance, the agriculture depart-ment's inspector general requested a validation match of 750,000 SSNs furnished by food stamp recipients in Illinois. About 130,000 numbers (over 17 percent) were invalid. A legal interpretation, which was later re-versed, led to a ruling that Federal privacy legislation would prohibit dis-closure of these contradictions from the SSA to the INS.

Since 1974, aliens *not* allowed to work in the United States have been issued a restricted Social Security card. They need one to report nonwage income from dividends and interests for tax purposes. Nevertheless, earnings of 326,280 persons were registered by February 1982 for credit to such "no employment authorized" SSNs.

No campaign has been under consideration to eliminate this large group of illegal wage earners and to deport them en masse. A manhunt of unprecedented proportion would be required to locate, charge, convict, and deport these persons. The federal courts would be clogged for years with appeals against hundreds of thousands of deportation orders. Federal prisons, already dangerously overcrowded with serious offenders, would be unable to handle the additional load.

A systematic investigation of these cases also would turn up many refugees from dictatorial countries. They could not be deported to Poland or Chile without violation of America's "political asylum" tradition.

A more efficient deterrent is needed than the prosecution of immigration law offenders who are detected by a discrepancy between their earning record and their immigration status prohibiting them from accepting gainful employment. Neither the INS nor the SSA have the resources to check out more than a few selected cases among the many persons with identity discrepancies. The Social Security system has to maintain some 240 million records, each one for a person who accumulated earnings under a unique personal number. Benefit payments must be mailed out periodically to over 36 million Old Age Social Insurance claimants. Approximately 4 million supplemental security income recipients, and more than 150 million reimbursed hospital and medical insurance claims must be processed each year. The SSA routinely handles about 7.5 million new claim applications and 13 million requests for new or replacement social security cards.

About $70 billion in wages could not be credited to the proper workers in 1981. The amount has risen since then to about $80 billion annually. In some cases the computer could not match reported earnings with the wage earner's stated SSN. In other cases, earnings were reported without any number. These unassignable earnings are placed in a suspense file.

The University of Pittsburgh discovered that the SSA lost a computer tape with its 1978 and 1979 reports on all employee earnings. Fortunately, the university could produce a replacement from its original files so that the data could be recorded.[9]

Until there is a major reform of the Social Security system, the news media will continue to feature human interest stories, such as the case where a computer-written letter informed a living person that he had died. Reliable data on the full cost of the misuse of the Social Security card are not available at the present time.

The Social Security system employs more than eighty thousand men and women. They serve directly or indirectly just about every living American. Many of the basic data assembled since the program began are still kept in conventional filing cabinets. The data processing system now in use needs to be modernized. Through the administration of several prior presidents and congresses, funds to update the system were withheld, though they were requested each year.

According to the current commissioner, John A. Svahn, "billions of dollars are wasted; services to beneficiaries are too often limited or nonexistent; opportunities for fraud and abuse too often exist. We are too often unable to respond to changes in law or procedures or to provide needed services."[10] As one reporter summed up the situation: "The computer system performed so badly that officials must now circumvent the system in twenty percent of the cases."[11]

The Social Security system will gradually acquire more of the needed computer capability to detect and correct some of its common data-processing defects, especially clerical errors, resulting from the transposition of numerical digits. But it has not been easy to recruit and to maintain properly qualified computer programmers and to pay them competitive wages. There are plans to spend $479 million by 1987 to update the central information system.

In spite of these administrative difficulties the Social Security system comes closer than any other federal agency to having a usable data base for expansion into a general national ID program. Its validity will not improve much without an ambitious and costly reissue of all outstanding documents. A number of administrative issues would have to be resolved.

1. All current holders of the old Social Security cards would have to provide detailed documentation about their identity. These breeder documents would then have to be verified carefully, especially birth certificates. This would require the hiring of additional staff. If biometric indicators were added, duplicate ID cards would become very rare.
2. New cards would only be issued on the basis of such a verification process. Those previously furnished would have to be replaced over a period of years by the more counterfeit-resistant version.
3. The verification process would lead to the discovery of holders of multiple SSNs, estimated in 1973 to exceed 4.2 million persons. Erroneous entries would have to be corrected, as much as possible, so that past contributions could be properly credited to each individual.
4. This identity verification process would also reveal administrative breakdowns that have accumulated over the years. Some frauds

would also be revealed. Procedures would have to be set up to decide when and how such cases would be handled, from simply correcting the error to criminal prosecution.
5. Cards would have to be issued to all persons, including those who do not have Social Security cards. Most of them are children and individuals in institutions who were never employed or who are without a taxable income.

The SSA takes the position that the cost of such a reissue process would not be a proper charge against its already overburdened budget. The agency would allegedly benefit only marginally from a more secure identification system in reducing errors in record keeping and instances of fraud. But similar benefits would accrue to most other federal and state organizations which use the SSN. A special appropriation by Congress might be the best way to resolve this budgetary issue.

The SSA has strict confidentiality standards. Employers, for instance, cannot obtain information about the age or prior earning records of an employee. SSA files contain the correct information, but it cannot be revealed to any casual inquirer. Confidentiality is enforced even to the extent of refusal by the SSA to sell lists of beneficiaries for commercial or for other mailing purposes. If the agency has to forward a letter to an individual, it has to be sent in care of the person's employer—the only address the SSA can rely on. However, it is up to each individual to respond. "One man, when contacted about an $8,000 dollar inheritance, told the SSA that it was worth losing the money to avoid beng re-united with his relatives."[12]

There have been several instances when private detectives were convicted for trying to bribe SSA employees to furnish incriminating information about a particular person. Officials in the early 1970s could recall only two cases—in 1947 and 1967—when officials made unauthorized disclosures of confidential information. In both cases they were prosecuted, convicted, fined, or jailed.

THE DE FACTO NATIONAL ID SYSTEM

No major American political leader is now advocating the adoption of a national ID system. But on a *de facto* basis, we already have one. This is illustrated by the accompanying table which shows the extensive use of the SSN in diverse programs administered both by private industry as well as by units of government.

Increasing Use of the Social Security Number (SSN)

Year	Responsible Authority	New Use for the SSN
1963	Treasury Dept.	Registers U.S. securities, other than savings bonds
1964	Treasury Dept.	Buyers of series H savings bonds required to provide their SSN
1964	Social Security Administration	Approves issuance of SSNs to ninth grade pupils if requested by a school
1965	Social Security Administration	Administer state Old Age Assistance programs
1965	Congress	Medicare legislation stipulates that clients provide their SSN
1965	Civil Service Commission	Administer civil service annuitant program
1966	Veterans Administration	Used for hospital admission and for record keeping
1967	Department of Defense	As the service number of military personnel
1962	Treasury Dept.	Banks, savings and loan associations, labor unions, and brokers required to obtain SSNs of their customers
1972	Congress	All recipients of benefits funded by the federal government were encouraged to provide their SSN.
1973	Treasury Dept.	Buyers of series E savings bonds required to provide their SSNs.
1974	Congress	The SSN became a requirement to receiving "Aid to Dependent Children" funding.
1976	Congress	Authorized states use the SSNs to administer tax, welfare, driver's licenses, and motor vehicle registration laws.

Within this authorized legislative framework, the SSN has become a common index to many personal records. This is how employment, health insurance, and tax files are differentiated from others with the same last name. Several states have adopted the SSN as one of the identifiers in their cooperative data-sharing network of law violations linked with the Federal Bureau of Investigations and the National Crime Information Center. The National Driver's Register of the U.S. Department of Transportation uses the SSN to match records and inquiries from participating states.

Students have to furnish the number when applying for a college board

admission test. Many institutions of learning also use this number for
record-keeping purposes. Credit bureaus use the SSN in their data
banks. The number is also needed to gain admission to a meeting or social
function at the White House, to join the Chamber of Commerce, to take
out most insurance policies, to check into a hospital, or to obtain a mort-
gage. The SSN is also used when people apply for a telephone installation, register to vote, donate blood or contribute to charity through a
payroll deduction plan. Supermarkets generally demand it from applicants for check-cashing privileges. Many health agencies use the National
Electronic Information Corporation to process claims on patients from
hospitals and doctors, relying on the SSN to keep accounts from becoming confused with files with similar names.

DATA BASE MATCHING

Data base matching is a way of comparing information in two or more different files of the same person. Such comparisons can aid administrative
efficiency, eradicate errors, and detect fraudulent statements. What wor-
ries civil liberty activists is the use of such procedures to construct comprehensive dossiers on everybody, or at least on selected persons for
unauthorized purposes.

Data pooling has been routine when a high security clearance is desired
or when someone is suspected of fraud. The technical ease and low cost
of extensive data base matching has led to a rapid multiplication of such
procedures. In January 1982, more than 85 officially sanctioned roster verification programs were reported to be under way in the federal government. State governments were in the process of making more than an
additional 120 searches to compare public assistance, unemployment
compensation, and other entitlement program records with bank deposits and employment files.

Federal government units have been reported to be maintaining more
than 856 personal data banks. The most comprehensive are the U.S. census, the Internal Revenue Service (IRS) and the SSA. There are also more
specialized data banks like those of the Selective Service system, the Veterans Adnministration, Medicare and other entitlement programs, and
Department of Commerce lists of business organizations. They maintain
mailing lists of persons to receive copies of the Consumer Price Index,
and other specialized reports. When state, local and private data banks
are added, the programs which keep computerized tabs would exceed a
thousand.

Each computerized data bank serves a specialized purpose. But almost
all of them can be matched using names, SSNs, age, and other personal

details. There are few legal restraints when this is done by private organizations and businesses. The Office of Management and Budgets (OMB) now requires government approval for such matching programs. And the public must be notified of the plan by publication in the *Federal Register*.

Since 1981, the SSA has begun to ferret out people who fraudulently collect supplemental benefits from among 4.6 million elderly, blind, and disabled persons have been receiving benefits. Applicants must file a statement about their resources in order to qualify for the benefits. Applicants must authorize the SSA to check with the IRS about dividend and interest earnings. The objective is to spot the occasional case with earnings well above the level at which Social Security payments would be warranted.

A challenge to this disclosure requirement was denied in Federal Court by District Judge Gerhard A. Gesell.[14] He ruled that it is unreasonable for the public to expect that eligibility for supplemental disability benefits be decided only on the basis of evidence provided by the applicant. The government has a responsibility for protecting the public by checking independent and collateral sources of information. Social Security would not only be checking tax returns filed by each applicant, but third-party reports from banks and businesses about payment they might have made to the welfare recipients. The court ruled that the latter had "no liberty or property" interests in these third party reports within the meaning of the Fifth Amendment which states that a person may not be deprived of "life, liberty and property without due process of law." In any event, due process was allegedly provided by first asking each recipient to sign an information waiver.

This ruling is being appealed by the National Senior Citizens Law Center challenging the power of the SSA to demand signed information releases under the threat of a cutoff in welfare benefits. Higher courts have been asked to weigh privacy and Fifth Amendment rights against the responsibility of public administrators to check benefit applications so that the limited subsidy funds are not being collected by criminals lacking in statutory entitlement to receive them.

Persons who now apply for supplemental benefits under one name and SSN but receive interests and dividends under another identity, will not yet be trapped by these procedures. They would be hurt only should Congress adopt a federally controlled identification procedure.

The SSN has also been used to track down debtors who fail to repay federal loans. Their bank assets and earnings can be examined electronically to verify their capacity to make loan repayments. A computer check of the records of 547,385 Massachusetts welfare recipients discovered that just over one per thousand, or 613 persons, had significant private assets; 87 accounts contained between $5,000 to $10,000 with one account having $89,000.

If the rate of false claims in this sample is representative of the nation as a whole, fraudulent claims for Aid To Dependent Children, Medicaid, Food stamps, General Public Assistance and Supplemental Assistance payments amounts to about $6.9 billion dollars. This is more than enough to pay for many social welfare programs that have been cut back to reduce the federal deficit.

Tax underpayments by the wealthy involve even larger hidden assets. If beneficiaries of business-oriented government programs were to be subjected to data base matching of their personal records similar to those used to search for welfare cheaters, much larger sums might be recovered. The 1982 Tax Reform Act tried to close one of these loopholes, used largely by the more wealthy segment of the U.S. population. Underpayment of taxes on interests and dividends would become rare if banks and corporations were required by law to withhold a minimum tax at the source. An unprecedented lobbying campaign by the banking industry led Congress to reverse itself after having enacted such provisions. The withholding tax had been estimated to have produced as much as twenty-five billion dollars in otherwise lost taxes.

Congress also has discouraged several proposals of the IRS to maximize its capacity to cross-check reports about earnings from different sources. The IRS wants to identify those who fail to report their full income or who collect government benefits to which they are not entitled. But the idea is being implemented piece meal. New sources of revenue are urgently needed as the federal deficit will exceed $200 billion in fiscal year 1985/86. Pressure is likely to mount on Congress to subject large taxpayers to the same data base matching surveillance now applied to persons suspected of abusing welfare programs.

A less controversial matching program involves procedures to locate unreported deaths or persons receiving pensions. A sample comparison of death records of the Medicare program of the Department of Health and Human services had disclosed 5,263 deceased persons who continued to receive benefit checks. Some were cashed by their surviving relatives or friends. Other discrepancies arose because of the inability of the SSA to update its records quickly, although it had been notified that a pensioner had, in fact, died.

Data base matching is not dependent on the availability of a common personal number. The Medical Information Bureau, which serves over 700 insurance companies in the United States and Canada, maintains a constantly changing data base on over 12 million insured individuals and corporations without the SSN. It can be done by relying on matching techniques such as by reliance on the first five or more letters of the surname and the six digits representing the date of birth. Files of the same person usually show the same birthdate and family name. There may be other aides to retrieving information, such as files on maiden names, aliases, and nicknames. But personal numbers reduce the likelihood of routine confusion of files with similar names. A unique personal number could do a lot to protect personal privacy by preventing such commonplace errors.

Opposition to an extension of the use of the SSN as a unique identifier cannot be dismissed out of hand. There have been unauthorized tappings of personal files, discussed in the next chapter. But those who would generally discourage the full use of the technology to produce valid tamper-resistant ID documents need to answer a difficult question: how weighty are privacy violations when compared to the commonplace abuses of both security and privacy by criminals? Why condone exploitation of the government and of unsuspecting private citizens through con-games and other uses of false identity records? There is no riskless trade-off.

LAW ENFORCEMENT EFFICIENCY

Law enforcement always involves issues of costs and benefits. Local police rarely invest much effort to trace stolen cars or personal minor burglaries. Only a small proportion of immigration law violations can be prosecuted. Some supporters of immigration reform would exempt small enterprises with less than five workers from the punitive provision of fining employers of illegal aliens. Families who now hire foreign domestic servants under the guise of being "guests" would not clutter court calendars.

A nationwide tamper-resistant system would provide a simple and inexpensive approach to reducing the number of law violators, without the need to build more jails and detention camps. Burglars in search of precious metals, objects, jewelry, or electronic equipment would be deterred if all second-hand dealers were required to first verify the seller's credentials. Repeated transactions by a person who is not a licensed dealer would subject him to a discreet investigation.

No simple device, like a tamper-resistant identity card, can defeat the underworld with its readiness to invest heavily in the technology of committing crimes. Valid Identification Program (VIP) cards will drive most forgers out of business. Even highly proficient operators may be discouraged from much of their counterfeiting. But the routine measures now under consideraton will not suffice.

At a hearing of the Senate Permanent Investigations Subcommittee, Newton Van Drunen, a convicted felon, testified that he perfected his skills at Sandstone Federal Prison in Minnesota, with relatively simple equipment.[15] He produced Texas birth certificates, baptismal certificates, and documents issued by the INS, including its new Alien Documentation Identification and Telecommunication (ADIT) card. The latter passed most visual checks. Only a few were picked up by border inspectors as being phony, but nearly all of them would have been spotted if they were equipped with portable digital readers. The latter would have rejected these counterfeit versions for lacking the built-in and—largely invisible—safety features, such as encrypted codes and fingerprints. Full testimony is reproduced in the Appendix.

CRIME DETERRENCE

The "Big Government" scare argument by those opposed to setting federal standards for ID documents is often countered by reference to the threat to freedom generated by such fraudulent enterprises. Misuses of false documents are far more common than the relatively rare abuses of data files by arrogant bureaucrats. Any real or alleged misuse can be counteracted in the courts, by Congress, and by administrative reform measures. By contrast, burglars, tax evaders, or individuals who violate immigration laws must first be caught before future such violations might be restrained. In 1982 close to 13 million crimes were reported to the FBI. 438,830 persons were in prison, at an annual cost to the public of 7.5 billion dollars. It is not known to what extent false documents and impersonation were involved. But they do facilitate the commission of a significant number of crimes and the efforts of those who perpetrate them to evade being caught.

In general, unreliable identity documents do more to protect the rights of criminals than those of the victims. A logical case can be made that improved validity in personal ID could have a direct quadruple impact on the deterrence of fraud and misrepresentation offenses:

1. Harassing potential terrorists and criminals: A person likely to commit an offense can now easily obtain a false driver's license, a stolen credit card, or a false passport. Such documents would become extremely difficult and often too expensive to copy for all but the very big operators and spies. Their use would also become quite risky, exposing them to detection.
2. Victim protection capability: Criminals will have to note that a potential victim has the means to protect himself against fraud and misrepresentation without resorting to the police. Electronic checking of credit cards would become more reliable than it is at present.

U.S. merchants could save much of the billion dollars in credit losses that they are currently experiencing annually.
3. Public participation in crime prevention: If someone is using a false identity, there is a simple way to alert law enforcement agencies. Legitimate persons whose identity is verified will have a vested interest against unauthorized use of their identity.
4. Law enforcement convenience: Law enforcement officers need not detain persons for long, if suspected of impersonation; computer data banks can make such checks within seconds or minutes. This is already being done in some states with automobile registration and drivers' license numbers. Citizens will be spared the inconvenience of being detained for investigation if there are doubts about their identity.

In spite of the widespread objections to gun control laws at both the federal and state levels, within 16 minutes the FBI was able to identify the shop in Dallas where the gun used to make an attempt on the life of President Kennedy was purchased. But with many of the ordinary crimes committed with a weapon, the available ID technology is underutilized. Certainly there are few ways to register people who deal in weapons, high explosives, and poisonous substances. False identity records are immensely useful to fugitives from justice or to those involved in the planning of acts of terrorism. In 1982, it was estimated that sixty million dollars worth of medical services were obtained by ineligible persons who used forged or stolen military ID cards. The Department of Defense has begun to test a Realtime Automated Personnel Identification System, abbreviated by the acronym *RAPIDS*. It is based on a carefully controlled credit card, accompanied by a photograph, a variety of magnetic stripes, and encoding devices. It is being issued to all military personnel and their dependents in the Tidewater, Virginia, area. Before someone is able to use their card, an Automated Machine Reader, like those used in banks, checks it against a list of approximately ten million persons entitled to receive military benefits or privileges.

The Department of Defense and certain companies engaged in classified projects have also begun to use retinal eye pattern indicators as does the Wells Fargo Corporation. Identification cards might also be used to make it more difficult for professional terrorists to hijack international flights. Preventive measures now consist largely of a personal inspection of passengers and their hand luggage. Some airlines also inspect freight carried in the hold.

By international agreement, passengers could be required to present their tamper-resistant ID card and have it checked against lists of known or suspected terrorist agents. Those lacking the required document would still be able to fly, but would first be subjected to a more thorough personal search. The kind of professional saboteur who attempted to assassinate the pope might well have been deterred from air travel by such a precaution.

There is no miracle cure to the excesses of the underworld. But their transnational movement can be limited, especially after their fingerprints or other digitally readable biometric features become known.

PROTECTING THE POOR

False identity papers also make it easier for con-artists to obtain fraudulent benefits from such entitlement programs as Aid for Dependent Children, Food Stamps, Medicare, and Disability Insurance. False and multiple claims have inflated program costs to levels where it has become politically popular to campaign in favor of cutting benefits to the truly needy.

In Washington, D.C., the city corporation counsel was notified of an average of 500 leads a month on cases of possible welfare fraud. An estimated $51 million in welfare benefits were paid out to ineligible recipients between 1978 and 1980.[16] The General Accounting Office found that not a single case was prosecuted. The prosecutor's office claimed it had more serious crimes to investigate.

The Federal Food Stamp Program has done much to prevent malnutrition among America's poor. But the fiscal base of this nutrition program has been threatened, not only by budget cuts, but also by the widespread fraud in issuing stamps and by outright theft. Two thousand fraudulent cards were confiscated in 1984. They are regarded to be only the tip of the iceberg. Old Illinois cards were reported by the Nilsen Report (June 1985) to be selling for $50 to $100 on the street. Some recipients were being issued up to 30 cards to replace those claimed lost. Precise data on the extent of such fraud is hard to obtain, but the leakage of funds through misused food stamps was estimated to have exceeded 25 percent in 1980.

As a counter-measure, the Department of Agriculture mandated in 1981 that identification cards be issued to eligible recipients in ten urban areas where fraud has been particularly widespread. The cards were prone to forgery. In 1985, the Department began using plastic cards with laser engraved photographs which can be digitally stored in a central file. This somewhat more fraud-proof card costs $3.50 each and a replacement can be made for about $2.00 from the stored data.

Many of the food stamp recipients were reported to approve of such security measures. Some have no other identification card. They do not drive a car and therefore have no drivers license. They never owned a passport. They generally do not have enough credit to be issued a bank credit card. As potential victims of the theft of food stamps destined for them, few objected to a procedure to make it more difficult for others to steal their entitlement.

Most people freely share their address by having it listed in the telephone book. Those in business distribute calling cards. But persons who have debts sometimes try to disappear. Such disappearances also complicate the collection of debts owed to the government. There are 358 federal long term loan programs. In 1981 the federal government was owed a staggering sum of $175 billion, close to what would be needed to balance the record 1985–86 federal deficit. Much of this debt is for development and business loans, which are not being repaid on schedule. In 1981 an estimated three billion dollars was needed to pay the interest on uncollected federal loans.[17]

People experiencing serious financial reverses have no choice but to postpone their debt repayment or to declare bankruptcy. That a borrower can become an impoverished debtor is part of the normal risk of the loan industry. But there is evidence that a proportion of federal debtors actually have the needed resources to repaying their loans. The deputy inspector general of the Veterans Administration illustrated this fact by noting that VA debtors included 48 federal employees earning in excess of $40,999 a year. The list included an assistant secretary of a federal department with a six year old debt of $173. 79,000 other federal employees were delinquent in repayment of loans totaling about $50 million. One quarter of Harvard's medical school graduates were behind in meeting their obligation to repay money they had borrowed, with a federal interest subsidy, to pay for their medical studies.

IMPROVED DEBT COLLECTION

Former Senator Charles H. Percy of Illinois, in 1973, had worked hard for the passage of the Privacy Act of 1974 and for passage of the Debt Collection Act of 1981 (S 1249) eight years later. It mandated the IRS to make an exception to its general requirement of keeping all tax information confidential. At the cost of about eleven cents a person, the IRS can locate the current address of most taxpayers who are delinquent in repaying a federal loan. This information is often sufficient to motivate delinquent debtors to pay up rather than to face the loss of their credit ratings and the risk of having their assets attached by a local court.

The insufficiency of governmental resources to engage in effective debt collection led to proposals to have it done commercially. This plan (Senate Bill 1249) would authorize the federal government to turn over uncollectible debts to commercial credit bureaus. They would be furnished with the delinquent's latest address secured from IRS data banks. The bill would also require all future loan applicants to include their SSN, making it easier to trace them.

John Shattuck, formerly of the Washington office of the American Civil Liberties Union (ACLU), testified against this plan. The proposed solution was seen as creating a new problem: an invasion of privacy by allowing the federal government to turn over the address of a delinquent borrower to a private debt collection agency. He warned that the credit industry would be handed a windfall profit by getting free access to credit information which could then be used to further their own business of rating people's credit worthiness. He also pointed to the erosion of confidentiality of federal taxpayer records, should the IRS become a customer of private collection agencies.

This constitutional objection did not appear to impress many legislators. Senator Percy, for instance, noted that in the private sector, no bank would lend money without the borrower furnishing his SSN. Why should the federal government, the world's largest credit institution, not be able to do the same? This new rule would close a loophole through which many persons can now escape repaying federal loans. Reduction in Federal debt delinquencies of billions of dollars could be used to reduce the federal deficit or to improve services to the truly needy. Or should losses be accepted in order to prevent the use of the SSN as an identifier to locate the address of financially well-heeled debtors? How many added taxes should the public be expected to pay in order to write off such unnecessary losses? It is estimated that the price is about $275 dollars for each taxpayer in the country.

DIMENSIONS OF PRIVACY

Prohibitions against the misuse of federal files seem to be well observed, if judged by the rarity of complaints about alleged violations. As of February 1982, only twenty-nine lawsuits were known to have been filed against the IRS claiming improper disclosure of confidential tax return data. In just one case an investigation of an alleged theft of oil, did a jury find in favor of the claimant.[18] The case is being appealed by the IRS. It denies that its official exceeded his responsibilities. The IRS is defending the claim that it acted properly in investigating a possible criminal act.

Of the other cases against the IRS, twelve were successfully defended. Eleven were still pending as of 1983. They generally involve charges that an IRS employee exceeded his authority in using information from a tax file when investigating serious charges of fraud.

The ACLU takes a different position. It values the rights of persons to privacy more than efficiency in collecting delinquent debts. In contrast, legislators tend to be more concerned with reducing the federal deficit. They are prepared to favor fair and prompt repayment of federal loans due from persons with assets sufficient to repay what they owe. This led to the introduction of the Debt Collection Act of 1981. It would further transform the IRS and the SSN into a general locator file for congressionally authorized purposes.

Those caught in this information web may feel outraged about such use of their personnel and tax files. But the failure of permanently employed borrowers to pay their debts is reducing the loan capital available for others who need such help. As an economy measure, federally guaranteed student loans were halted for months in all schools where more than twenty five percent of those who had graduated were in default. The administrators were enjoined to use greater care in recommending students for loans and to use their influence to get delinquent alumni to pay up. Such collective punishments, however, rest on shaky constitutional grounds and this practice was subsequently discontinued.

Separated and divorced single parents often find themselves being abandoned by their former spouses who simply disappear, leaving no forwarding address. Court-ordered financial contributions for the care and maintenance of their offspring are ignored. Congress authorized the Social Security System to locate and disclose the addresses of delinquent parents to state and local agencies responsible for the collection of overdue child support payments. A court warrant can then be served to force the delinquent parent to live up to their support obligations.

In New York state, federal, state and local welfare programs were able to recoup six million dollars in federal tax refunds that were impounded from people owing child support payments under the authority of the revised Social Security Act of 1981. Additional funds have become available after New York State passed legislation authorizing withholding of state and local tax refunds and of unemployment insurance checks.[19]

Do these and other intrusive procedures violate the constitutional prohibition against Fifth Amendment self-incrimination? A case for this position can be made, and has been made. But who is threatened by this address verification program; debtors who have the resources to pay, criminals who evade taxes, individuals who live under assumed names, and illegal aliens who earn money from which taxes were deducted by the employer. Is the state entitled to use its data bases to locate such law evaders? At what point should a democratic government refrain from using its capabilities to trace the movement of persons accused of, or suspected of, even more threatening law violations, like kidnapping and terrorism?

A substantial group of public opinion leaders question the legality of employing these search procedures. Their commitment to law enforcement is balanced against concerns that there is too much government. Congress did not enact a proposal by Representative Burgener in 1982 to require the attorney general to conduct a feasibility study of issuing a tamper-resistant and machine readable plastic covered social security card,[20] which would have improved the technical capability of authorized officials to locate fugitives from justice. The topic will soon be systematically addressed, under provisions of the recently enacted Comprehensive Crime Control Act of 1984. It mandates the president to make recommendations on how to improve the management of federal data files through technical changes in the quality and the consistency of terminology of identification documents.

FEDERAL ID CARDS ARE HERE TO STAY

There are at least sixteen separate projects to develop tamper-resistant identification programs in the federal government. Six are sponsored by the Department of Defense and two each by the U.S. Postal Service, the Department of State and the Department of Agriculture. Two of them impact on large segments of the population—the Social Security card and the Medicaid card.

Efficiency experts might decry this multiplicity of exploration as an illustration of alleged uncoordinated big government. The professionals who provide technical and administrative leadership in each of these programs are aware of at least some of the projects in other units of the federal government. But in the absence of recognition in the Office of the President that a coordinate strategy is both needed and feasible, it is inevitable that responsible officials throughout many units of the government would proceed independently with projects to meet the specialized needs of their organization. The diversity of purposes is apparent from the following listing, adapted from the *Nilsen Report* of June 1984:

Department of Defense

1. Reissue of 10–12 million identity cards of military personnel, the Realtime Automated Personal ID System. (RAPIDS)
2. Access on line eligibility of military personnel, to be used together with the RAPIDS program: the Defense Eligibility Enrollment Reporting System (DEERS).
3. The Defense Communication Agency (DCA), designed to upgrade the use of photo-ID cards.

4. The Army Food Management Information System (AFMIS), to manage a control card system for mess halls at 1,500 facilities.
5. A test of hand geometry as the basis for accessing army Automatic Teller Machines (ATM's), as a way of paying personnel without having to issue checks. This program is being tried out by the Army Payroll Department in cooperation with the Treasury Department.
6. A hospital card/tag system, for the Department of Defense health system, to provide an automated medical and personal history file for each employee.

Postal Service

7. Develop capacity to collect, edit and forward time and attendance data for employees nationwide, the Source Time and Attendance Recording System. (STARS)
8. Development of an access control card system for 3,000 employees in Indianapolis using a "passthrough" reader. Employees will have to carry a Postal Access card.

Department of State

9. Creation of an electronic or intelligent passport, the Machine Readable Passport (MRP), in conformity to recently adopted worldwide technical specifications.
10. Development of an access control system for U.S. embassies worldwide (DOS).

Social Security Administration

11. Replacement of current Social Security cards with a more tamper-resistant version.
12. Development of a secure recipient ID card to be used by states in the administration of their Medicare program.

Department of Agriculture

13. Development of photo ID cards for food stamp recipients for use in major urban areas.
14. Development of an on-line machine-readable plastic card ID system, also for use in monitoring the food stamp program.

Department of Justice

15. Automation of the record keeping system of the INS by adoption of the Alien Documentation, Identification and Telecommunication system (ADIT). All current immigrants are to be issued a machine readable ADIT. Gradually, aliens already in the country would also

be given such a document, to facilitate computer storage and retrieval of their files, anywhere in the country. Files now have to be
transferred physically, whenever an alien moves to a new location.

Veterans Administration

16. Development of an access control system for Veterans hospitals
    and for protecting the security of its computer systems.

Each of these projects works with a private contractor. The acquired experience should be useful if and when a policy decision is made to adopt a
uniform and multipurpose national data system. The shortcomings of existing ID programs are widely recognized, but without political leadership, proliferation of specialized ID programs is likely to increase.

Multiple programs and computer hardware make comparisons of data
stored in different files only marginally more complicated. Protective
measures against privacy violations would be most effectively administered in a uniform system. Cost effectiveness is also likely to maximize.

ANONYMITY AND SECURITY

Most people feel they are more than a number. But this is the most anonymous way to store data about themselves. Clerks can handle numbered
files without ever knowing anyone's name. They would not necessarily
have to know when they are handling the record of their neighbor or
someone who is a public figure. Computer-stored data can also be electronically scrambled and can be made safe from being accessed by unauthorized persons than the usual name-indexed files now used for most
administrative purposes.

There is a growing tendency to adopt additional technical security features. More and more states issue drivers' licenses with a signature and
photograph fused into a plastic card. The credit card industry, through an
International Association of Credit Card Investigators (IACCI) and the
National Bureau of Standards in Gaitherburg, Maryland, are monitoring
new technical developments to enhance card security. They also cooperate in sharing private data files to track the users of overdrawn credit
cards or those which were stolen. While biometric indicators are not fully
used, they are increasingly employed in special purpose identity programs.

The criminal underworld also keeps pace with the development of this
ID technology. This can be inferred from the volume and ingenuity of
computer crimes. Public policy determinations are needed to decide how
quickly and with what restraints by privacy considerations, public and

business agencies can proceed to use this same technology for improvements in the efficiency, accuracy and security of documents used in transactions involving trust.

INACTION IS COSTLY

In 1982 President Reagan's OMB opposed proposals to issue a federal work entitlement document. By 1985 this opposition had given way to a readiness to support immigration reform legislation. Congress avoided agreeing to a joint version of a Immigration Reform and Control Act in 1984. Both houses had passed it with some different provisions. One of the opposition arguments was the allegedly high cost of administering an ID data bank for 230 million living Americans. Estimated costs ranged widely, from many millions to billions. New expenditures are not something to be undertaken readily when the United States generates the largest deficit in its history.

Those who favor a nationwide identification procedure, nevertheless, counter with a simple message: the status quo is also costly, even *more* costly. The United States has a vast underground economy. Huge sums are earned from drug traffic, smuggling, rackets, gambling, prostitution, illegal immigration, the sale of stolen goods, and many types of "ordinary" fraud. These criminal industries, estimated in 1981 at roughly $124 billions, go largely untaxed.[21] They exercise a corroding influence on society, corrupting labor unions and multinational corporations. Double bookkeeping and the bribing of public officials are common. There are no reliable statistics, but the taxes due on these earnings would go a long way toward reducing America's budget deficit.

The criminal underworld is the principal beneficiary of America's chaotic approach to personal identity documentation. How much aid do they deserve from the rest of us who make an honest living, pay taxes, and worry about civil liberties? A joint study of the SSA and the INS in Denver concluded that 50% of the INS documents were false for establishing eligibility for Social Security cards and for various benefits.[22]

Some states are making symbolic efforts to counteract these abuses. Dealers in precious metals in Texas must keep a record of who sells them merchandise. In Michigan, no sales of precious metals can be consummated unless the seller is willing to be fingerprinted. But little is known about the utility of these isolated efforts. Neither state has the capability to use these data to discourage burglaries by making it risky to turn stolen goods into cash. The absence of a nationally coordinated program makes it easy for burglars to evade the controls of relatively tough states by disposing of their loot in more permissive jurisdictions.

False ID documents enabled one enterprising New Yorker to process 60 false guaranteed student loan applications, totaling $140,000. In Rhode Island, a cooperative project with the INS and the Department of Education identified twenty-seven ineligible aliens who had fraudulently received student benefits. There were twenty-two convictions, one dismissal and four fugitive defendants.[23]

Sample surveys indicate that such frauds are widespread. In Illinois, the applications of 198 aliens for unemployment benefits were cross-checked with INS Service records. Fifty-one percent were found to be using a phony document. When a similar one day sample study was conducted on a statewide basis, 119 out of 257 alien applicants were found to be using false green cards (46%).[24] Misuses of entitlement and government support programs for business are also prevalent among the native born. This inflates their cost considerably.

Fraudulent use of multiple identity documents does not require much skill. One couple in Connecticut created sixteen fictitious identities, three women and thirteen children, by illegally applying for and receiving, SSNs on the basis of counterfeit baptismal certificates. Blank forms can be purchased in any church supply store. During four years, the couple defrauded the government out of $67,000. When caught, they were in the process of setting up an identical scheme in Florida.

Nationwide losses, involving nine entitlement programs for which a SSN is required, were estimated to add up to $15 billions a year. Leakage through fraudulent business transactions, domestic and worldwide, is much more costly. Comprehensive data are hard to come by because of bank secrecy practices and the ease with which funds can be transferred to surveillance-safe havens in Switzerland, Lichtenstein, Lebanon, the Bahamas, and elsewhere. No one has a reliable count of the extent to which false and counterfeit identity documents are useful for laundering illegally acquired funds. Many U.S. banks are under investigation for having illegally transferred sums in excess of $10,000 overseas without the required reporting forms. International criminals can enter and leave the country under varied pseudonyms. There are few who question that identity misrepresentation is a major challenge to orderly and trustworthy government and business.

Unreliable identifiers do more than to invite fraud. They lead to other types of victimization. Some people, and not always a divorced parent without custody rights, kidnap a young child and keep him. Over 28,000 such cases were reported last year. The FBI National Crime Information Center opened 780,000 missing person files between 1975 and 1982, 76 percent of whom were children and juveniles. In addition, there are about 1,000 unidentified deceased persons annually.

Introduction of a tamper-resistant ID system will cost money. Many administrative problems will have to be resolved. But these new expenditures need to be compared to a cost often ignored in public affairs: *the cost of doing nothing.*

Savings through ID card related fraud could reach the level of tens of billions. Immigration is only one illustration of the general law enforcement preference for a *prevention* strategy. VIP has the potential for facilitating significant improvements in public administration. The benefits of prevention are discounted, however, in the view of many responsible persons concerned about the alleged risk to privacy rights guaranteed by the American constitution. This issue will be addressed in detail in the next chapter.

REFERENCES

1. *The Personal Identification News* vol. 1, no. 1, April 1985; Health Management Systems, Inc. *LifeCard*, Baltimore, Maryland; Blue Cross and Blue Shield of Maryland, 1985.

2. Nilsen, Spenser H., *Nilsen Report*, no. 377, Aug. 1984.

3. Workers Defense League, *Preliminary Report on Slavery and Peonage Practices in the United States in 1981*, Nov. 12, 1981.

4. Clark, Cathy, *The Paper Trip I: For New You Through New I.D.*, Fountain Valley: Eden Press, 1977.

5. Reid, Barry, *Ways to Disappear and Live Free*, Rev. ed., 1978. Fountain Valley: Eden Press.

6. Author not identified. *The Road Back*, Torrance: The Noontide Press, (no date).

7. Comptroller General of the United States, 1976, *Smugglers, Illicit Documents and Schemes Are Undermining Control Over Immigration*, Washington, D.C., GGD–76–83:18.

8. Edelhertz, Herbert and Charles Rogovin, *A National Strategy For Containing White Collar Crime*, Lexington: Lexington Books, 1980.

9. University of Pittsburgh, Memorandum from Paul Soyan to Faculty and Staff on "Social Security Administration" February 22, 1982.

10. Commissioner John A. Svahn, personal statement.

11. Rich, Spencer, *Washington Post*, March 3, 1982.

12. Westin, Alan F. and Michael A. Baker, *Databanks in a Free Society: Computers, Record Keeping and Privacy*, New York: Quadrangle Books, 1970: 32–39.

13. Ibid:39.

14. *New York Times*. July 13, 1982:A18.

15. Van Drunen, Newton, U.S. Congress, Hearing of the Senate Permanent Investigation Subcommittee. June 15, 1982.

16. Clark, Timothy B., *Washington Post*, ca June 1982:3.

17. Unites States Senate, April 23, and June 17, 1981.

18. *Rodgers* vs. *Larry C. Hyatt* (A Chief of the Criminal Investigation Division of the Internal Revenue Service), Personal Correspondence.

19. *New York Times*, August 4, 1982:81.

20. Illegal Immigration Control Act of 1982, HR156.

21. Senator Guy Nunn, *Congressional Record*, Washington, D.C., March 7, 1981:S2301. His remarks are based on the report *Illegal Narcotics Profits*, U.S. Senate Report No. 96–887, Washington, D.C., U.S. Government Printing Office, August 4, 1981.

22. Senator William V. Roth Jr., U.S. Congress, Senate Permanent Subcommittee on Investigations, *Oversight Hearings on Fraudulent Identification Documents and Penetration of Benefit Programs*, Washington, D.C., June 15, 1982.

23. Thomas, James Jr., Inspector General Department of Education, testimony before the Senate Permanent Subcommittee Investigations, ibid., June 16, 1982.

24. Fahner, Tyrone, Attorney General of the State of Illinois, ibid., June 16, 1982.

CHAPTER 5

THE CASE AGAINST
A VIP CARD

THE "BIG BROTHER" SYNDROME

Opponents of the Valid Identity Program (VIP) rarely question its utility. Their unequivocal opposition is based primarily on the fear that it could lead to a universal card and totalitarianism.[1] How justified are these fears? Private investigators are now able to steal confidential information or to bribe others for it if facts are needed for nefarious purposes. Computers can also be put to such use. Such abuses in American information systems, while rare, are being monitored by Robert Ellis Smith, the "Ralph Nader of Privacy," and publisher of the *Privacy Journal*.

These rights have been abused. After World War II, many a dedicated public figure was subjected to government harassment during the Eisenhower administration on the basis of unverified and often false information. 527 persons were later notified by the Department of Justice that they had been a target of COINTELPRO, a program of calculated defamation. This acronym for a now prohibited domestic counterintelligence program included "dirty tricks," such as the spreading of false rumors. Organizations regarded as subversive by the FBI were disrupted by secret agents. These constitutional rights violations were reversed, but not until much damage had been done. Opponents of a national ID system are concerned that its establishment might somehow lead to a repetition of such abuses.

No one can dismiss such a concern lightly. Ever since the Alien and Sedition Act of 1878, the prevalence of lynchings and the periodic discovery that government agencies have engaged in human rights violations, has led the public to accept the dictum that vigilance is indeed a price of liberty.[2]

During the *Watergate* scandal, officials close to President Richard Nixon secretly were able to access FBI, tax, and other records to intimidate individuals regarded as political enemies. However, public opinion and Congress forced President Nixon's resignation. Without a pardon from his successor, the former president would have been prosecuted and possibly jailed. Several of his key staff did indeed go to prison, including Attorney General John Mitchell, the country's chief law enforcement official.

J. Edgar Hoover might have met the same fate, but for his death. The number three man of his inner administrative circle disclosed that Hoover often leaked useful information to politicians he favored, so as to help defeat those he despised. Incriminating data on prominent persons were kept in four special rooms of the FBI headquarters building for Mr. Hoover's personal use. For instance, the FBI boss injected himself into the primary campaign between Thomas Dewey and Harold Stassen. Mr. Hoover ordered FBI officials to draft reports issued under Dewey's name making him appear more up-to-date on Communist threats than Stassen. Anti-Kennedy stories were leaked to the press during the close campaign against Richard Nixon. A defamation campaign was launched secretly against Martin Luther King Jr., whos public stature the director of the FBI wanted to tarnish. Franklin D. Roosevelt and Lyndon B. Johnson also used the FBI to investigate political opponents. Could not another Edgar J. Hoover gain the power to keep politically incriminating dossiers on targeted persons?

THE PUBLIC OPINION FACTOR

Unlike taxes, highway construction, and national defense, the question of a national ID card is of concern to only a few special interest groups. Within the public at large, few persons have first hand knowledge or care much about this technical question. Public opinion on this topic has never been investigated in depth. But there are many people who have feelings and vague impressions, which are expressed in public opinion polls.

In California, according to a 1982 Field Institute Poll, it was a substantial majority (65 percent) which opposed reliance on a general ID card "as a way to tighten up on immigration." The opposition was highest for whites and hispanic respondents. Blacks were almost evenly divided. This regional viewpoint was more negative than three nationwide public opinion polls in which a majority voiced support for a general tamper-resistant ID program.

A 1977 Roper Poll disclosed that 51 percent of a nationwide sample favored a mandatory ID card for everybody, citizens as well as for aliens. Of those opposed, 29 percent were ready to favor issuance of a tamper-resistant Social Security card in place of the current version. In other words, 4 out of 5 of this sample preferred replacing easily counterfeited

ID documents with a federal card that would be technically more trustworthy. Similarly supportive views were expressed in a 1980 Gallup Poll by most subcategories of a national survey. College graduates and white collar workers were most inclined to disapprove of the idea. Some of these opponents have voiced quite passionate views. They really worry that a Big Brother computer in America could provide a data base for the tyrannization of our society.

TOTALITARIAN ID PATTERNS

The Soviet control system relies heavily on personal documents. Each resident is issued an internal passport at age sixteen. The document includes the bearer's picture, name, and date of birth. Since the Soviet Union views itself to be a multinational state, each person is required to identify himself with *one* nationality, even the children of a mixed marriage.

The passport is apt to be used to enforce discriminatory practices against certain nationalities, such as Jews and Volga Germans. Their children are not likely to be accepted in a training program for a diplomatic or military career though they might be well qualified. The top universities, like the University of Moscow, are known to be admitting few applicants from these stigmatized minority groups. Those allowed to enter will be carefully watched for manifestations of independence and dissidence.

The internal passport also includes data on compulsory military service, place of residence, marital status and minor dependents. Passports are taken away from prisoners and military personnel, a fact which facilitates the detections of escapees and AWOL (Absent Without Official Leave) soldiers.

The document will provide officials with basic personal data which can be used to enforce existing travel restrictions. No one can visit anywhere for more than seventy-two hours, without police permission. Popular cities like Moscow, Leningrad, Kiev and the Baltic capitals are closed to travelers, except for someone who marries a local resident or has skills needed by a local enterprise. The secret police (the KGB) can insert restrictions in the document, effectively preventing a passport holder from travelling, and risking arrest if he does so.

Before the 1970s, passports were generally withheld from collective farmers. This prevented them from drifting to the cities. They were "just as effectively chained to the soil as were the serfs of the last century."[3]

An additional personal document is maintained at the place of employment – the *Workbook*. It includes many details of a person's work assignment, pay, promotions, transfers, demotions, commendations, and disciplinary actions. By law, a Soviet citizen cannot change his job without first submitting his workbook to the new employer. Most enterprises cooperate with persons who wish to change jobs. Political dissidents cannot, however, apply for a new post without their prospective employer knowing all about their records. During the Stalin era, withholding the workbook was commonplace. This document provides the Soviet State with another powerful control mechanism.

Finally, each urban resident is likely to be watched by the *Upravdom* (warden) of his apartment building, a state employee who serves as concierge, janitor, rent collector, and informant to the local police. He will also spy for the secret police, if they request surveillance of a particular person. The *Upravdom* maintains a register of all tenants, including visitors.

The control of this triple ID system over 265 million people is now moderated only by its inefficiency. As far as is known, there does not seem to be a central Soviet agency where information from different personel rosters is matched automatically. But the Soviet Union is likely to acquire such a capability soon.

Shortly after Yuri V. Andropov became the Soviet head of state, he ordered the police to crack down on the common practice of workers leaving their job for several hours during the day. The police were instructed to raid stores, bars, and eating places to check the identity documents of the customers. Those who could not prove that they were off duty were taken to the police station to be booked. The employer was notified and urged to reprimand the culprit.

In all nations, capitalist as well as socialist, workers are expected to be optimally productive. Time clocks are sometimes used to record the precise number of hours spent on a job. Chairman Andropov added an additional deterrent to absenteeism on the job: police surveillance.

The People's Republic of China also enforces similar limitations on travel and residence on over a billion people, a quarter of the world's population. Identity cards are needed to purchase many items, even a train ticket. China's current documents could be easily forged, but it does not appear to happen very often. The entire population is organized in job-focused Danwei (work place) groupings. Their approval is needed to get a place to live, to travel, and even to get married. Each Danwei is directed by a Communist Party official. Hotels will not provide a room without a letter from the Danwei secretary who also distributes coupons for rationed food. Even foreigners living in the country must be part of a Danwei.

These practices may be modified now, as the People's Republic of China is moving quickly from the repressive practices of the Red Guard. Certainly then, and probably even now, each Danwei keeps a confidential dossier. It includes evidence of foreign contacts, a person's class background for three generations, and data on any alleged moral offenses like pre-marital sex or suspected opposition to the regime. People have no right to access these files, to correct misrepresentations of errors that may be included. Severe abuses were justified by these secret files during the Cultural Revolution, when some of the country's most irresponsible Red Guard members turned the social system upside down. Millions were turned into traitors, and non-persons overnight; they were imprisoned, exiled, forced to do physical labor in the countryside or executed, often after being tortured.

The control of the Danwei is supplemented by street committees which watch people in their apartments. The committee men are a cross between building superintendant, police informer, social worker, and union hall hiring boss. They are nominally elected, but often subtly nominated by the Communist party machinery. They are not paid a salary, but depend on small gifts of meat, vegetables, and rice from residents who want to be on good terms with them. They can enter someone's home at any time without prior notice. A couple engaged in a marital dispute at night may find themselves chastized for not resolving their problem. These committees also help enforce the prohibition against having more than one child per family. Some neighborhood monitors even chide people for not washing their dishes or for not keeping their quarters clean.

The Chinese government has begun to ease some of these controls, giving the population greater freedom to change jobs and travel while giving local authorities more decision-making power. But, there is as yet no evidence that protection of privacy is a policy issue. The Government believes that it is in the public's best interest that the state continue to be involved in many matters that would be outside its scope in most Western nations.

It would be inaccurate to suggest that these invasive surveillance systems are *the cause* of Communist tyranny. Most Western democracies have better administered data banks, including a mandatory identity card, personnel files at work, and a doorman at the more expensive places of residence. But they also have strong traditions and laws to protect personal privacy. They tend to be well enforced.

THE ID CARD AND PREJUDICE

The FBI maintains fingerprint and other personal information on roughly 30 percent of the population. The Social Security system has a file on every employee and taxpayer. The U.S. census maintains a file on every person. There are more than 858 federal data banks in the Department of Health and Human Services, the Veterans Administration (VA), the Department of Commerce and in many other government agencies. Each roster is subject to restrictions to minimize potential abuses of privacy. But in the minds of some people, these growing electronic data processing capabilities emit a red light warning that liberty and privacy are in danger.

Should Congress enact an employer liability provision, subjecting anyone knowingly hiring an alien without a work permit to a heavy fine? Employers would become the first echelon of enforcing the employment restrictions against aliens. Spokespersons for Mexican-American groups fear that people with Spanish surnames or Latin features would be more thoroughly screened, both by potential employers and by agents of the Immigration and Naturalization Service (INS). Blacks, Chicanos, youths with long hair, and homosexuals are among the minorities who are often singled out for special attention by law enforcement officials. Discrimination may increase if employers are required to check the employment entitlement of all new job-holders. Indeed, such persons are already the object of employment discrimination, except for the most unskilled and dead-end jobs. Will the use of tamper-resistant ID cards add to this burden of discrimination? Or will there be a decline, if all American workers, irrespective of race, age, citizenship or other characteristics must document their employment entitlement before accepting a position? Would some employers who now hire without discrimination policies, adopt them because of the ID requirement?

Estimates are sharply divided on this subject. Spokespersons who anticipate a reduction in minority employment opportunities are countered by others who doubt that this would happen. Few of the employers who run sweatshops and industrial farms are known for their compassion for unusual people. They hire the handicapped, illegal aliens, black skinned, fat people, and others because they are inclined to accept jobs that pay poorly. These minorities have limited labor market options and therefore will often tolerate difficult and dangerous working conditions.

Such minority group members with a work permit are likely to find a VIP document a distinct asset. Many of them have no other trustworthy ID document. Credit cards may be beyond their reach because they do not have any credit. Some do not have a car and therefore need no driver's license. A security prone document, like the Alien Documentation Identification Telecommunication (ADIT) card can protect them against false detainment or arrest, when law enforcement officials stop them for identification. By contrast, illegal aliens would find it almost impossible to conduct any business with government agencies or to get a driver's license.

Federal and state affirmative action legislation is already on the books. Its enforcement would be aided by the fact that whenever a position is being filled, an employer could keep a computerized record of all applicants. The ID cards of all applicants could be recorded. In the event of an accusation that discrimination was a factor in the choice of the final candidate, they would be able to contest the accusation by comparing the selected person and his qualification against all others who had been considered.

Some employers carefully build up a record of minority group applicants but then interpret their job requirements in such a way that they are almost never hired. Such evasive tactics are uncommon, however, when filling unskilled and low paying jobs. Prejudiced employers prefer to hire people they regard as "inferior."

In Europe the necessity to present an ID as a condition of employment has not prevented the massive influx of millions of migrant workers—Turks in Germany, Finns in Sweden, Algerians in France, and Moroccans in Spain. However, the mandatory identification and registration system enforced in these nations makes it possible to keep track of these newcomers, who can be easily located, if their employment is terminated. Those who were able to enter these countries with a permanent residency permit will find their documents a protection against being denied unemployment and for other welfare benefits due them.

DISTRUST OF GOVERNMENT

Concern that the government will know too much is rooted deeply in human history. Even before the Romans invented the census to count males and their property for taxation and conscription, population counts were undertaken in many ancient nations—in China, Babylonia, Persia, Israel and Egypt, to exploit people or to recruit forced workers and soldiers.

The exploitative emphasis has changed with the inception of the welfare state. Modern governments devote large resources to *help* their residents. A sizable portion of the revenues is redistributed in forms of public service and benefit programs. A reliable ID is needed not only for law enforcement and taxation but also to administer human service programs equitably, with a minimum of fraud.

A century ago, most Americans could function quite well without any identity document. They were known among their peers and neighbors. Those who moved about had to put up with a lengthy period of establishing trust among their new acquaintances and neighbors. Modern life cannot function this way. A young woman, leaving home for the first time for a distant city in order to find work, will quickly have to resolve many identity-related issues. She needs to rent an apartment. What land-lord will give her a lease without credit and cash, without a discrete in-quiry whether she is single, married, with or without children? She may be asked questions — about her education, prior work, family, or religious affiliation. For every charge account or driver's license, she will have to reveal much personal information. No physician can treat her without learning much about her medical and family background. Voting, school attendance, an application of accident insurance, or signing up with a computer dating service all are conditional on sharing personal infor-mation.

Privacy is one of the personal attributes that most people cherish. We want control over who can get to know us well. We also would prefer to protect ourselves from being misunderstood or abused. The basic distrust between many citizens and their government or other large organizations remains. It is hard to love or trust a "system". A few draft registers have publicly burned their registration cards. There also are occasional in-stances of computer sabotage. But these modern day Luddites are not likely to succeed in stifling one of the world's most rapidly growing industries — information technology.

Even those inclined to favor reforms in the way ID documents are now issued, urge that caution be exercised before any program is authorized that could become a basis for a national identification system. Senator Mark O. Hatfield of the state of Washington, advocated a plan for a se-cure system of employment eligibility; but he urged that limits be placed on its general use — congressional participation in the planning the de-tails. (S. 529):

> There is no consensus among our citizens, let alone among the members
> of Congress, that a national identification card is desirable. I am aware that
> S.529 limits the use of any identification document that may evolve from
> this bill, and I remind you that when the Social Security card was instituted,
> its use was similarly restricted. I deeply resent the extent to which the Social
> Security card has become a nationwide identifier, and I am mindful of how
> this new card could precipitate a gross invasion of privacy.

THE RIGHT TO CONFIDENTIALITY

The Constitution includes no direct reference to a right to privacy, but many of its guarantees have been so interpreted by the federal courts and by Congress. The Privacy Protection Study Commission of 1977 decided against a more tamper-resistant Social Security numbering system with-out appropriate safeguards against its abuse by government officials or by others. An even stronger stand against this idea was taken by a Secretary Advisory Committee on Automated Personal Data Systems study of the Department of Health, Education and Welfare:[5]

> A permanent SSN issued at birth could create an incentive for institutions to pool or link their records, thereby making it possible to bring a lifetime of information to bear on any decision about a given indvidual. American culture is rich in the belief that an individual can pull up stakes and make a fresh start, but a universal identified (person) might become a prisoner of his recorded past.

In a brief for the American Civil Liberties Union (ACLU), its then legislative director John Shattuck, concluded that the proposal for a tamper-resistant work identifier "would merely exchange one problem for a different and more serious problem."[6] Shattuck pointed out that the position of his organization was in agreement with the view of the late Senator Sam J. Ervin, when he proposed what was later enacted as the *Privacy Act of 1974*:

> There must be limits upon what the government can know about each of its citizens. Each time we give up a bit of information about ourselves to the government, we give up some of our freedom. For the more the government or any institution knows about us, the more power it has over us. When the government knows all of our secrets, we stand naked before official power, stripped of our privacy. We lose our rights and privileges. The Bill of Rights then becomes just so many words.

In a related brief, the ACLU staff testified against the adoption of an employment verification system as part of the proposed Immigration Reform and Control Act of 1982:[7]

> First, in the case of a National Identity Card, by creating a new de facto domestic passport, the possession of which, if required, could have the effect of substantially expanding the government's power to stop, question and search without a warrant—a power which is now fortunately, confined to the narrow area of highway safety and the regulation of drivers' licenses.
>
> Second, a secure verification system would very likely be built on a national population data bank which would centralize personal data about all persons authorized to work in the United States, so that their movements and characteristics could be followed by employers and other authorized users of the system.
>
> Third, to the extent that this database is used over time to further other important government programs and policies unrelated to immigration control, it would become a means for tracking and controlling the activities of millions of citizens and lawful residents of the United States.

The ACLU concerns are more widespread than its membership. Similar fears have been the basis of rejection of various proposals for adopting more secure national identifiers, both in the United States, in England, and elsewhere. This view was summarized in an editorial in the *Wall Street Journal*:[8]

> Now that the Simpson-Mazzoli immigration bill has overwhelmingly passed the Senate and moves over to the House, maybe someone can figure out exactly what it says. The Reagan administration actively supports the bill, opposes a national identity card, but can't quite decide whether the immigration bill would or wouldn't lead to one.
>
> Annelise Anderson, associate director of the Office of Management and Budget, apparently thinks it could. In a newspaper interview last week, she said the administration opposed the section of the Senate bill calling for a "secure system to determine employment eligibility" three years after enactment. But OMB promptly issued a press release saying Mrs. Anderson was expressing only her personal views. Meanwhile, it says, the administration will push ahead with clarifying amendments to make sure the bill doesn't require a national ID.
>
> The Senate language is ambiguous. It calls for an identification system "resistant to counterfeiting and tampering." However, existing documents such as birth certificates and driver's licenses—which vary from state to state—and even Social Security Cards are a cinch to fake. It's hard to imagine a difficult-to-counterfeit system without an expensive national ID system—either some kind of nationally issued working papers or an electronic call-in data bank.
>
> The specter of a national ID card sends shivers down liberty-loving spines. It conjures up images of Soviet and Nazi tyranny, of South African pass laws, or, on a more benign level, of French bureaucrats imagining they're some kind of Napoleon every time they ask to see your papers. It raises fears that arrest records, credit ratings, even secret FBI reports, will be kept in central files on each individual—that some minor functionary in Baltimore will stop you from closing a condominium deal until you pay your overdue parking tickets in Kansas City.
>
> Messrs. Simpson and Mazzoli have tried to assuage these fears by including specific safeguards against using the IDs for law enforcement or for any purpose other than "verifying that the individual is not an unauthorized alien." Still, civil libertarians are afraid the ID would be a precedent for an internal passport. To avoid charges of discrimination against legal residents who look foreign, the government would have to require that everyone in the labor force carry work authorization papers, making the system a tempting target for other uses.
>
> The most convincing arguments we've heard against the Simpson-Mazzoli bill come from Hispanic groups, which say its provisions—particularly employer sanctions—cannot be seriously enforced without massive expenditures on policing and without identification measures that public

opinion will most likely not accept. Before the bill goes any further, it might be a good idea to consider whether this nation is willing to pay the costs of enforcement, including a possible infringement on individual liberties.

An even more passionate plea against a national identification system by William Safire was serialized nationally:[9]

> In a well meaning effort to curb the employment of illegal aliens, and with the hearty good wishes of editorialists who ordinarily pride themselves on guarding against the intrusion of government into the private lives of individual Americans, Congress is about to take this generation's longest step toward totalitarianism.
>
> There is no 'slippery slope' toward loss of liberties" insists Senator Alan Simpson of Wyoming, author of the latest immigration bill, "only a long staircase where each step downward must be first tolerated by the American people and their leaders."
>
> The first step downward on the Simpson staircase to Big-Brotherdom is the requirement that within three years the federal government come up with a "secure system to determine employment eligibility in the United States."
>
> Despite denials, that means a national identity card. Nobody who is pushing this bill admits that—on the contrary, all sorts of "safeguards" and rhetorical warnings about not having to carry an identity card on one's person at all times are festooned on the bill. Much is made of the use of passports, Social Security cards and driver's licenses as "preferred" forms of identification, but anyone who takes the trouble to read this legislation can see that the disclaimers are intended to help the medicine go down.
>
> Most American citizens are being led to believe that only aliens will be required to show "papers." But how can a prospective employer tell who is an alien? If the applicant could say, "I'm an American, I don't have any card," the new control system would immediately break down. The very basis of the proposed law is the notion that individuals must carry verifiable papers —more likely, a card keyed to a "new government data bank"—to prove eligibility for work.
>
> No big deal, say those who consider illegal immigration more fearsome than the coming of an internal passport; if you're legitimate, you shouldn't object. And shucks, law-enforcement officials won't use it for anything else, nosirree—at least not until the nation is ready for another legislated step down the staircase.
>
> Most Americans see no danger at all in a national identity card. Most people even like the idea of a piece of plastic that tells the world, and themselves, who they are.
>
> "I'm me," says the little card. "I'm entitled to all the benefits that go with being provably and demonstrably me." Good citizens—the ones who vote regularly, and who don't get into auto accidents might get a gold card.
>
> Once the down staircase is set in place, the temptation to take each next step will be irresistible. Certainly every business would want to ask custom-

ers to insert their identity cards into the whizbang credit checker. Banks, phone companies, schools, hotels would all take advantage of the obvious utility of the document that could not be counterfeited. Law enforcement and tax collection would surely be easier, because the federal government would know at all times exactly where everybody was and what they were spending.

And then you might as well live in the Soviet Union. One of the great differences between free and enslaved societies is the right of the individual to live and work without the government knowing his every move. There can sometimes be privacy without freedom, as those in solitary confinement know, but there can be no freedom without privacy.

When Patty Hearst managed to remain a fugitive for 591 days, that did not mean the FBI was bad at catching fugitives; it meant that America was a free society. In China or the Soviet Union she would have been captured in days, because it is impossible for ordinary citizens to move about without permission. If our values mean anything at all, they mean that it is better to tolerate the illegal movement of aliens and even criminals than to tolerate the constant surveillance of the free.

The attorney general, who evidently has no grasp of libertarian conservative principles, will not fight this legislation. When an outside adviser, Martin Anderson—who with his wife, Annelise, at OMB represent what is left of the conservative conscience of the Reagan administration—objected in a Cabinet meeting to this danger of federal intrusion, William French Smith was forced to tell Congress of "a small but serious objection" to the identity card clause. He later made his objection meaningless by pretending it was "inappropriate to presume" he would have to do what the bill mandates him to do—come up with a foolproof identity system.

We are entering the computer age. Combined with a national identity card—an abuse of power that Peter Rodino professes to oppose in the House, as he makes it inevitable—government computers and data banks pose a threat to personal liberty. Though aimed against "undocumented workers," the computer tattoo will be pressed on you and me.

Critics of ID card improvement programs often fail to address the fact that even without a national basic identity card, the government and business already have the capability to collect, store, and retrieve very sensitive and detailed information about every individual. The Civil Service Commission, the FBI, and others in the government have for a long time been empowered to undertake investigations in which the life of every person is subjected to scrutiny from the cradle to the grave.

EXCESSIVE VIGILANCE

In large cities people are often afraid to walk in their own neighborhood. Many live behind bolted doors; some keep guns for their personal defense. In response to such fears, the police department of Lenaxa, Kansas induced businessmen and landlords to inform them when hiring a new employee or offering an apartment for rent. The purpose of this strategy was to "keep an eye on who is coming into town." Most landlords and businessmen were glad to cooperate, since the police chief used this information to check the names with a computerized "ALERT" information system kept by the nearby Kansas City Police Department on persons with a criminal record. One could also be included in this roster for other reasons; for instance, being involved in demonstrations for politically unpopular causes. The practice was stopped and procedures were adopted to minimize the risk of privacy abuse.[10]

Privacy rights have always been threatened whenever government or private organizations or individuals have information that could be used in an unreasonable fashion. Since the publication of Arthur R. Miller's *Assault on Privacy*,[11] a revised version could no doubt be compiled with more recent illustrations of privacy abuses. But the interest of society in making effective use of personal data for crime control, welfare program administration, and tax collection as well as for commercial uses, generates growing pressure for maximizing data base accuracy. This preference for verified information also enhances the risk of misuse by officials of available dossiers for personal gain or political purposes.

There is no simple answer to this dilemma. More and more information is needed to conduct our personal and public affairs. This requirement also entails the risk that information be abused when it comes into the wrong hands.

DOCUMENTARY SELF-INCRIMINATION

Commercial and computer crimes, income tax evasion, and many other offenses are generally discovered through inconsistencies between different data files. Law enforcement could be strengthened by periodic mass screening of data bases to identify categories of persons who might be involved in underreporting of their income, the laundering of money through indirect transactions, or making contradictory statements about their personal circumstances. When would such law enforcement techniques turn into "surreptitious snooping?"

Is it a violation of the Fourth Amendment to search files on transactions of an investment firm officer suspected of having stolen funds from customer accounts? What about a now commonplace screening of bank assets of candidates for appointment to a responsible public post or of persons who have applied for food stamps? Are these procedures a form of entrapment? The U.S. courts have not favored such an interpretation.

But these legal issues arise repeatedly, as data base matching is becoming an increasingly common procedure. It can improve administrative efficiency and minimize error, but it also provides data about possible violations of the law.

A two day Senate Committee hearing was held in 1982 under the chairmanship of William S. Cohen of Maine on Oversight of Computer Matching To Detect Fraud and Mismanagement in Government Programs. These issues were dissected in extensive testimony. It was made clear that there is a problem of balancing personal and public interests. No one who testified at these hearings was ready to defend the idea that the federal government be authorized to maintain lists of persons who included payments to a psychiatrist among their medical deductions when submitting their income tax. At the same time, the Department of State and the CIA have reasons to exclude from sensitive security positions persons with a history of severe or chronic mental illness. Would it then be proper to check the personal files of job applicants for evidence of a psychiatric illness?

Tax returns of physicians are now being checked by the IRS to verify that they fully report their earnings, sometimes by matching them against reports by patients, hospitals, and insurance providers. Since data base matching is already being used to detect people who apply for welfare entitlements on the basis of nonexisting (false) SSNs, it would be unpopular to oppose similar roster verification procedures to target white collar crimes. In recent years, the inspector general of the Department of Health and Human Services found as follows:[12]

> There are complex laboratory tests that can normally be performed only within a hospital. In five locations, computer searches of billings to Medicare/Medicaid disclosed claims for allegedly doing such tests in physicians' offices.
>
> Physicians can reasonably charge higher fees for a first visit because they need to spend more time with a new patient than during subsequent visits dealing with the same problem. A data matching project in just one location was able to unearth more than half a million dollars in excessive claims by billing follow-up visits at the same high rate as the initial examination.

Similar comparisons of rosters could no doubt disclose other inconsistencies in claims, billings, and disbursement. This procedure was questioned on four constitutional grounds by John Shattuck for the ACLU[13]:

> 1. Fourth Amendment objections against "unreasonable searches and seizures." While no house to house searches were conducted to locate evidence of possible wrong-doing, the results are quite the same: "A massive dragnet into the private affairs of a huge number of persons."

2. People are entitled to be presumed innocent until proven guilty. They should not be expected to justify their conduct, whenever the government may choose to investigate them without prior and specific evidence of wrongdoing. In Massachusetts, welfare officials automatically cancelled allocations to persons who were discovered to have bank accounts above a given size. Some of them were later able to prove that they continued to be entitled to their public welfare checks. While such automatic cut-off procedures have been discontinued, this incident illustrates a potential abuse that can occur when computer data are used without first checking on their accuracy and relevancy.

3. The *Privacy Act of 1974* advocated the principle that individuals have a right to control the use of information about themselves. They should be able to prevent its use without their consent for purposes wholly unrelated to those for which it had been originally obtained. But this legislation also sanctions the use of personal data files in the investigation of specific violations of the law. How these conflicting principles are to be balanced is left unclear.

4. When a computer-matching program locates information that implicates a person in an illegal act, does this constitute a violation of due process procedures? Such suspects are located without a warrant being issued or without any particular person being under suspicion. An entire category of persons, like food stamp recipients, are checked out—in a "fishing expedition"—which can lead to the discovery of persons who have income from wages well above a level that would entitle them to food stamps.

Constitutional objections could be met by requiring physicians to sign a waiver authorizing data base matching of their billings and related files as a condition of receiving health insurances payments. The same can be done with defense contractors, whose billing practices are coming under increasingly close surveillance in view of the evidence that billions of dollars of unjustified charges have been added to "cost plus" contracts in recent years.

Defenders of computer matching point out that it is a non-intrusive procedure of protecting the public interest. No one need to search the home of a subject or detain them for investigation. Data base matching allows accountants to proceed systematically in checking out clues of possible law violations or misrepresentation of evidence. The U.S. federal, state, and local income tax collection procedures would break down without this feature.

Data base matching procedures have been routine for years in some businesses, especially in the banking and insurance industry. A person who repeatedly travelled in the Middle East was refused life insurance. Banks are apt to check the credit rating of an applicant for a loan. Blue Shield disallows fees to physicians whose patients fail to confirm that an alleged service was actually rendered. People who claim a full paycheck may be tripped by a time-clock that fails to show they had been at work during some of the pay period.

Secure identity documents make it possible to introduce preventive techniques to minimize white collar crimes and other law violations that involve fraudulent records. But information power, like all power, needs to be administered under policies that can be defended as being clearly within the public interest.

Privacy rights deserve protection against unreasonable uses of the contradictions, lapses in memory, and errors that will always occur when fallible human beings provide data. It must also be remembered that the information is coded and recorded by human operators who can become tired, bored, or careless. The *Bill of Rights* will need to be updated to differentiate more clearly than is now possible between publicly sanctioned roster searches and circumstances when they should be forbidden as a form of involuntary self-incrimination.

CUMULATIVE INFORMATION ANALYSIS

The Central Intelligence Agency, (CIA) is prohibited by law from engaging in domestic activities. But there are no prohibitions against another type of "CIA"—*Cumulative Information Analysis*. Only criminals and those who have carefully constructed a trail of false identity (like FBI undercover agents) can exempt themselves from such a procedure.

Candidates for high public office are expected to disclose the most intimate facts of their private life, including several years tax returns. The public learned that President Ronald Reagan who had urged Americans to take up the slack in government welfare programs, was personally "tight" in making charitable contributions. Senator Eagleton of Missouri was pressured to withdraw as a vice-presidential candidate after details of his private medical record were disclosed. Background information can be assembled with great speed with more details than can be recalled by the subject.

The complexity of making such an analysis—routinely performed by private investigators or the FBI—is being reduced. Personal data files are becoming increasingly computerized. It is routine for people to give consent for having their files checked if they want a job or a bank loan. Nothing new would be added to this already available volume of data by any of the proposed national identity procedures that have been under consideration.

It is simply not true that a national identity document would be needed to enable the feared "Big Brother" to tyrannize the public. The machinery for close surveillance of people already exists. What keeps it and Cumulative Information Analysis under control are America's strong traditions in favor of privacy, reinforced by legislation so that an aggrieved person, damaged by the unauthorized release of personal data, can sue for compensation in a court of law. However, the growing use of credit cards and checkless transfer of funds through digital channels provides a basis for an even more intrusive pattern of surveillance: an illustration of what might soon become possible was provided by the publishers of *Computers and People*.[14]

Daily Surveillance Sheet—Confidential
July 13, 1984

Subject: John Q. Public, 4 Home Street, Anywhere, USA. Male, age 40, Married, Electrical engineer.

Purchases: Wall Street Journal, $1.00;

   Breakfast, $2.25;

   Gasoline, $6.00; Phone (111-1234), $.25;

   Lunch, $4.00; Cocktail, 1.50;

   Bank (cash withdrawal) $200.00;

   Lingerie, $135.67; Phone (111-8769), .85; Phone (869-1111), $.80; Bourbon, $12.53; *Boston Globe*, $.50.

Preliminary Analysis

   Owns stock (90 percent probability).

   Heavy starch breakfast—probably overweight.

   Bought $6.00 gasoline. Owns VW. So far this week, subject has bought $25.00 worth of gasoline.

   Obviously doing something besides driving 9 miles to work.

   Bought gasoline at 7:57 at gas station 6 miles from work.

   Subject probably late for work.

   Third such occurrence this week.

   Phone number 111-1234 belongs to Joe Book. Book was arrested for illegal book making in 1970, 1978 and 1982.

   No convictions. Phone number 222-5678 belongs to expensive men's barber shop specializing in hair restoration.

   Drinks during lunch. Withdrew $200.00 in cash.

   Very unusual since all legal purchases can be made using a Uniform Federal Funds Transfer Card.

   Cash usually used for illegal purchases.

   Bought expensive lingerie. Not his wife's size.

   Phone No. 111-8769 belongs to Jane Doe.

   Phone No. 869-1111. Reservation for Las Vegas (without wife).

   Third trip in last three months to Las Vegas (without wife).

No job related firms in Las Vegas. Will scan file to see if anyone has gone to Las Vegas at the same time and compare to subject's phone call numbers.

Purchased Bourbon. Third bottle this month. Either heavy drinker or must be entertaining.

Subject left work at 4 PM. He purchased Bourbon 1 mile from his job at 4:10 PM. (Opposite direction from his house).

Subject bought newspaper at 6:30 PM near his house.

Unaccountable 2.5 hours.

Subject made 3 purchases today from young blondes.

(Statistical 1 chance in 78.)

Probably has weakness for young blondes.

(Jane Doe is a young blonde).

The accumulation of such intrusive information is technically feasible. Divorce lawyers and private investigators can sometimes accumulate such a dossier, but in order to do it well, a warrant would be required. Such privacy invasive accumulation of data has been used to investigate fraud and other crimes. The New York State Commission on Featherbedding Practices was able to document that fraudulent practices are commonplace in the New York construction industry. For instance, one operating engineer—a person who operates a bulldozer, a crane or other heavy equipment—was collecting wages of $400,000 a year. He had submitted vouchers for regular pay and overtime; telephone calls proved beyond doubt that he was vacationing in such places as Acapulco, St. Maartin, in Europe, and elsewhere. It is comonplace for workers to claim pay and overtime for periods when they are not working. Construction companies acquiesce to avoid conflict with local unions.[15]

Credit card agencies do not normally compile such detailed profiles. The time when purchases are made is rarely recorded. Many department stores, the Warner AMEX Corporation, and probably other cable TV systems have adopted privacy protection procedures. Warner AMEX promises to keep information about cable TV viewing preferences only as long as needed for billing purposes. Subscribers would be notified, if this is legally permitted, should a Government agency obtain a court order to see their file.[16] The kind of data used in the above fictitious "Daily Surveillance Sheet" is not being collected, except when an individual is under intensive observation by a number of private or public detectives. Only in a dictatorship could conditions be created to collect such information routinely.

Technically, a web of surveillance procedures could be spun around any person targeted by the government or an individual willing to hire a crew of private detectives. Existing legislation is too vague to limit such Comprehensive Information Analysis to cases where the public interest clearly overrides such gross violations of personal privacy. But the ordinary day-to-day risks of storage of personal data are much more mundane.

In the view of most policy analysts, the fact that technology can be misused does not justify a refusal to employ it. Millions of people have installed burglar alarm systems, designed to spy on their own living quarters. The National Security Agency is reputed to have the technical capacity to monitor 54,000 telephones transmissions to and from the United States, but existing legislation to prohibit unauthorized tapping of telephones by private persons or government agencies work quite well.

There are no neat boundaries between the right to privacy and the needs of national security. Wherever the line is drawn, technological changes require that this balance be reviewed periodically as more efficient intrusive procedures come into common use.

CURRENT U.S. POLICIES

Governments enjoy special powers. Their use would be immoral and unlawful if exercised by any individual: *Governments can and do assume* the right to misrepresent, to lie—even to kill. Secret services, even in democracies, can issue a false identity document to some of their agents. Criminals are occasionally entrapped into supplying evidence that can convict them, as in ABSCAM and in other false front operations. The United States government routinely protects key witnesses or escaped foreign spies by issuing a false ID document, backed up by a fraudulent birth certificate or whatever else is needed to make the camouflaged identity creditable.

The propriety of these exceptions to the moral code is in part based on the infrequency of their use. No democracy can function well without enjoying creditability. A move toward organized mass surveillance would run into strong public opinion opposition. Most Americans favor minimal interference in their personal affairs by the government. But their viewpoint shifts radically if the targets of surveillance are criminals or unpopular social movements.

Governments are generally expected to be vigilant in using their resources to minimize crime. The Constitution does, however, subject this power to many limitations. A warrant must be issued by a court before a person's home or files can be searched for possible evidence of alleged wrongdoing. This judicial restraint does not apply to data stored in files of voluntary organizations and private businesses. Physicians, lawyers, national security agencies, the U.S. census bureau and others have not been able to enforce their claim to keep confidential files.

The Federal Advisory Committee on False Identification (FACFI) recommended that the security of existing documents be upgraded. It opposed the use of biometric indicators for general use in ID documents. It also spoke out strongly against proposals for a national ID system:[17]

> It is certain that any new system designed to verify and store identity information on over 200 million people would be extremely expensive and require a major national effort. It is highly probable that proposals for such a system would be opposed politically. If such a system were implemented despite these difficulties, it would be subject to defeat by imposters and counterfeiters taking advantage of the careless inspection of documents or through corruption of officials. Occasional errors would also occur in such a system that could adversely affect innocent people. Organized crime would take advantage of any national ID system because of the presumption of validity surrounding such a large system. Criminals could reap benefits far greater than they obtain under the current multi-faceted system of identification.

As previously noted, the proposed Simpson-Mazzoli Immigration Reform and Control Act is contrary to this recommendation. The bill includes a provision for a nationwide work entitlement procedure; but in the years since the FACFI report was first conceived, technological improvement in the accuracy of ID documents has outdated many of its factual considerations. The FACFI and its staff failed to investigate the cost and privacy safeguards that could be built into a new ID procedure to greatly cut down on identity frauds. Congress also authorized a growing number and variety of new ID systems, but in an uncoordinated way with regard to standards of safety for issuing them.

The case for and against a VIP document needs to be reconsidered in the light of the current state of technological development. In 1982 there were already 15,000 computers and a work force of more than 100,000 computer specialists in the federal government.[18] The volume of information they can store and retrieve about nearly every American is staggering. A large part of the country's population could be subjected to intrusive surveillance procedures. But this potential for repression is not being utilized. Existing legal barriers against such abuses work well most of the time. Many Americans are, however, concerned about the clandestine adoption of such devices by government security services or private investigators.

One data source that may be useful to policy makers in reviewing this controversial issue is the experiences of Western democracies. Most of them have a nationwide ID program. Some of their experiences and practices will be reviewed in the next chapter.

REFERENCES

1. Whyte, William H. "The Case for the Universal Card", *Fortune,* April 1954:137–232.

2. Morgan, Richard E., *Domestic Intelligence: Monitoring Dissent In America,* Austin and London: University of Texas Press, 1980; Athan, Theoris, *Spying on Americans: Political Surveillance From Hoover to the Houston Plan,* Philadelphia: Temple University Press, April 1978: 137–232.

3. Barron, John, *KGB: The Secret Work of the Soviet Secret Agents,* New York: Bantam Books 1974, 127–138.

4. Butterfield, Fox, *China, Alive in the Bitter Sea,* Toronto and New York: Bantam Books, 1982.

5. Department of Health, Education and Welfare. Study of "Secretary Advisory Committee on Automated Personal Data Systems." July 1973, 111–112.

6. Shattuck, John, May 6, 1981:11,120 Congressional Record, 12646; 1974.

7. Shattuck, John H. and Wade J. Henderson "Statement on The Immigration Reform and Control Act of 1982," H.R. 5872/S.2222, American Civil Liberties Union, April 1, 1982, p. 7.

8. *Wall Street Journal.* Sept. 2, 1982.

9. Safire, William, *Pittsburgh Post Gazette,* September 10, 1982:6.

10. Westin, Alan F. and Michael A. Baker, *Databanks in a Free Society: Computers Record Keeping and Privacy,* New York: Quadrangle Books, 1972:80–88.

11. Miller, Arthur R., *The Assault on Privacy,* Ann Arbor: University of Michigan Press, 1971.

12. Inspector General of the Department of Health and Human Services.

13. Shattuck, John, American Civil Liberties Union, December 15, 1982.

14. Massachusetts Berkeley Enterprises, Inc., *Computers and People.* Vol. 24, 1975.

15. *New York Times,* June 12, 1985.

16. Westin, Alan F., "Home Information Systems: The Privacy Debate", *Datamation,* vol. 28, no. 7, July 1982:100–113.

17. Federal Advisory Committee on False Identification, *The Criminal Use of False Identification,* Washington, D.C.; U.S. Government Printing Office, 1976: 74–75.

18. Head, Robert V., *Federal Information System Management,* Washington, D.C.: The Brookings Institution, 1982, 4. U.S. Government Printing Office, November 1976:75.

CHAPTER SIX

IDENTIFICATION AND DEMOCRACY

PEOPLE NUMBERING

Most modern nations and an increasing proportion of developing countries have a comprehensive population register. Iceland pioneered with the first modern census in 1703 (an honor also claimed by Sweden) and was the first nation to publish data from its 1750 census. The Scandinavian national registers and many others are based on a coordinated birth and death registration system, something lacking in the United States. Each person is assigned a unique "birth number" for use in the Central Personal Register. It is constructed of three parts on the basis of following principles: 1. Six digits representing the day, month, and year of birth. 2. Three digits to designate sex, century of birth, and citizenship status. 3. Two algorithms calculated on the basis of the other nine digits. This secret code, it is estimated, will disclose all but one mistake in an average of one hundred thousand incorrect numbers.

Identity documents contain limited and largely innocuous personal status data. But there are also more extensive files in a central register with additional information. It goes well beyond what would be needed for verifying one's personal identity. Included are data on parentage, successive places of residence, schooling, occupation, citizenship, and religion. In Sweden, the registers are also used to collect church taxes from all wage earners except those who officially opt out of any religious affiliation.

Strong objections have been voiced to the use of the personal number in files kept for business purposes. The reason given is that data base matching might be made too easy. Others do not like the fact that the birth number reveals the card owner's age. Denmark recently required its banks to withdraw all credit cards that had used the birth number. But other people seem to prefer the convenience of having to memorize only one number for many different purposes.

The procurement and use of a false ID card is less common in Europe than in America. Casual and short-term forgeries occur when cashing a check with a false ID or when entering a country with a false passport. But it is difficult to establish a new identity or to maintain several of them simultaneously. Someone would have to construct an entire set of fake ancestors, school attendance, church records, marital history, and changes of address. Once these records become fully computerized, it will become even more difficult for anyone who expects to use a false, stolen, or counterfeited ID document for any length of time.

In some Western countries like Austria, where the population registers have been administered locally, a proposal for its nationalization is under discussion. In France and in West Germany the central roster procedure was carefully considered but rejected. The opposition believes that localized records would inhibit the matching of ID records with information in health, welfare, and national security files. However, when file comparisons are needed for national security or crime prevention purposes, the local population rosters are open to the authorities. Matching procedures are just a bit more expensive and inconvenient.

Europeans have never experienced the anonymity of the frontier. People never could move around without informing the local authorities. It is taken for granted that government bodies need to have an up-to-date population roster. The secure ID card technology is well developed. European manufacturers compete aggressively in the race for new patents. But there also are lively social policy debates about the question: how much should any government be allowed to know about the private personal affairs of its citizens? What can be done to prevent abuses of the data now available to the keeper of personal data files? What use, if any, should be made of the data card technology to produce tamper-resistant, interactive, and machine readable ID documents?

Japan has a system of hand-written genealogical records maintained for generations by local authorities. They are accessible to the public. Families whose children wish to marry someone not well known in the community are likely to check the records of the intended spouse and his kinship group. Ethnocentricism is still pronounced in Japan, in spite of its democratic constitution.

Few families would be agreeable to a marriage with a Korean or a member of a Barakumin family, social outcasts since the Tokugawa period. These stigmatized persons cannot be physically distinguished from other Japanese. But they are regarded as socially inferior. They will rarely be given a good government job or a position in industry. The misuses of birth and death records in Japan are similar to those in the United States: of a few decades ago when it was not uncommon to search records to identify persons who had a black ancestor, although they and their family were "passing" as white.

As Japanese public records become better computerized, there may not be any change in what is recorded. Family history could, however, be protected from unauthorized use within legislatively mandated standards of privacy. This would make it easier for the government to implement its policy of counteracting widespread discriminatory practices against the Koreans and the Barakumin. Computerization does not necessarily increase the risk of data abuse.

The secret police in dictatorships have little difficulty in using conventional data sources to find their victims. During World War II the Japanese used telephone books in Indonesia to locate Dutch and Indonesian leaders whom they wanted to intern or kill after occupying the country. During the German occupation of much of Europe, the Nazis used population registers and personal identity documents to deport and ultimately kill anti-Nazis, many Gypsies, and nearly all Jews. But when these records were not available, the Gestapo was able to use quisling informants and synagogue records for locating many of their victims.

A belief in the administrative utility of national personal identification rosters in all these victimized nations led to their postwar continuation in spite of frightening abuses. France, West Germany, Belgium and others continue to issue an identity document to everyone. Even where the law does not require it, most people carry an ID card on their person for ready use, when signing for a certified letter, when cashing a check, when applying for a job or when registering in a hotel.

In Israel, residents over sixteen are required to carry their ID document at all times when away from home. The document facilitates occasional security checks conducted without prior notice. ID cards are also required of all adults in Luxembourg and Greece. In Switzerland, about half the population has a nationally issued document. In England, Austria and a few other countries, there is no general ID requirement. People can use any one of several IDs—a passport, a drivers license, a personal identity card or a Dienstausweis, a special ID document issued to civil servants. All of them include a photograph, the name, and birthday of the holder.

There are additional registers for health insurance, welfare entitlements and tax purposes. In general, it is easy for European governments to locate individuals and retrieve detailed information about their personal and family history. But unlike the Nazi period, such uses are now circumscribed by privacy regulations in at least eleven nations and enforced by officers with extensive powers. Consequently, few abuses are being reported. Reports from the German Democratic Republic indicate that regulations are under consideration affecting data protection. But according to Wilhelm Steinmueller, they seem to be focused on data *security* to protect state interests, not on the *protection* of individuals.[1]

The Norwegian Research Center for Computers and Law noted a few cases of citizens who refused to provide information required by the country's 1972 census. In only one instance did the objector refer to her concern for privacy of computerized information systems. Another individual based his objection on recollections of forced enlistments under German occupation. The Norwegian public at large appeared to accept their national identity system as normal and useful.[2]

Many of the world's ID documents are still printed on simple paper. Few are machine readable. None are interactive, capable of storing information on how they are used. There is reluctance about moving quickly to utilize the available technology to produce more reliable documents out of concern that a centralized and computerized system might give the government too much information about the life of the average citizen. This cautious approach to technological updating is likely to change over the next decade. In West Germany, the Federal Printing Office has been commissioned to develop a laminated identity card, with the following features:

1. Special paper, microdots, algorithms and other electronically readable safety features.
2. Alteration security, so that a card will tear if one tries to change the photograph or other data once it has been issued and laminated.
3. Procedures to prevent theft of empty forms from local offices where they may be stored.
4. Machine readability so that people could be digitally checked at busy airports, border stations, or harbors.

Sweden manufactures highly tamper-resistant personal identity documents for other countries, for banks and for other agencies, but its passports lack biometric indicators and can be forged as easily as those of most other nations. Special precautions have been under discussion, but they have not yet been adopted. More attention is given to security features in Finland. While no one is required to carry a national ID card, citizens are expected to prove their identity to authorities upon request. Most people have ID documents. The data on which they are based are kept locally. Records are not computerized, but because of the small size of the country and moderate population mobility, it is easy to verify information like citizenship status and place of residence manually.

IDENTITY AS A NUMBER

A coordinated Personal Identification Numbering (PIN) system device for differentiating residents by other than name was introduced in all the Scandinavian countries. In Sweden the family records are kept by the about 2,500 Lutheran parish offices. Weekly up-dating reports are forwarded to the National Central Bureau of Statistics. New addresses, births, deaths, and other information are immediately recorded giving the country a relatively up-to-date total population registry. The government of Sweden considered abolishing the PIN (Personal Identification Number) as part of a campaign to minimize privacy abuses. After careful study of the technical and social issues involved, it was decided to keep it as the basis its National Central Bureau of Statistics and of 114 different personal data files. Much of the information is kept in encrypted form, to prevent data leakage.

West Germany has more computers than any other European nation. After an extensive debate in its parliament, the government opted in favor of a meaningless and randomly chosen identity number to differentiate persons who might have an identical name. This ID number, (Personenkennzeichen), unlike the SSN in America, cannot be used legally by other government agencies or private organizations as an index for computer storage and retrieval of information. Powerful subgroups thought that the widespread use of one number would encourage excessive data base matching. No action was taken, however, to significantly reduce the powers of the police and state security services to access personal data files in pursuit of specific investigations. This includes three extensive public information systems available to authorized officials as needed:[3] 1. The social and health insurance system, the "Social Data Information System of the Federal Republic of Germany". 2. The security files NADIS and DISPOL, combined data bases of federal and state organs to protect the constitution, to serve the West German military and intelligence services, and to monitor traffic across the country's borders. 3. Mandatory population registers in about 4000 localities, which are coordinated nationally to register data on major life events, including birth, education, changes in residence, marriage status, and death.

England represents a significant exception to the administrative use of a general population register. A national identity card had been in use during the Battle for Britain, largely for rationing purposes. It was discontinued after victory was won. As in the United States, there is widespread distrust of government. The right to withhold identity information is cherished by English civil liberty advocates. But in reality the technology is already available enabling the security services to link many of the over 200 separate British personal data files, including those of the Inland Revenue (tax) unit, the Department of Health and Social Security, the Department of Employment and of M-15, the British equivalent of the FBI and CIA.[4] A combined search of these files is possible by using a person's name and national insurance number.

France instituted a personal registry in Paris in 1792, primarily to locate nobility hiding from the revolutionaries. Later, this practice was extended to the whole country, registers being kept in each district. After World War I, the procedures were centralized in the Institut National de la Statisticque et des Etudes Economiques (National Institute of Statistics and Economic Research). Each person was given a unique identity number. Recently, after more than a decade of study, a modernized procedure was adopted to store the information centrally on magnetic tapes and to issue nearly tamper-proof plastic cards. But the Socialist Government, which came into power in 1981, canceled this program. It also eliminated mandatory fingerprints. French companies hold many of the basic patents of the micro-chip ("smart") card technology. But the policy to maintain the status quo with regard to ID card administration reflects concern that a centralized and computerized system would give the French authorities too much privacy-sensitive information.

In West Germany and in the Netherlands, parliament also considered legislation to shift to a nationally supervised registry. No action has been taken so far. There is a keen interest in enhancing the speed and accuracy of personal IDs. But many legislators seemed to fear that centralization of local lists of residents into a single nationwide roster would give the police too much power. Yet, comprehensive and centrally available personal data already exist in all but form, on a need to know basis. Credit and other business organizations also have been able to accumulate comprehensive files on most of the adult population.

THE ID CARD CURTAIN

Amid democratically governed areas, Hong Kong adopted what is probably the most diversified use of an ID system in a democratic society. ID cards are used as a device to limit population growth through illegal immigration. Hong Kong has about 5.5 million people crowded into 1000 square kilometers, including many mountainous and uninhabitable islands. Not until 1949 did the government require travel documents from mainland Chinese who wanted to enter the Crown Colony. Most of them were destitute refugees fleeing from abject poverty and tyranny.

As a first control measure, a fence was strung along the border, heavily guarded by British troops. But there was a never ending supply of young and desperate Chinese ready to risk drowning or being killed by sharks while swimming onto a Hong Kong Beach. In 1979, for instance, 89,900 illegal immigrants were apprehended and returned to mainland China. But another 107,700 illegals were later found to have evaded capture where the government had to face the limits of its resources to provide additional refugees with housing, employment, and other necessities.

A carrot and stick policy was adopted. The government announced that all illegal immigrants would henceforth be returned to China, but offered amnesty to all those who had arrived before October 24, 1982, provided they registered within three days. Each was given an identity card entitling them to remain.

Enforcement of this provision required that all residents, even those living in Hong Kong for many generations, have an identity card. After a period of grace, anyone lacking such a document would be presumed to have entered the country illegally. They could not obtain or keep a job, register their children in school, or receive any of the colony's many welfare benefits other than emergency medical services. They would be deported immediately to nearby China.

Illegal immigration dropped immediately and now is down to a trickle. Hong Kong is replacing its formerly easily counterfeited ID document with a version that is close to being tamper-proof. The only border crossers who can overstay their leave are Chinese in Hong Kong staying with relatives, who feed and house them so they need never come to the attention of the authorities. Periodically this policy leads to tragic choices, like that of parents who were not allowed to keep a child they had smuggled into the colony. This had occurred after the amnesty deadline had expired.

Hong Kong has not closed its borders to political refugees. More than any other political entity, it has helped to rescue many Vietnamese boat people. They might have perished on the high seas but for the willingness of Hong Kong to let them land. 93,000 of them were admitted to permanent residency. Another 12,000 were kept in special camps with the expectation that other nations would grant them asylum.

Is Hong Kong a model of what is likely to happen in the few remaining nations where immigrants are still welcome, at least in moderate numbers? The United States, Canada, Israel, West Germany, Australia, South Africa and some of the South American nations continue to maintain an "open door" policy for selected and limited numbers of immigrants. All wish to control who is to be admitted and who is to be kept out.

In Canada, unlike the United States, both the employer and the illegal aliens whom he might hire, violate the law. Nevertheless, only sixteen percent of the illegal aliens in a Toronto sample were found to be using their own proper ID card. The rest obtained employment without an ID card or by providing a hard-to-verify and easily counterfeited Social Insurance Number (SIN).

How Illegal Immigrants Qualify for Work
Toronto Sample Survey*

Documents Presented To Claim Job Entitlement

A borrowed but valid SIN card	14%
A stolen or counterfeit card	10%
Presented a fictitious SIN number	4%
Presented neither SIN card nor number, but was given employment	55%
Total using an illegal procedure to obtain employment	83%
Total using a valid Social Insurance (SIN) card that had been issued to the alien.	16%

*W. G. Robinson, Special Advisor, "A Report to the Honorable Lloyd Axworthy, Minister of Employment and Immigration on *Illegal Immigrants in Canada*, submitted in June 1983, House of Commons: pp. 96–97.

It is apparent that Canada has accepted many migrants without proper ID papers. They live clandestinely and therefore must often work under unfavorable and marginal conditions. If they are apprehended, there is much public ambivalence about treating them harshly. They have violated immigration laws, but they are rarely viewed as having transgressed moral norms. As in the United States, the opposition to illegal immigration is tempered by empathy for the individual who is trying to better life for himself and his family. But Canada already requires employers to screen the job entitlement of all new employees.

CITIZEN RIGHTS' PROTECTION

The United States Congress developed privacy protection procedures during the 1970s in reaction to the Watergate scandal disclosures when civil rights violations were conspired at the highest level of the government. Europe also responded, although to less dramatic evidence, that personal files could be abused. The Dutch government, for instance, keeps detailed records regarding the personal affairs of every resident, including data on close blood relationships of husband and wife, inheritance provisions, tax law responsibilities, and the occasional removal of children from parental care. Most people seem to accept this fact as unavoidable in a welfare state where each person's circumstances affect their entitlements to extensive social services and income maintenance programs.

Privacy has been protected by limited access of officials to these data on a need-to-know basis. Birth, marriage, and death registers are separate from health and welfare programs, as are records about divorce, and health data related to a stillborn birth. There is no general identity card in Holland, but just about every adult has a drivers license, health insurance, or other document, verified against his basic registration file.

Further strengthening of privacy rights may soon take place in accordance with a proposal to establish a Dutch Citizen's Supervisory Board. The board would be appointed by Royal Decree for a term of four years. It would report directly to the minister of justice. Some of the board members would be chosen for their technical knowledge about administrative automation, civil service administration, and laws related to human rights. They would be responsible for protecting access by each person to information about himself, in part to verify its accuracy. There would also be much control over the sharing of data with third parties. This is now authorized by law for many purposes, including provisions for the equitable distribution of living space, the administration of public health programs, taxation, national defense, the tracing of delinquents, and certain financial transactions.

A Central Population Registry (CPR), now under consideration, could be operated with much less personal information than the already existing data banks. The CPR would be prohibited from storing or collating information of a "legal, police, political, medical, racial, financial and religious nature or data concerning physical or mental characteristics."[5]

A Dutch resident who believes himself damaged by any action of the CPR could appeal to the supervisory board for an award of damages. In addition, officials who administer the data banks would become personally liable for violations of the law and could be subject to imprisonment for up to three months or by a fine not to exceed 2,000 guilders upon conviction.

Somewhat different controls over potential population data bank abuse are already in force in West Germany. Basic identity files are not centralized. They are kept at the state (Land) level. The following information is stored and updated:

1. Family name and previous names
2. First names
3. Highest academic degree
4. Artistic or other pseudonyms
5. Day and place of birth
6. Sex
7. Guardian, if any, including name, academic degree, and address
8. Citizenship

9. A photograph
10. Membership in a judicially recognized religious body
11. Former and present places of residence including main and second residences
12. Spouse, including their name, academic degree, and date of birth
13. Address and date of marriage, including dissolution by divorce or death
14. Minor children, their names, and dates of birth
15. Number of the personal identity card, its place and date of issue
16. Right to vote
17. Tax data
18. Information about official actions to refuse a passport or to withdraw one which had been issued
19. Information about compulsory military service eligibility (males only)
20. Day and place of death

Each person is issued an ID document, an Ausweis, at age sixteen. It need not be carried, but many people keep it on their person because of its utility. It must be renewed every ten years. It includes only a small portion of the information stored in the locally kept data file.

Unlike France, Spain, and Greece, West Germany prohibits the inclusion of fingerprints. Information coded serial numbers based on the age or other personal facts of the document holder are also prohibited. The ID card number cannot be used to open any other file or to search other data banks, except for reasons of crime control and national security. The technical capabilities to produce tamper-resistant and interactive ID cards is well developed, but not utilized.

There was considerable legislative discussion during the 1970s about changing these restrictive practices. Computer experts and researchers lobbied for easier access to the locally kept data files to facilitate administrative efficiency. A personal number, uniform for keeping all public records, was proposed. Its use would eliminate the occasional clerical errors due to the similarity of names. Five percent of German males are called Hans. Twenty-five percent have one of ten common first names. Five percent of all persons have one of thirteen popular family names.

Parliament discussed but was deadlocked on this issue. The proposal of nationwide assignment of a birth number was finally dropped although 70 percent of a representative sample of Germans over the age of 18 favored the idea in a poll taken in December 1971. Only 16 percent were in opposition. 14 percent said they could not make up their mind.

Citizens' rights are now monitored by inspectors (Datenschutz ombudsmaenner). There is one in each Land (state). There also is a federal ombudsman at the national level. They and their staff have jurisdiction over both public and private data banks. They must give approval before information is exchanged between them. Controls have at times been so tight as to generate complaints that effective administration as well as legitimate research projects are needlessly impeded.

The mere existence of a nationwide system of personal registration has been questioned by some as a threat to Germany's democratic way of life.[6] Other citizens are quick to rise to its defense because of its utility, especially for crime prevention purposes. Excessive restrictions on data base matching also inhibits the collection of demographic statistics and health information crucial for the conduct of social, economic and political research. Such studies can be undertaken without risk of releasing information about any particular person. When an occasional case of data bank abuse is reported, the responsible Data Protection Ombudsman quickly gets involved.

Individuals have been hurt by data bank disclosures through refusal of employment for which they were qualified.[7] But more commonly the uses of such documents are widely appreciated. There also is much support for strong security measures against terrorism. The country has been plagued by violent anti-establishment groups like the Baader-Meinhof and Neo-Nazis. The government is expected to use all available and legal measures to combat them, including access to their ID files. Wilhelm Steinmuller's review of the situation concludes that no major change in the right to exercise these powers should be expected in the near future.[8]

Israel is replacing its easily counterfeited ID documents with less tamper-prone ID cards. The Knesseth (parliament) passed a privacy protection law by a large majority in 1981.[9] It covers both public and private data banks. It addresses the complex issue of how to combine the right to privacy with the public right to information. Invasion of privacy is defined as spying on or harassing a person, or publishing a photograph or film that could be viewed as humiliating. The unauthorized use of a person's name, picture, or voice for commercial purposes is also forbidden. Reproducing the content of a private letter without permission of the sender or the recipient is unlawful, as is the transmission of information on a person's private affairs for other than the purposes for which it was given. However, a distinction is drawn between such violations of privacy and the publication or broadcast of newsworthy details in circumstances that are within the proper domain of public interest. These protective measures sanction but also limit the rights of news media to use information. Only the future will tell how the Israeli courts will balance a person's entitlement to privacy with the right of the public to be kept informed by the media.

Israelis are guaranteed the right to inspect information kept about them in a data base, other than those of the police, the armed forces intelligence services, and the public security services. Tax investigations, issues involving the foreign relations of the country, or the disclosure of the identity of informants can also be kept secret by the government. The law does not forbid exchanges of information between government agencies but persons have the right to insist on the correction or deletion of erroneous data from any of their files.

Similar protective legislation is either being discussed or has been adopted in other democratic countries. The result is a deliberate underutilization of the available tamper-resistance technology. The following policy issues often arise:

1. How to provide residents with evidence of their identity, with optimum protection against having information counterfeited, stolen, or otherwise misused.
2. How to protect personal privacy and satisfy the public's right-to-know even when dissemination of information could be detrimental to a particular individual.
3. How to enforce laws and to protect the public from being victimized by criminals or terrorists or from unreasonable acts committed by public officials who have access to personal data banks.
4. How to collect and update demographic data for public program planning, taxation, the military services, and other functions.
5. How to balance the preference of individuals for privacy with the necessity of insuring optimum accuracy about certain major decision points affecting the society as a whole. This includes registration of birth, death, marriage, and divorce; acquisition of licenses to practice a skill or a profession; establishment of a business or the dispensing of entitlement programs.

"BIG BROTHER" IS UNDER CONTROL

The International Police (INTERPOL), headquartered in Paris, is supported by 135 nations, many of them dictatorships. It provides support to national police organizations to counteract transnational crime conspiracies. Data about illegally acquired or traded objects are now being computerized, such as the serial numbers of counterfeit bank notes, stolen art objects, and data related to drug trafficking. But the international committee which monitors INTERPOL's activities has not sanctioned the maintenance of computerized files on suspected criminals.

The committee thinks modernizing INTERPOL's outdated data exchange procedures should be preceded by an international compact to guarantee standards of privacy protection that are acceptable to democratic nations. Although information continues to be shared among INTERPOL officials, the organization is particularly sensitive to the possibility that some authoritarian regimes might wish to use INTERPOL for reprisals against political dissidents who fled persecution.

A Council of European Commmunities' specialist, on the basis of a thorough survey, concluded that much of the impetus for privacy legislation in Europe is generated by prior discussions of these topics in the United States: "Almost every issue that arose in Europe was also an issue in the United States, but at an earlier time."[10] Sweden has had a decade of experience with extensive data sharing, while maintaining a high standard of privacy protection. It enacted Europe's first Data Act, which licensed the operators of public and private data banks. Tyranny is not about to take over any of the Western democracies.

These facts have not, however, silenced active minorities who worry about the potential for abuse by power hungry officials. As previously mentioned, there have been occasional fanatic cliques, who like the nineteenth-century Luddites, used violent means on behalf of their cause.

Modern counterparts, like a self-styled "Committee for the Liquidation of Computers" bombed the Government computer center in Toulouse, France on January 28, 1983. The Duesseldorf offices of IBM and of Control Data were bombed in 1982, as were the Sperry Rand offices in West Berlin and an IBM office in Harrison, New York. But such acts of terrorism have not halted the rapidly growing reliance on machine readable identity documents. Their utility generates a never ending stream of technological improvements. Among large segments of the European public, there remains a high sense of trust that both the government and business are generally reasonable in their use of rapid, cheap, and comprehensive data storage and retrieval.

France enacted legislation "Concerning Computerized Indices and the Protection of Liberties" on January 6, 1978 (Act No. 78-17). It also provided for the establishment of a "National Commission for Data Processing and the Liberties" to enforce the new law. Both public and private personal data banks must conform to the standards set by this Commission. They can receive and act on complaints from the public. But on matters affecting state interests, the *Conseil d'État* (State Executive Council) can waive the protective provisions.

The election of President François Mitterand in 1981 led to a sudden reversal of a previously adopted policy to centralize France's ID system and to replace existing ID cards with machine readable documents. Three prefects in Paris had to recall them, after some had already been distributed. The new centralized system was abandoned in favor of the preexisting reliance on documents, printed on easily counterfeited yellow paper. The Mitterand government preferred to continue a high risk of counterfeiting to "a trend toward diminished privacy."

From a civil rights viewpoint this dramatic *no* to France's ID reform program means very little. France has had the capacity for nearly two centuries of keeping track of its residents. A biometric indicator, a fingerprint, was used in the identification document until quite recently, as in several other European nations including Spain. But there is enough public distrust in the government to have made it a popular political move to keep the old system, even at a loss in revenue. The Ministry of Interior had invested about 50 million francs ($7,260,000 dollars) in this abandoned data quality improvement project. The Mitterand policy reversal was a statement that privacy warrants a high priority. It was made in spite of the fact that 8-10 percent of all ID cards in France are lost or stolen each year.[11]

A status quo policy preference also enjoys support in West Germany. Its census was temporarily postponed by the Federal Constitutional Court. The Bundestag had adopted a law authorizing the census to compare its files with those of the population registers kept by local authorities. This matching of data bases would have made it possible to improve the accuracy of both of these major personal data files. The small but vociferous Green party feared that this procedure would lead to privacy abuses, including increased ease in locating illegal aliens.

Privacy can never be an absolute norm. It is a compromise between security and the administrative need to have information about people, and the right to optimum privacy. West Europeans share more information about themselves than is commonplace in the United States, but they also enforce more explicit restrictions on the management of both private and public data banks. Machine readable safety features are well developed but are not yet widely used in ID card verification.

THE WORLD CARD IDEA

Private industry issues machine-readable cards. Visa, Mastercard, American Express, Diners Club and Eurocheck cards already enjoy creditability in almost every nation of the world. Their utility is backed up by a worldwide communication system that verifies the creditworthiness of each cardholder, transmits bills, and transfers funds. Information stored in one language can be retrieved, within certain limits, in another. The binary system through which such storage and retrieval are accomplished is the same everywhere.

An internordic certificate of change of address exists. Denmark, Norway, Finland, Iceland, and Sweden already cooperate closely in their population registry procedures. Uniformity in population registry data has also been under discussion in the European economic community. In principle, a committee of ministers resolved on September 28, 1977 to adopt common technical standards. But many details remain to be worked out. There are also negotiations for a passport union, a compact for a machine-readable passport for use in 120 nations.

In May 1973, some of the larger European and American banks organized SWIFT, the Society for World Wide Interbank Financial Telecommunications. It is a cooperative society chartered in Belgium with more than 1300 member banks in 35 countries. It can provide a high degree of privacy for financial transactions between member banks. Information about each transaction is scrambled and transmitted by a secret code. Banks can communicate with each other directly through satellite communication centers in Belgium and Maryland. In excess of $70 billion on an average day are cleared through SWIFT. A minimal number actual dollars or gold bars have to be shipped back and forth.

The network that links American banks with the Federal Reserve System turns over more than the total volume of the national debt every few days. Companies that have been producing and selling controlled bank note paper are confronting a decline in their business. Massive electronic transfers of funds reduce the need for cash. The companies are gearing up to manufacture and sell basic plastic stock for producing tamper-resistant identity documents to governments, to the credit industry, and to various other types of organizations.

Interest in worldwide cooperation has also been expressed at meetings of the International Civil Aviation Organization (ICAO). After 12 years of study and multilateral negotiations, the ICAO adopted a plan for a uniform machine-readable passport. A committee including representatives from Australia, Canada, France, the Federal Republic of Germany, India, Kenya, Sweden, the United Kingdom, the United States, and the Union of Soviet Socialists Republics recommended that all nations proceed to issue machine readable passports as soon as is practical. This would accelerate the clearance of passengers at international airports and border crossings. Uniform technical standards were adopted so that a single digital reader could process passports of all nations. The following characteristics were agreed upon.

Width: No less than 87.8 mm (3.46 inches) and no more than 88.2 mm (3.47 inches).

Length: No less than 124 mm (4.91 inches) and no more than 125.2 mm (4.91 inches).

Thickness: Excluding other booklet pages, the machine readable portion of the passport should be no less than 0.254 mm (0.025 inches) and no more than 0.635 mm (0.025 inches).

The committee also agreed on information that should be contained in each passport, at a designated machine-readable zone:

1. A symbol to designate the machine-readable passport
2. Code of the state which issued the passport
3. Passport number
4. Surname
5. Given names
6. Nationality of passport holder
7. Birthdate according to the Gregorian calendar
8. Personal number or an assigned registration number (optional).
9. Sex
10. Place of birth
11. Date of issue
12. Date of expiration

Standards were also adopted to secure the passports against alterations by using such materials as a controlled paper stock, special inks, and a plastic covering.

The issuance of machine readable passports already has begun in the United States. Commercial credit cards are using common standards so that those issued in one country are likely to be usable in others. This is a form of international money that is competing increasingly with travelers checks.

Valid and easily verifiable ID cards have become a necessity in the electronic age. Personally written letters, files, and checks are being replaced by electronic impulses; an urgent message can be left on our computer while we sleep. Information sources as extensive as the resources of many libraries can be accessed through data bank sources like *DIALOGE* or the *New York Times Index*.

The machine-readable world card idea is pregnant with the possibility that fugitives from justice in one country will experience much greater difficulty in international travel. Even without computers, INTERPOL can already issue international crime alerts. But the greater ease with which future suspects might be flagged at inspection points increases the significance of exercising political judgment.

The European Community Commission is very conscious of the need to balance movement toward a machine-readable European passport with explicit protection measures to prevent privacy abuses.[12] The British parliament is currently considering enacting protective legislation before joining a European passport union, a proposal which has been under negotiations for about a decade. Among the issues that will have to be resolved by the democratic nations is the acceptance of a criminal alert from an East European or from other nondemocratic nations when the accused is a political refugee. Tamper-resistant cards are neutral instruments. Their uses for good or evil are functions of how they are used.

World cards are providing added conveniences to international travelers. These conveniences will keep their use high on the agenda of transnational policy review.

Many of the world's nations have centralized identity systems, maintained as an administrative convenience. They vary greatly in their regard for human rights, but this aspect is unrelated to the degree to which the secure ID card technology is utilized. Tyranny is not inherent in the mere existence of a national ID document, nor on the use of computers to store personal data. The new technology can be programmed in support of any cause, to protect people's privacy or to invade it.

A basic international ID card/passport is on the horizon. Its development will take time. International compacts are slow in being negotiated. Each nation has its legislature and the need to achieve domestic consensus. In spite of these delays, however, a treaty will soon be adopted. It will shift the power to determine how passports are to be issued to a supra-national commission.

It is doubtful that the rapidly growing technology for ID card safety will remain underutilized for much longer. This forecast is based on evidence of growing public concern with protective measures against crime, terrorism, and other privacy abuses. The available administrative options, which promise to achieve both privacy and security, will be reviewed in the remainder of the book.

REFERENCES

1. Steinmuller, Wilhelm. "New Technologies and the Protection of Liberties." *Vergleichende Rechtswissenschaft*. Verlag Gesellschaft-Recht und Wirtschaft, GMBH, 1982.

2. *Research Center for Computers and Law*, Oslo: University of Oslo, 1982.

3. Das "Melderechtsrahmengesetz" MRRG (Registration Law), *Bundesgesetzblatt*, Teil I, 22 August 1980, no. 50; also Hans-Dietrich Genscher, "Das Bundeseinheitliche Personenkenn zeichen: Argumente und Informationen zu einem Aktuellen Thema," *IBM Nachrichten*, October 1972:258–265.

4. *New Statesman*. March 5, 1982, vol. 103, No. 2659:6–8.

5. Ministry of Home Affairs, The Hague, Netherlands, 1974, p. 19.

6. Taeger, Jurgen, *Der Neue Personalausweis*, Reinbek bei Hamburg, Rowohlt Taschenbuch Verlag, 1984.

7. Cobler, Sebastian, "Buerger im Wuergegriff der Computer", *Stern*, February 12, 1981, Heft Nummer 8.

8. Steinmueller, Wilhelm, "New Technologies and the Protection of Liberties", *Vergleichende Rechtswissenschaften*, Heidelberg, Verlagsgesellschaft Recht und Wirtschaft G.M.B.H., 1982.

9. Jerusalem, Israel, *Sefer Ha-Chukim*, (Legal Register), no. 1011, March 11, 1981 and an explanatory note in *Hatzaoth Chok* (Legal Commentaries), No. 1453, p. 206; Aryeh Rubinstein, "A Curb on Big Brother", *Jerusalem Post Magazine*, Friday May 3, 1985: 5.

10. Hondius, Frits, *Emerging Data Protection in Europe,* Amsterdam and New York: North Holland Publishing Company, 1975:6.

11. *Le Point,* no. 431, December 22, 1980.

12. European Communities Commission, *Towards European Citizenship: A Passport Union; The Granting of Special Rights,* Luxembourg, Boite Postale 1003, July 3, 1975.

CHAPTER SEVEN

WEIGHING THE BALANCE

THE COST OF DOING SOMETHING

A national ID system will cost money. The U.S. Chamber of Commerce lobbied against the idea in part because of allegedly excessive cost. Senator Alan K. Simpson of Wyoming claimed that the Chamber's professional staff cited high cost estimates, when "more objective sources present less alarming figures." He admits, however, that "$100 million to $300 million a year" would not be a small budget item.[1]

The out-of-pocket cost of full installation of a computerized Alien Documentation Identification and Telecommunication (ADIT) system was estimated at $62 millions in 1979.[2] This amount is small when compared to the billions of dollars needed for antifraud law enforcement. Since it is profitable for the airlines to operate a computerized reservation system instead of the manual and telephone program that was in prior use, this should be even more true of large governmental bureaucracies. Their records management system often breaks down and clerical and administrative staff have to be assigned to perform tasks that could be completed more cheaply and accurately by digital equipment.

As previously noted, the Social Security Administration expects to spend close to a half a billion dollars to fully computerize its record system. Data on immigrants, collected at considerable cost, are often not available or get lost. Border inspectors must manually check the names of all border crossers against the "look-out" list of inadmissible persons or of those carrying invalidated, stolen, or otherwise improper documents. Nevertheless, in the interest of alleged "economy," most funds to computerize the check-up system were eliminated repeatedly by Congress since they were first requested in the 1970s.

Cost effectiveness was also stressed in an American Civil Liberties Union (ACLU) opposition brief:[3]

> The projected cost of implementing a system of secure, counterfeit-proof documents or a general population registry, the two most frequently sug-

gested verification systems, could be staggering: one reads about estimates from $5–$10 up to $100 million for development of the registry; from $1 million to $230 million annually for its operation; and from $100 to $850 million for the issuance of new counterfeit resistant Social Security cards or identity documents.

The SSA provided even larger cost estimates—at least $850 millions—for issuing counterfeit-prone cards to roughly 200 million card holders. Years rather than months will be required. The administrative problem is complicated by the fact that the SSA does not have a current address for most of the people to whom a card was issued.

The high cost estimates produced by government agencies contrast sharply with the data provided by Blue Cross/Blue Shield of Maryland. This health insurance agency will soon issue a Life Card to its 1.6 million subscribers. Each card will contain 800 pages of information about each patient's medical history, a digitalized photograph of the holder, and his digitally coded signature. Also retrievable from the card will be such data as an electrocardiagram, a chest X-ray, a list of medicines that have been prescribed, insurance coverage, and a list of physicians who regularly treat the patient. The card will be carried by each person, if they so desire. It also will be updated after each use. The code number of each provider making an entry on the card, as well as the machine used for this purpose, can also be recorded. The cost per card is estimated to range between $1.25 to $1.50. The equipment needed to read each card can be purchased by health providers for under $1,200. Doctors and patients will be saved much time in medical history taking, especially in the event the patient is admitted under emergency conditions where he or she might not be able to convey this information.

A national ID card would contain much less information. Demographic data also changes less often than medical conditions. The card itself should therefore be no more expensive. The heaviest cost will be for administration to verify the breeder documents supplied by each applicant before a new identity card can be issued.

"Excessive cost" is in any event a questionable basis for opposition of the idea of a national identifier. If properly organized, the Valid Identification Program (VIP) system could become self-supporting, if not a source of revenue. The cost argument is, however, a useful political tactic for groups opposed to the idea as such. The United States Chamber of Commerce, the ACLU, and organizations representing Mexican-Americans are not "balanced budget" interest groups. They refer to the cost factor to buttress their opposition on other grounds. The fact that such an ID program would also cost money gives these groups a basis for an appeal to otherwise uninvolved but budget-minded legislators.

Social Security officials have claimed it would be unreasonable to burden their budget with the total cost of providing Americans with a tamper-resistant identity document. More valid ID cards, so they claim, would benefit their program only marginally "because perpetrating fraud against the Social Security system by mere possession of a counterfeit or fraudulently obtained Social Security card is practically impossible."[4]

The big beneficiaries would be other organizations—public and private —which use Social Security numbers (SSNs) as unique personal identifyers to minimize confusion in their records about persons with similar names. A sizable reduction in the now widespread employment of illegal aliens would also be highly likely, in addition to the 326,280 unauthorized workers, who had reported earnings although they had been issued "No employment is authorized" SSNs[5] for which wages had been reported.

European ID card production costs have been reported to be much lower than those estimated for the United States. In Switzerland, cards are issued by each Canton (state) at costs ranging from $4.70 to $5.55. In Finland, the cost is only $2.00, with a mere $250,000 budget to manufacture and to distribute them. West Germany estimates that it will cost $3.4 millions to replace its domestic passports with a more tamper-proof version by 1986.[6] France invested about $7,260,000 to computerize its entire national ID system. The government canceled this technological reform when it had just begun to be implemented. No data are therefore available on how much more it would have cost to issue tamper-resistant documents to every French resident and to operate the already completed central data bank.

It is not known just what costs were included in these low European estimates. They probably exclude the cost of administration, which would be sizeable in the U.S. because there is no existing national identification system. How much money will actually have to be allocated will depend on four major administrative options: 1. level of desired security, 2. scope of the card's use, 3. fee charges, 4. compliance time.

1. *Security of the document:* Skilled manpower would be needed to check the breeder documents offered before a more valid identity card could be issued. Costs will be higher if the validity of birth certificates, voting registration cards, passports, and baptismal records were to be enhanced by biometric indicators and checked by trained officials to spot as many as possible of the false documents now in use. Most outstanding Social Security cards were issued *without any verification* of information supplied by the applicant, often by mail.

Reissuance occurs now under new and more stringent security precautions. Social Security cards are now issued only on the basis of convincing evidence of age, citizenship, or alien status, and true identity. In general, applicants must appear in person when applying for a new or replacement card. But Cathy Clark, who edited a forger's manual reassures her readers that these safeguards can often be circumvented. She cites many loopholes in the way Social Security cards are issued under the new procedure:

> Here is the real story of the Social Security administrator's 'in depth' interview. Stop by your local Social Security office during the first week of the month or during lunch hour. Things are so hectic at this time that it is easier for Paper Tripper to just 'slip through.'

Interviews tend to be perfunctory. Ms. Clark suggests that:

> "Big Brother" (as she designates the government) just doesn't have the time or the manpower to hassle SSN applicants. If you are cool, getting the number is a breeze. Breeder documents are rarely verified. Prosecutions for false applications are rare.[7]

The production cost of each card will also go up if biometric indicators will be used. Digital readers will have to be available at many locations. They will be needed to verify such items as signatures, fingerprints, retinal eye patterns, and voiceprints. The machines have to be serviced and periodically replaced. But each cost factor must be weighed in terms of how the incidence of document fraud is reduced. Machines tend to be more accurate than people; they can also perform a validation function at relatively low cost. They don't unionize, demand vacations, and can be made to work a twenty-four hour day until they blow a silicon chip.

2. *Scope of its use:* The Simpson-Mazzoli Immigration Reform and Control Act of 1982 included a provision to limit the use of any new ID procedure to just one purpose: *verification of work entitlement.* Government agencies and private business would be forbidden to use it as a general identifier.

If the same document could also be used for other purposes—getting a marriage license or applying for new credit cards—the cost of maintaining a readily accessible verification procedure would be offset. The cost of maintaining the central file could also be shared by airlines, which would use the ID card to register passengers and to discourage terrorists and hijackers. Persons with a tamper-resistant document would be well identified without having to fill out any forms. Their unique biometric index would also be on record, in case of an accident or if they attempt to engage in air piracy. Passengers without the ID card would be thoroughly screened. After a few years, once the system is put in operation worldwide, hijackers would no longer be able to enjoy the anonymity that facilitates the operation of international terror cells. Their agents could no longer travel freely without great risk of being apprehended.

Domestically, the ID card could be used to reduce fraudulent insurance claims. Entitlement programs for veterans benefits, food stamps, aid for dependent children, and federally guaranteed business loans could be policed more easily against misrepresentation. Certain tax evasion practices and credit card misrepresentation routines would also be made more difficult. Costs could be further reduced because of the centralization of periodic updating normally required in personal data files. When changing one's home address, getting married, or obtaining a new telephone number, one entry can correct the same item in many files. At present, the Social Security System, the armed forces and many others must separately pay for the cost of correcting their respective master files.

3. *Fee charges:* A new issue office would have to be set up quickly to handle the many tens of millions who are likely to apply for such a document. Poor people would be underrepresented if a fee were to be charged. The ADIT card is issued without cost, as is the Social Security Card. But Americans are paying for most of their other ID documents. An American passport costs $35.00. A driver's license may soon cost as much in many a revenue-starved state. Credit cards are now being issued upon payment of an annual fee, $15.00 and up.

The ID overhead cost would also be affected by the decision as to whether it would be generally mandatory or whether it would be needed only when people apply for a new job. A voluntary program would not need an enforcement division staffed by lawyers. It would be less costly to administer than a mandatory program. No one would have to be prosecuted should they be unwilling to apply for a VIP document.

A potentially large source of revenue would be fees for verifying documents needed for commercial transactions, like property title registrations, or credentials of an applicant for a senior level position in government or industry. Notary public fees would gradually be replaced by the more trustworthy process of computerized verification of digitally readable biometric indicators, stored in the central population registry.

4. *Compliance time:* Any new program would be less costly if introduced gradually than if many people had to be recertified quickly. West Germany expects to take five years to do the job to replace its current ID documents with a tamper-resistant version that is also machine readable. The Immigration Reform and Control Act provided for a three year transition period during which the president could explore different options for providing the public with a tamper-resistant identification procedure.

Whatever the balance of cost and income producing factors, a VIP type

ID system would add a new federal administrative function. The General Accounting Office (GAO) opposed a proposal whereby the Immigration and Naturalization Service (INS) would purchase automated digital reading machines for its new ADIT cards.[8] The GAO thought the equipment would only marginally benefit what they regarded as the main mission of the INS, the prevention of illegal immigration. This opinion ignores the utility of the new card for improving the general efficiency of administration. A machine readable ADIT card would help the INS to computerize its record system.

Persons who have been using false documents would be exposed. Provisions would have to be made for the adjudication of such cases which would range in the millions. Neither the INS or other Federal Law Enforcement agencies could handle such a large number of violators. This is one reason, along with the humanitarian disinclination to launch a mass deportation program, why all current proposals for immigration law reform include an amnesty provision.

THE HIDDEN COST OF THE STATUS QUO

The high price of the status quo, of doing nothing, was ignored in the General Accounting Office (GAO) calculations when it concluded that the use of ADIT cards by the INS was not cost effective. It is expensive to apprehend, detain, and deport illegal aliens. Losses from the use of stolen Automatic Teller Machine (ATM) cards in 1984 were estimated at between $70 and $100 millions. There also are sizable credit card losses and costly computer crimes in excess of a billion dollars a year. Significant reductions in these losses due to the use of near tamper- and theft-proof identity documents must be balanced against the cost of issuing them.

Reductions in losses do not show up in a normal balance sheet. The cost of crime to its victims is not a federal budget item. Accidents which are prevented do not balance the books of traffic law enforcement costs. The Environmental Protection Agency does not evaluate its budget by the billions which are saved by preventing environmental pollution.

Without such social accounting principles, the expense of introducing a nationwide tamper-resistant ID program would be assessed against an artificially narrow view of its utility. Upgrading of the quality of U.S. identity documents promises to have a broad administrative impact. It would increase administrative efficiency, enhance public safety, contribute to the overall reduction of fraud, and reduce the incidence of substandard working conditions. It would bring a sizable part of the untaxed economy to the surface and discourage illegal border-crossers.

These probable utilities of ID program reform are irrelevant to persons for whom a national identity roster is an *a priori* danger. They prefer the status quo. At present, Americans can choose between using a variety of ID documents or none. Those willing to pay cash can function most of the time without being asked to identify themselves, except when they drive a car, seek a job, or want a business license. They must also compromise their opposition to presenting credentials if they wish to qualify for a civil service job with a residential restriction or to obtain admission to a state university at the more favorable "in state" tuition charge.

Cost calculations would take on a different character if a voluntary nationally monitored and tamper-resistant ID document were to be adopted. The government and business would be tempted to expand its use. This is what happened to the SSN, after an executive order was issued in November 1943.[9]

Irrespective of how Congress will resolve the national ID Card controversy 1985, the expansion of computer use is forcing more reliance on machine-readable and verifiable identifiers. How quickly this process will proceed and with what safeguards against abuses of privacy, is an issue that can no longer be avoided. Technically feasible alternatives must be weighed within the awareness that the availability of easily forged documents represents a threat to people's privacy. It is all too easy for imposters to victimize the public.

The national ID card controversy is an illustration of Alvin Toffler's *Future Shock:*[10] widespread public concern about the unknown. All innovations require that people adapt to rapid changes. Some people react to the uncertainties of planning for the future with fear, anger, and confusion. The prospects of a national ID card generates such feelings among a number of Americans. These concerns will need to be addressed if a VIP tamper resistant ID program is to be developed with the necessary public support.

FREEDOM OF INFORMATION VERSUS PRIVACY

Most personal data are revealed voluntarily. U.S. politicians, from the president down, make their income tax public. Parents must provide a copy of their tax return if their children are to become eligible for a subsidized low-interest loan. Interactive cable television will further reduce our privacy; yet people pay a monthly fee for these intrusive devices. Applicants for most federal posts are fingerprinted and fill out a detailed life history form to facilitate a security check of their background. All presidents since Franklin D. Roosevelt, with the exception of Ronald Reagan, were fingerprinted for the civilian file kept by the FBI because they held a prior federal job.

Students of the computer revolution generally agree that standards of privacy in the twentieth century have to be modified by the fact that we share a great deal of information about ourselves in return for professional services, business opportunities, and welfare entitlement programs. Even the plumber needs to know who and how many people live in a home before recommending the size of a new water heater which he might be installing. The quick and easy storage and retrieval of such information and the well developed technology for data base matching far exceed the human capacity to memorize the details of past circumstances. All democratic nations are concerned about the balance between privacy rights and the administrative and national security need to have personal information available about its residents.

Freedom and privacy are treasured in every society. Can there be too much of either? Civil libertarians find themselves on *both* sides of this issue. They favor freedom of information and of the press. But they also want to defend privacy rights of the individual against humiliation, defamation, and unwelcome disclosures of his private life. The *New York Times* takes pride in the slogan that it carries "all the news that's fit to print." Reporters work hard to get a story by accessing computerized personal data banks, including the *New York Times Index*, which can retrieve sensitive personal details that may have appeared in print decades ago.

The United States Constitution is explicit in guaranteeing freedom of information. Congress shall make no law "abridging the freedom of speech or of the press" reads the first amendment. The word *privacy* is never mentioned, but is implied in the Fourth Amendment. It guarantees "the right of the people to be secure in their persons, houses, papers and effects against unreasonable searches and seizures." The courts and legislatures have had to work out an acceptable pattern of co-existence with these conflicting basic values. The dean of privacy research, Alan Westin, noted that the courts tend to interpret privacy rights narrowly. Civil libertarians have had to look for protection to legislation, at both the state and federal level.[12] There is little protection against surreptitious snooping or defamatory leakage of personal data.

The dilemma about revealing too much data, but providing enough information, is illustrated by a reversal of attitudes during the last few decades on the recording of racial, ethnic, and sex characteristics. It has become routine for public and private agencies to advertise that they are equal opportunity employers. Race, age, sex, and ethnic status will not be a basis of employment rejection or acceptance when qualified applicants are considered for a position. To make this policy creditable, personnel departments began first to delete such questions from their application blanks. Photographs disappeared from many personnel files, lest they might influence who would be hired.

The adoption of affirmative action programs forced a reversal of this policy. In order to document compliance with laws against institutional racism, and other forms of discrimination, employers were asked to document that special efforts were being made to locate applicants from to these previously disadvantaged population groups. Government agencies demanded statistics, along with evidence of how many minority group persons had applied, were rejected, or hired. Failure to present data might be viewed as an evasive tactic, which would make an agency's employment policy suspect.

Questions on race, age, and ethnicity reappeared on job applications. The 1980 census was much more explicit than any previous one in inquiring about the racial and ethnic identity of the individual. "Private" information of an earlier decade had become essential data urgently needed to monitor public policy implementation.

Much the same issue comes up in crime reporting. Media stories used to stress racial characteristics of both victims and the suspected and convicted criminals, especially when heinous acts were committed— rape, murder, and robbery. But journalistic codes of ethics led to avoidance of such stigmatization. The public's interest in a celebrated case or the need to generate potentially useful information from witnesses can still be served by publishing a picture of the offender or by having an artist draw one, clearly showing the racial characteristics of a suspect.

Do people have a right to keep their sexual preference and marital status private? There are no simple answers to such a question. When it comes to hiring school teachers, diplomats and CIA agents, there are vocal and powerful interest groups who justify the exclusion of homosexuals from such posts.

Most employers would deny the allegation that they discriminate against married people or pregnant women, but many will informally consider this fact when filling a vacant job. Some believe it is risky to staff a job with a married woman if it requires frequent long distance travel. Some fear her marriage will be placed under stress because of her employment and adversely affect her performance. These considerations are not likely to surface, however, when men are hired. It is rare for any employer to inquire about the pending birth of a child when hiring a traveling salesman.

Employers need not share with those they hire all of the available information that might be useful in evaluating a job offer. People have been known to move at their own expense to take a job when the employer was already considering a declaration of bankruptcy. Conversely, why should employees be expected to share details about their personal life with an employer? They could be—and often are—used for purposes inimical to a worker's interests.

Should the federal government impose a one-sided identity disclosure process on job applicants, without requiring parallel candor from employers about their organizational circumstances that could have a bearing on a worker's decision to accept employment? Should job applicants have to be told they are filling a temporary job, while someone is on leave who will be entitled to return to their job? Should they be informed that most people will be fired before they accumulate seniority to become eligible for a vested company pension?

Inequities in what the two negotiating sides are expected to disclose are often mentioned by those opposed to excessive ID document security. They prefer the status quo under which job applicants are free to decide when to disclose their actual age, health, marital status, and other personal data to a company or government agency.

Should the right to privacy be extended to include the option to withhold one's true identity? On one issue, federal law pronounces a clear *yes.* For tax purposes, employees must reveal who they are. But this requirement is easily evaded by persons ready to use stolen or counterfeit Social Security cards. Is this a "civil liberty" that warrants protection?

THE BATTLE FOR CONFIDENTIALITY

Companies with in-house medical care programs have at times been suspected of accessing confidential medical files before making decisions about promotion and retention. Businessmen routinely use birth and death registration files as leads to locate potential customers for selling insurance or offering investment opportunities. Information from allegedly confidential educational or credit files is sometimes available for the preparation of mailing lists and for other purposes quite different from those for which it was assembled.

Technically, little stands in the way of creating an extensive dossier on every person, except protective laws and regulations which can be designed to protect governmental and private information files. The computer is very neutral: it is a matter of public policy of how it will be programmed.

When one considers how many thousands of organizations keep files about imtimate details of our lives, it seems remarkable that most of them seem to be quite effective in limiting their access to unauthorized persons.

In 1977, the U.S. Privacy Protection Commission recommended additional legal measures, along with voluntary safeguards. Some organizations have instituted such measures voluntarily, if only to protect themselves against expensive litigation from persons who could claim that their privacy was unreasonably violated.

Additional safety precautions will need to be legislated. Forty-one percent of a sampling of corporations indicated they had no policy disclosing information from employee files to a governmental agency. Eighty-five percent disclosed information to creditors without subpoenas being issued, as compared to 49 percent to landlords and 22 percent to charitable organizations. Additional precautions may be needed to limit the access of the credit granting community. It must be noted, however, that a large proportion of such inquiries are based on signed authorizations by the person who is willing to have his employer contacted in order to get a bank loan or credit card.

There is no neat way of drawing a border between where utility ends and risk begins in the use of any national identifier. Congress has passed privacy legislation. It has limited disclosure of information stored by the U.S. census, the IRS, and the FBI. But as already noted, it also has authorized data clearance procedures among different data files to locate people who fail to pay their debts, who evade the draft, or who engage in other, often more serious violations of the law.

It is easy to generate a heated discussion between those favoring administratively useful data sharing practices and others who oppose them as invasions of personal privacy and as violations of due process. In West Germany this has become a major issue of political controversy between the Green Party, which favor severe restrictions on computerized information storage, and the ruling coalition, which wants to utilize its capabilities under less restrictive privacy guarantee standards. More needs to be known about the consequences for people and for society when information is restricted or used freely—as advocated by representatives of the news media who favor freedom of information legislation.

Few would defend the idea that our tastes in movies, seen at home via closed television, be made public or shared with mailing list firms. Should every person be entitled to know what kind of charitable contributions are made by an individual? Should the FBI have access to data on the happiness of someone's marriage by viewing the files of a social counselling agency? Such data may be relevant to solving a crime. When there is incriminating information, it is apt to be leaked about people who run for public office. Such information may not be routinely asked when someone applies for employment.[13] But talent search firms engaged in screening people for top level executive positions will provide such data to the corporations which they serve. The fact that a divorced man is paying alimony is considered in granting a bank loan. Within hours after the killing of a black youth during a police check of a poolroom in Miami in 1983, news media had information about the unfortunate victim, his prior education, employment and plus information about his gun. Similar details were available about the Hispanic policeman who shot him. Reporters used the data to make a CIA-type comprehensive information analysis.

Privacy and freedom of information are two sides of the same civil liberty coin. Both sides are highly regarded. Their balance involves tough policy choices. Some are made legislatively. Others are decided by the courts, the news media, or by administrators of data files. A residue remains with each individual who can decide when information is to be shared or kept in a safe, a locked diary, or freely shared with others.

"RED TAPE"

Opponents of the national ID card have cited the inefficiencies of the current Social Security card system to illustrate the risk that a national identity program would also be inefficient:[14]

> Government recordkeeping, of course, is so abysmal that it's hard to imagine the ID system working anyhow. Anyone who thinks the Immigration and Naturalization Service is going to do an efficient job keeping track of 100 million Americans in the work force might take a look at the Internal Revenue Service, which wants a withholding tax on interests and dividends because it can't keep its own records straight. At the Social Security Administration, individual files are kept in manila envelopes in storage centers that spread for acres.

Supporters of the ID concept would not question the *Wall Street Journal* observation that there is administrative inefficiency in the management of government data banks. When asked why they cannot achieve the level of productivity of commercial credit card files or airline reservation data banks, it must be noted that congress repeatedly blocked the purchase of computer equipment and on-line terminals. Without them government records cannot be fully automated.

On the other side of the argument, there are those who worry that a national VIP program could work if many data banks were to become effectively coordinated. In the salty language of the same *Wall Street Journal* editorial:

It raises fears that arrest records, credit ratings, even secret FBI reports, will be kept in central files on each individual – that some minor functionary in Baltimore will stop you from closing a condominium deal until you pay your overdue parking tickets in Kansas City.

Absolute privacy was surrendered when *homo sapiens* invented writing, started to keep records and, live in organized social groups. But the incidence of error in personal data files can be reduced when well programmed computer resources are manned by properly trained personnel under policies balancing security needs and privacy rights.

PRIVACY VS. PRIVACY - AN ETHICAL DILEMMA

Leading American politicians seem to prefer acceptance of criminal misuse of identity cards in preference to making active use of the tamper-resistant ID technology. On several occasions Congress has declined to approve proposals for optimum use of computer information systems. A carefully prepared Tax Administrtion System (TAS) proposal was voted down. It would have enabled the Internal Revenue Service to collect more taxes by adding to its data base matching capacity to detect tax evasions, inhibit fraud, and notice innocently overlooked tax obligations.[15] Safeguards had been included in the proposed legislation to protect taxpayer information, in conformity with the Privacy Act of 1974 and related measures.

Repeated proposals to Congress for legislative sanctions for coordinated federal data banks such as the FEDNAT Plan, were also disapproved.[16] This plan was scuttled, in part, by disclosures that an occasional over-committed crime fighter or politician had tampered with the constitutional rights of their adversaries. They had clandestinely operated programs like the FBI Counter Intelligence Program against unpopular and allegedly subversive groups.[17]

Gut-level opposition to a nationwide personal identifier was cogently summarized by Senator Barry Goldwater, when he joined with Senator Percy in proposing an amendment to Bill S3418 to halt the use of SSNs as a universal population identifier.[18]

Mr. President, when parents cannot open bank accounts for their children without obtaining social security numbers for them; when all school children in certain ninth grade classes are compelled to apply for social security numbers; when a World War I veteran is asked to furnish his social security number in order to enter a Veterans Administration hospital; and when the account number is used and required for numerous other purposes totally unrelated to the social security program, then it is time for society to stop this drift towards reducing each person to a number.

Once the social security number is set as a universal identifier, each person would leave a trail of personal data behind him for all of his life which could be immediately reassembled to confront him. Once we can be identified to the administration in government or in business by an exclusive number, we can be pinpointed wherever we are, we can be more easily manipulated, we can be more easily conditioned and we can be more easily coerced.

Just over half of the Father Hesburgh Commission on Immigration Reform voted for the national work entitlement verification system included in its final report, eight in favor and seven against. Privacy concerns were a major reason given by the opposition. Both sides of this issue express strong support for human rights and the constitutional guarantees of freedom. But they differed in their assessment of what would be the best tactic to protect these goals. Their positions can be summarized as follows:[19]

Right of United States to discover illegal aliens: U.S. tax laws require that Social Security numbers be issued to aliens who earn taxable dividends and interest. If such a SSN is used to register earnings from employment, the government is required to prosecute.

Protection of illegal alien against self-incrimination: Wage taxes of an alien, even if he is not legally entitled to accept employment, should not be used to entrap him. It violates the constitutional rights against self-incrimination. Social Security files should be confidential.

Right of children to receive court mandated child support payments: Title IVd of the Social Security Act authorizes child support enforcement officials all over the United States to search SSA and other data banks to locate the address of parents who have disappeared. They can then be served with a warrant for failing to make court mandated child support payments.

Right to keep one's address secret to maximize personal privacy.

Employer Responsibility to avoid hiring for a position of public trust known criminals or dangerously unstable persons: Numerous state and federal laws require background checks to screen out persons with a history of crime or mental illness from being given assignments affecting the security of the United States, the well-being of children, or other positions of trust. IRS records can be checked by government attorneys to screen prospective jurors in certain cases.

Rights of discharged criminal and ex-mental patients to privacy on the grounds that they have paid their debt to society.

No country should offer asylum to criminals.

No sovereign nation should enforce foreign laws.

The United States has negotiated extradition treaties with many countries. Information on bank accounts held under a false name, or on deposits of persons accused of a crime in the United States, will be provided to the U.S. government. There is much resentment that nations like Switzerland, Lichtenstein, the Cayman Islands and others have bank secrecy laws that protect depositors, even if they are known to be criminals.

When two rights are in conflict—and this often happens—the United States Supreme Court and political leaders must make difficult choices. Quite often, it is a choice between "right" and "right," not between "right or wrong." Decisions are most likely to stand the test of time if one can first review evidence related to this issue.

The National Board of the ACLU resolved in 1977 to oppose the use of Social Security cards and other government documents as a condition of employment. It argued that such a practice, in effect, creates an "employment passport," which creates a universal identifier for all persons in the United States. In 1981 the national legislative director of the ACLU justified this resolution in a thought provoking brief.[20] Sixteen months later, the Privacy Committee of the same organization recommended that this policy be revised.

Well reasoned arguments can be put forth on all sides of this privacy versus privacy controversy. Thomas E. Rainert summarized the policy issue noting: "Informational privacy is not an absolute social goal. There are social and institutional needs for information to enable efficient decision making."[21] He cites the case of *Peller* vs. *Retail Credit Corporation,* where an adolescent was refused a position in a retail store after taking a polygraph test. The test allegedly indicated that he had used and sold illegal drugs. The young man denied this allegation. Nevertheless, the retail credit firm sold the information to a local credit reporting agency. Peller sued after he was fired from a subsequent job with an accounting firm after they had received a credit report which they had ordered. The young man's career was certainly damaged. If he had really been a drug addict and drug pusher, would this constitute a legitimate basis for denying him a position where he was likely to have access to confidential information about clients?

How should these competing rights be weighed? They involve a difficult choice between *freedom versus tyranny, security and privacy.* They involve the question of the trustworthiness of polygraphs. Whose rights need priority, those of an alleged criminal or of a potential victim?

Summary of the National ID Card Controversy

Opposition Rationale	Support Rationale

VIP As a De Facto Domestic Passport

A domestic passport would identify persons better than any existing document. This would have the effect of substantially expanding the government's power to stop and question suspects and search for evidence.

This power is now confined to the narrow area of highway safety and the checking of car registrations and car licenses. Police and other government officials would be given too much power over anyone they chose to stop and ask for his/her identity.

Most people have several ID cards, including a drivers license and a Social Security card. But both are easily counterfeited. Improvements in their security have nothing to do with the domestic passport issue. No new powers are delegated to any official to stop, question, and search persons without a warrant, or to check on their citizenship status.

A Valid Identity Program (VIP) would actually protect people against being detained for investigation of their alleged identity.

National Population Data Bank

A secure identification system would require the maintenance of a central population data bank about all persons authorized to work in the United States or those who would be excluded. The movements and the characteristics of nearly all U.S. adults could be checked by employers and by other authorized users of the system. Irrespective of any legally mandated user limits, a national ID program would result in a significant reduction of existing privacy rights.

Such public data banks already exist and are administered by the U.S. Census, the Bureau of Internal Revenue and the Social Security System. They are supplemented by many private personal data files. Privacy has been well protected by Congress. When abuses were discovered, findings led to legislative or administrative remedies. The U.S. census has been kept free of unauthorized leaks. Could this not also be true of the proposed Valid Identification Program.

Broadening Use of ID Data Banks

An employment entitlement identification data bank would gradually be used by other government programs, unrelated to immigration controls. It could become a means for tracking and controlling the activities of millions of citizens and legal residents alien of the United States.

Data banks already exist with more personnel information than needed for a secure ID card or a control identity file. Congress has and can continue to limit their use for other purposes and prevent unreasonable surveillance of citizens and lawful U.S. residents by the government and the private sector. Opponents of secure ID documents exaggerate their threat to privacy standards.

Risk of Ethnic-Racial Discrimination

Employers will scrutinize the identification papers of minority groups more closely than the documents of nonminority workers. More ethnic-racial discrimination is a likely consequence.

The proposed employment identification system will place aliens and citizens, minority and non-minority persons on an equal footing. Everybody will have the same document certifying to their right to accept a job.

DISTRUST OF GOVERNMENT

Distrust of the government is commonplace. It is no accident that the United States and Great Britain are without a national ID system. In both countries there is what many regard as healthy skepticism about the claims of benevolence by government. Its officials must be watched and constrained by constitutional and legal procedures.

This distrust of centralized government may be related to a preference for local control of personal records. Birth and death records are kept at the village or city level. Only since World War II, as computers developed a capacity for speedier storage and retrieval of data, has there been consideration of an alternative. As a result, many local merchants now give credit on nationwide and international credit cards—Visa, MasterCard, Diners Club, and American Express. There is more and more cooperation between local, state, and federal tax collecting bureaus and traffic enforcement agencies.

The positive experience of business with nationwide information systems has generated pressure on the government to consider their expanded use. In *Privacy and Freedom*, Alan Westin anticipated fifteen years ago that the growing computer industry would exercise such an influence:[22]

> For planning, efficiency and social control, these government data centers, computerized (private) transaction systems and central records of the future could bring enormous benefits to society. But unless safeguards for privacy are placed carefully in the planning and administration of systems that most computer experts feel to be inevitable developments of the next two decades, the growth in data surveillance will be awesome. Meanwhile, the present dossiers and computerized information systems continue to increase, without many legal or administrative guidelines as yet to cope with the issues of privacy that they raise.

It is commonplace for technological innovation to proceed more quickly than administrative procedures to limit their negative impact. This has been true of automobiles, atomic energy, and chemical pesticides. It is also the case with tamper-resistant ID cards. The Bill of Rights can be protected by the same computer technology that has been used to threaten it. As will be detailed in Chapter 9, data protection procedures can be very much strengthened. Legislatively adopted standards can be translated into administrative procedures by the companies which produce ID cards and the agencies which use their product to maintain personal files.

The changing technology for storing and retrieving computerized information calls for appropriate adaptations to utilize the silicon chip to provide both information and a reasonable degree of privacy. In a society where information is a commodity of growing commercial and administrative utility, privacy protection must be geared to these new realities.

REFERENCES

1. Simpson, Alan K., *New York Times*, August 10, 1982.

2. Comptroller General of the United States, *New Alien Identification Systems Little Help in Stopping Illegal Aliens*. Washington, D.C., General Accounting Office of the United States. GGD-49-44, 1979.

3. Shattuck, John H. F. and Henderson, Wade J., "Statement on the Immigration Reform and Control Act of 1982" (H.R. 5872/S222) American Civil Liberties Union, Washington, D.C., April 1, 1982.

4. Comptroller General of the United States, *Reissuing Tamper-Resistant Cards Will Not Eliminate Misuse of Social Security Numbers*, HRD-81-20. December 23, 1980:25.

5. Federation For American Immigration Reforms' "Fair Immigration Report," April 1983, Washington, D.C.

6. Stahlberg, Jurgen, "Der Neue Pesonalausweis," *Wechselwirkung*. NR. 17, November 1980.

7. Clark, Cathy, *The New Paper Trip*, Fountain Valley, Eden Press, 1977.

8. Comptroller General of the United States, *Information on the Enforcement of Laws Regarding Employment of Aliens in Selected Countries*, Washington, D.C. GAO/GGD August 31, 1982.

9. Executive Order No. 9379, November 1943.

10. Toffler, Alvin, *Future Shock*, New York: Bantam Books, 1970.

11. Flaherty, David H., *Privacy and Government Data Banks: An International Perspective*, London: Mansell, 1979.

12. Westin, Alan, Comment at a Faculty Seminar at Columbia University on January 20, 1983, after a presentation of the author's preliminary findings reported in this book.

13. Linowes, David F., "Is Business Giving Employees Privacy?" *Business and Privacy*, Winter 1980:47–49.

14. *Wall Street Journal*, September 2, 1981.

15. Comptroller General of the United States, *Safeguarding Taxpayer Information—An Evaluation of the Proposed Computerized Tax Administration System*, Washington, D.C.: U.S. Government Printing Office, LCD 76–115, January 17, 1977.

16. United States Senate, *Surveillance Technology*, Joint Hearings Before the Subcommittee of Constitutional Rights of the Committee on the Judiciary and the Special Subcommittee on Science Technology and Commerce of the Committee of Commerce. Washington, D.C.: U.S. Government Printing Office, June 23, September 9 and 10, 1975:3–9.

17. Select Committee to Study Governmental Operations with Respect to Intelligence Activities, 1976.

18. 94th Congress, 2nd Session, *Legislative History of the Privacy Act of 1974*: 759.

19. Father Hesburgh, Chairman, *U.S. Immigration Policy and the National Interest The Final Report and Recommendations of the Select Commission on Immigration and Refugee Policy*, Washington, D.C., March 1981, National Board of the American Civil Liberties Union, Board Minutes, June 18–19, 1976.

20. Shattuck, John H. F. and Henderson, Wade J., "Statement on Work Authorization Systems and Immigration Policy," October 2, 1981, American Civil Liberties Union.

21. Reinert, Thomas E. "Federal Protection of Employment Record Privacy" *Harvard Journal of Legislation*, Winter 1981:207–251.

22. Westin, Allen F., *Privacy and Freedom*, New York: Atheneum Books, 1967:157–158.

CHAPTER EIGHT

POLICY ALTERNATIVES

FIVE ADMINISTRATIVE DIMENSIONS

No major interest group is on record in favor of unreliable identity documents. But there is a wide range of views about what should be done to achieve a higher level of validity.

There is the *centralization* question. Should there be a basic tamper-resistant document and a central file against which all other ID cards can be verified by telephone or computer? Should the system be federalized or should it be administered by local and/or state governments, a public utility, or a public service corporation?

There also is the question of *voluntarism*. Should people be free to secure or reject a tamper-resistant document? Or should it be mandatory?

For what purposes should such a document be authorized or required: when soliciting a new job, when getting a marriage license or when renting an apartment? Should it be carried at all times or be required for presentation only for certain purposes, like filing a lawsuit, when qualifying for a job, or applying for a driver's license?

Are there circumstances under which it would be expressly forbidden to require the use of a national ID card, for instance on admission to the emergency room of a hospital, when protesting an action of a government agency, or when renting a motel room?

There also is the question, about how much *information* is to be included in the ID document. Citizenship would be relevant if a document is to be used crossing an international border. Age will affect eligibility for many entitlement programs. What about the level of education? Many people would be reluctant to reveal this information to a stranger. A basic identity document need not serve as a passport where all border crossings are recorded, nor need it replace a drivers license, which would include entries about serious traffic violations.

Technical security features are also a matter of controversy. An unduplicated number makes it easy to differentiate between persons who might have the same name or other similarities in their identity. This number could be associated with a biometric characteristic like a signature or a fingerprint, which can be digitally verified. With only these two features a document can be used with little risk of being counterfeited or used by a thief.

Finally, there is the question of *data utilization*. Who should be permitted to access personal information data banks. For what purposes? Should different data banks be allowed to compare information under their jurisdiction? Under what circumstances should standards of confidentiality be enforced? When can they be waived?

Proposals for tamper-resistant ID programs need to consider each of these five administrative policy choices. They are universal in scope. Travel, worldwide credit, and checkless transfer of funds are illustrative of the growing variety of functions in which it is important to consider implications of these policy alternatives.

THE CENTRALIZATION ISSUE

Unlike birth certificates and drivers licenses, the production of the Alien Documentation Identification and Telecommunication (ADIT) card is centralized at the Immigration and Naturalization Service (INS) facility in Arlington, Texas. Request for documents can be initiated in any INS facility in the United States or overseas. It is followed by a five stage process to maximize validity:

1. Interviewing of the applicant
2. Verification of breeder documents (birth certificates or baptismal records)
3. Production of the card
4. Delivery of the cards to the proper applicant
5. Verification of proper use of the document to exclude alterations, theft, or other improper use

Precautions are mandated at each step to minimize fraud and misrepresentation. What is done will also affect the cost of production and use.

At present, the INS exercises much care in monitoring the first four steps. Trained officials inspect the breeder documents that are offered. Some forged certificates may escape their notice, but suspicious applicants can be checked by contacting the originating local office. A picture and fingerprint of the applicant is taken. An INS official then witnesses the signature, which will be placed on the person's ADIT card. These records are then shipped to the Arlington card facility, where the ID document is then produced under high security conditions. The completed card is hand-delivered at a U.S. border station or mailed if the applicant has a permanent address in the United States.

Additional security precautions could be included, if the INS had the needed money and manpower. Birth certificates could be checked with the office that issued them. In doubtful cases the Bureau of the Census could be asked by the applicant for a Certificate of Enumeration. It would verify that the information provided by the applicant was found in previous census enumerations. The card could then be delivered only after its owner satisfies a government official that he looks like the picture on the document, produces the same signature, and has a fingerprint which matches that on the card.

Congress has not yet appropriated funds to make it possible to have ID cards read digitally. The built-in security features, (and others that could be added) would further reduce the possibility that a card could be used by someone other than the person to whom it was issued. At present, ADIT cards can only be inspected visually. Poorly trained, tired, or busy inspectors have on occasions missed crudely made forgeries, which lack the ADIT card's built-in electronic features and machine-readability.

The public gets the quality of inspections it is willing to finance. This is not only true in the INS. Because there are only 220 food inspectors monitoring roughly 66,000 food processing plants in the United States, an average inspector is responsible for 300 enterprises. How often can he afford to visit any one of them, when he works only about 240 days a year and needs time for administrative chores?

The United States is a forger's dream.[1] It is easy and cheap to get a perfectly valid copy of someone else's birth certificate. Baptismal records can be produced in the name of an even larger number of real or alleged churches. There also are no national standards for issuing drivers' licenses. Credit cards and other identity documents can be used without anyone comparing information on the document with the characteristics of the bearer.

Social Security cards may soon be issued on banknote paper less easily counterfeited than the present version. But as previously noted, it was not a crime until recently to counterfeit, alter, lend, or sell a card. Only the reproduction of the seal of the Department of Health and Human Services was expressly forbidden (U.S. 18 Code 506).

The budget of a federally coordinated system would probably be insignificant when measured against the utility of replacing the many unreliable American ID documents with an almost tamper-proof ID card. Each of the approximately eight thousand independent units which now issue vital statistics documents need to maintain a separate administrative staff. This is costly and inefficient.

The Parliaments of France and Germany debated the centralization is-

sue for several years. Both decided against altering their locally administered mandatory registration system, under political pressure from activists concerned that a centralized file would place too much information at
the disposal of the government. In West Germany, public concern about
these issues is illustrated by the publication of ten pocketbooks, to sum
up the case against what the authors think of as an excessive access by
state agencies to personal data files. The anticentralization decisions were
welcomed as a political victory by a vocal minority who had campaigned
for this viewpoint.

Technically there are no grounds for assuming that a locally administered registration system would provide more privacy. The opposite is
probably the case. It is easier to enforce privacy guarantees in one central
system than in thousands of local setups. German and French officials
continue to be able to access local personal registers, when this is deemed
to be necessary to investigate a crime, to prevent a security mishap, or to
check on someone's eligibility regarding an entitlement program. Protection against misuse of an information system is not a matter of where the
information is stored. It requires affirmative administrative measures,
mandated by law and monitored by a vigilant public.

If a federally issued basic ID document were to be adopted, a decision
would have to be made where this new function would be administered.
The FBI is identified in the public view with crime control. The INS deals
only with the foreign born and foreign visitors. The IRS and SSA already
have comprehensive files on all U.S. residents who work or who earn dividends and interest. A case could also be made for adding this function to
the data analysis-oriented Bureau of Vital Statistics. Or should an entirely
new administrative unit be created?

Some policy makers might prefer to delegate this function to a public
utility, using private capital, but operating under close supervision of a
presidentially appointed board that would enforce security and privacy
standards; or the government could set up a public corporation. They
would be licensed to generate income from the sale of ID cards and from
verification services to businesses or individuals. In important transactions, a properly organized ID system will be a far more reliable basis of
authentification than a notary public stamp. The corporation could be required to furnish free ID cards to certain categories of the public. Fees
could be regulated to prevent price gouging. Such a corporation, some
will argue, can operate this projected service more cheaply than a government agency. The corporation would also have a strong vested interest to
uphold security and privacy standards. Violations could lead to costly
fines or, in the event of severe negligence, to a loss of their license to
operate.

Centralization, whether under public or private enterprise auspices, will be questioned by some on ideological grounds. Those who assert that there is too much "Big Government" will be confronting other policy makers who favor expanded government initiative to combat crime, misrepresentation, tax evasion, and to protect the security of computer data banks.

Americans are in ever growing need of trustworthy identification. Almost half of the population over five years of age moved between 1975 and 1980, many of them several times. Identification is clearly an interstate activity. Personal documents are used on a nationwide and international basis. Keeping addresses and mailing lists current is a complex clerical job which computers are well designed to handle. The system could be accessed from anywhere in the world, but with security features far more reliable than any of those now in use.

Privacy violations are not a major problem at the present time in spite of the fact that data exchange programs are becoming commonplace. The federal government, local authorities, and private industry have been authorized to engage in a good deal of data pooling. Geographic dispersal of personal files has not precluded data bank comparisons or the collection dossiers when authorized by law. With a modem and a telephone, data banks anywhere can communicate with ease. Only legislative restrictions, when properly enforced, can limit roster matching to situations where this is done with an acceptable balance of privacy rights.

VOLUNTARY OR MANDATORY IDS?

Participation in a census is mandatory, but there are always individuals missed by its enumerators. Some categories of persons are systematically undercounted. This includes illegal immigrants, poor people, urban ghetto inhabitants and non-English speaking residents. Demographic data have been collected decennially since 1790, but for more than two hundred years, the United States has functioned without a national ID system. This voluntaristic tradition has all but disappeared in view of a growing number of mandatory requirements. Motor vehicle drivers must qualify for and carry a drivers license. New employees must have a Social Security Number (SSN). No one can travel abroad without a U.S. passport, except to Mexico, to Canada and to some of the Caribbean Islands.

Voters may be asked for a voter registration card. Access to the worksite is often based on being able to display a special card. Many other documents—marriage licenses, graduation certificates and Blue Cross-Blue Shield health insurance cards—are needed in the conduct of our daily lives. But as previously noted, there are many mandatory identity documents, but few are so controlled to be reliable.

The proposal for a mandatory central identifier remains controversial, nevertheless. It will almost certainly be challenged in the federal courts. A mandatory provision would also add a law enforcement burden to an already overextended Federal Bureau of Investigation.

Under a voluntary system freedom to dissent would be preserved. Opponents would be free to decline being included in the system. They would retain the right to put up with the inconvenience of repeatedly explaining to credit card companies why they do not have a federal ID document. They would have to rely on less trustworthy documents.

A general federal population roster would gradually emerge, encompassing almost everybody. To a large extent, such a roster already exists in the Social Security system. But if it were to utilize the current technology to produce good ID documents, Congress will be tempted to make use of it for additional administrative purposes. It would provide a roster more up-to-date and more complete than the decennial census.

Opposition to such a de facto comprehensive national personnel roster will be strong. Provisions would have to be made to reassure those who fear its misuse. Even if the present chaotic ID system is maintained, such protective procedures will need to be considered. Fortunately, the technology that will facilitate the use of a national roster for generating relatively current demographic data for research and planning purposes can also be used to give each individual much more control than he can now exercise about the accuracy of information about him stored in any information system.

SURVEILLANCE CONTROL

Policemen enforce the law under many constitutional restrictions. They cannot stop a person in the street or in an automobile just to check on who he is. In most circumstances, a search warrant is needed to investigate where a violation of the law is suspected.

There are exceptions. In emergencies, such as the aftermath of a forest fire or flood, access to some areas may be closed to all but persons who live in the area. All travellers can and will be stopped unless they have proof that they reside in an otherwise closed area. Within twenty-five miles of a U.S. border individuals can also be stopped to document their citizenship. But free nations have generally well enforced legal restraints on the use of personal data. Any program to improve the quality of identity documents would need to be balanced by well enforced sanctions to restrict their use for surveillance purposes.

For instance, electronic devices can be used to check where people are located at any given point in time. Physicians, plumbers, and others who travel while working carry beepers that permit them to receive messages. Animals in the forest can be equipped with an electronic device that will reveal information about their whereabouts and way of life under natural conditions.

A proposal is under consideration to use this technology as an alternative to full time imprisonment. Nonviolent offenders could have some or all of their sentence converted to a partial loss of freedom, in the form of an evening or weekend home arrest. They would be allowed to work, but would be confined to their quarters at all other times except when an absence is authorized by their parole officer or during a medical emergency. Conformity to these conditions could be monitored centrally by means of an electronic bracelet worn by each person. They could also be required to check in periodically by placing their finger or eyes on an electronic reader installed in their home to register their fingerprint or retina pattern. These reports would be recorded automatically at police headquarters.

The idea might be welcomed by convicted offenders. They would be able to hold a regular job, live with their family, and sometimes save enough money to compensate the victim(s) of their crime. The procedure would also save taxpayer funds. In 1982 thirty-one states were under court orders to reduce overcrowded conditions in their prisons. There would be less pressure to build new jails and prison.

This proposal, however, also has serious implications for personal privacy. In Communist countries and in South Africa this technique could be used to monitor house arrest sentences imposed on political dissidents. Some businesses might be tempted to use such electronic spy devices to check on employees.

This intrusive technology can be either progressive or repressive. It will work only when the monitored person is willing to cooperate. Each must wear the electronic unit and check in periodically to prove that the right person is actually wearing the device which is assigned to him. Protective standards will need to be adopted to regulate these devices, to prevent invasions of privacy and violations of human rights. Like telephone tapping and other surveillance techniques, the computer confinement technology must be subjected to a strict process of licensing, with publicly approved standards.

Nationwide ID files could provide other relatively nonintrusive forms of surveillance to help law enforcement. Thieves can be incriminated by accessing their bank accounts to investigate suspicious deposits or disbursements. A bigamist need not be caught living in several residences; more than one marriage license, in the absence of divorce papers, will suffice to get an investigation launched. This nonintrusive capability is already being used widely to detect persons who illegally claim a public entitlement.

A HUMAN FRAILTY ALLOWANCE

Some data inconsistencies are inevitable because of coding errors, lapses in memory, changes in personal status over time, and socially acceptable white lies. Matching of data bases will reveal these discrepancies. They must not be allowed to become an automatic indicator of wrongdoing. Many inconsistencies reflect the fallibility of the human condition. This issue has yet to be fully addressed at the legislative level.

If this has not yet become a major political issue, it is because most operators of data banks refrain from sharing their information, ever mindful that the public retains a good deal of power over what and to whom information is revealed about their personal life. A hospital will accept a pregnant woman's statement of being married without checking where the marriage took place. It is really no one's business whether the child was conceived in or out of wedlock.

No individual can be expected to have instant and precise recall of detailed events in the past. Occasional errors are unavoidable. Computers can outperform them when it comes to being precise and consistent. An employment application to the government or a statement of assets and liabilities made to a bank will require detailed information few people have at their fingertips. How many are able to list all residential addresses and telephone numbers since birth? In a physical examination to qualify for life insurance, a questionnaire may ask about all ailments and diseases since birth. Lapses in memory and confusion of details are part of the human condition.

The cumulative effect of collecting data on such lapses of any individual would constitute a serious burden. Yet, this is deemed to be a suitable investigative technique when someone is suspected of income tax evasion or some other crime, where evidence must be thoroughly reviewed. Computers cannot differentiate, however, between a lapse in memory, a white lie without criminal consequences, and a fraudulent misrepresentation designed to victimize the public. Yet such distinctions are important.

This issue poses an administrative challenge which requires public attention. Both saints and sinners are tarnished in real life by the fact that the human brain does not function like a computer. This differentiation between people who generate inconsistent data about themselves for criminal reasons and the majority who are just human and fallible is important.

No candidate for public office can be expected to have a record without error. Legal as well as administrative procedures will have to be devised to limit the public disclosure of such routine inconsistencies, except in circumstances where there is evidence of criminal intent or an item of compelling public interest.

The technical perfection of computers must be balanced by a human frailty allowance, much like that which operates in normal social life. The balance between privacy, efficiency, and accuracy is not clearly marked. But the issue needs to be addressed at the legislative and public policy level.

THE OPTIMUM IN NONINTRUSIVE SECURITY

Opposition to the national ID card concept is also fired by the vision that too many nosy officials might be empowered to inquire about our age, sex life, race, educational level and many other personal facts even when it is irrelevant to their official function. There is no necessity that such data be made available to them. Biometric and ID numbers are the most neutral of all identification characteristics, less subject to prejudice than photographs, signatures and voiceprints.

Most ID cards however are inspected visually rather than digitally. For this purpose additional information is needed, such as a person's first and last name, sex, age, a photograph, and a signature. Specialized data are added to conform to particularistic uses of different ID documents. On birth certificates, information about the parents of the child, place and time of birth and—in some places—the marital status and age of the parents and their race are included. Bank cards often have a code about the credit limit of the holder. A growing number of individuals carry cards with a detailed medical history for use in an emergency, should they lose consciousness. The card will alert those who treat this patient about allergies, blood type, and other medically relevant facts.

Few would question the need to reduce the risk of unauthorized access to security sensitive installations. All White House employees are fingerprinted. Access to atomic weapons has to be carefully controlled through foolproof identification. Most municipalities will hire policemen only after they are fingerprinted, something also true of the FBI and CIA. Banks like to check employees with access to money, and child care agencies often check out persons who will work closely with children.

The Department of Justice fingerprint ID data bank was originally established for crime control purposes. But the FBI also maintains a separate noncriminal fingerprint unit for identification purposes. Fingerprints of all persons subjected to security clearance for a responsible post are kept there. Those of celebrities are filed separately, under extra security precautions.

The Department of Justice Fingerprint Identification Data Banks were set up in 1924, although some fingerprint records were being used as far back as 1896. The FBI offers free clearance services to banks, credit agencies, police, nursery schools, children's institutions, and other organizations. They can check out prospective employees considered for jobs where trust is an important consideration.

The importance attached to this service became apparent to agencies authorized to use it when the FBI had to discontinue its civilian clearance service in 1981, due to an overload of work and lack of personnel. During a one-year stoppage, there was a flood of complaints to the FBI and to Congress. Civilian agencies protested, sometimes citing horror stories about persons who had been hired in capacities of trust, who turned out to have criminal histories. Most graphic was the discovery by a day care center that a new employee had previously been convicted for throwing a baby into an incinerator.

Fingerprints can be forged by specialists. It is technically possible to impersonate someone by obtaining a copy of his actual fingerprint from an object such as a glass. The print can then be transferred to a cellophane strip and placed over the proper finger like a bandaid. The digital reader would then respond to this facsimile, rather than to the criminal's own finger pattern. One tragic case is known in which this technique was used to frame an innocent man with a bank robbery. He served two years until a private investigator was able to unearth the evidence to free him. The victim had been framed by the director of the local crime laboratory who had stolen his fingerprint from a file card under his care.

Fingerprints have recently enjoyed a burst of popularity due to the fact that about 28,000 American children disappeared in 1985. Most of them ran away from home, but thousands were kidnapped or murdered. About 1,000 young dead were unnamed and unclaimed in the country's morgues. Legislation was passed in 1982 for a national clearing house of missing children. "If stolen cars are kept on a computerized file, why not missing children?" noted one of the sponsors of the bill.[2]

Voluntary fingerprinting of children by their parents has become common in a growing number of communities to help identify them in the event of amnesia, disappearance, or foul play. Very few parents object when such a program is offered in their locality. Babies born are generally footprinted in hospitals as a protection against identity mix-ups. Footprint configurations remain the same for life, but they are administratively cumbersome. They could be matched against a child's fingerprint when the first ID card is issued, after the child is a few years old. At birth, babies' fingers are too smooth to get a good digitally readable line pattern.

Technological changes often produce exaggerated anxieties when their implications are not well understood. The public has reason to be concerned about the development of electronic eavesdropping and other surreptitious surveillance techniques that are being used by governments or by private persons to spy on someone else. Biometric indicators, however, as well as electronic security codes which can be digitally checked involve data that are neither personal nor culturally sensitive and they differentiate people without revealing anything about their private affairs.

STIGMA AVOIDANCE

Stored personal data vary in privacy-related sensitivity. People also differ in their readiness to share facts about themselves. It is therefore useful to review levels of stigma potential of facts to see how they might be handled administratively:

1. Minor stigmatization potential, such as last name, first name, place of birth, signature, telephone number, SSN, color of eyes, and fingerprint.
2. Major stigmatization potential such as race, sex, religion, citizenship, nationality, income, debts, or medical data.
3. Political data on party affiliation, current or prior membership in social and political action agencies.
4. Status loss data such as prior arrests, convictions, bankruptcy, slow-payment record, unusual sexual preference, mental illness, family breakup or career setback.
5. Status gain data such as holding public office, ownership of a business, employment in a prestigious post, academic degrees or prizes awarded, membership in professional organizations, honors received, good credit record, or career advancement.

A national ID document could exclude most stigma sensitive data. Most stigma sensitive categories of information could be protected by a special code to limit its revelation to carefully designated persons.

Who these officials are, and when they could access the data file would no longer have to be secret. Except during a court ordered investigation of a possible crime, individuals could have access to the identity of the persons who can review their record, just as hospital patients can know which physicians and nurses can review their medical records.

Printing presses can spread malicious slander, yet few Americans would favor censorship being used as a countermeasure. There are security restrictions on the free flow of information in the democracies, but they have to be justified on legal and constitutional grounds. Neither "the right to privacy" nor the "public's right to know" are absolute.

An administrative machinery to resolve privacy controversies needs to be perfected. Such resolution relies excessively on litigation. An administrative review could resolve many problems speedily and at modest cost. A strategy needs to be adopted to maximize security and protection of privacy in the light of the technology that can be used for both. Some of the relevant legislative and administrative features will be explained in the next chapter.

REFERENCES

1. "Reissuing Tamper-Resistant Cards Will Not Eliminate Misuse of Social Security Numbers," Washington, D.C., U.S. General Accounting Office, HRD 81–20, December 23, 1980.

2. *New York Times*. June 12, 1982: 30.

CHAPTER NINE

MODERNIZING THE BILL OF RIGHTS

CONTROLLING THE GOLEM

There is a recurrent theme in medieval Hebrew mysticism of the power of holy men to create a robot to perform routine tasks. This Golem must be watched lest he runs amok and endanger people. He is strong but lacks a creative mind and a contemplative soul.

Is the tamper-resistant ID card such a Golem? Will the card compete with our real identity? Will bureaucracies deal with individuals, even more than they do now, as computerizable categories rather than as dynamic persons?

In any record, manual or digital, some erroneous entries will be made. It is not easy to keep them updated. Data banks need to be carefully monitored against being accessed by malevolent persons. An inaccuracy in a data bank can leave a person stranded without credit, resulting in job loss or a false arrest. In the case of *Collins* vs. *Retail Credit Company* a report based on unverified rumor and idle speculation led to a rejection of Ms. Collins's request for automobile insurance on false allegations of her being an excessive drinker and sexually promiscuous.[1] She took the credit agency to court and was awarded $321,750 in actual and punitive damages, plus attorneys' fees.

Redress of error through judicial proceedings is rare, except when the injured party can afford to finance legal proceedings or when a clear case of defamation occurs, which a lawyer is willing to handle on a contingency basis.

In democratic countries, therefore, there is a tendency to rely on less expensive protective measures. Twelve major approaches are in use. They are not mutually exclusive. They provide an alternative to the view of some civil libertarians that the best strategy against possible invasions of privacy is to limit the maintenance of files about people and to reduce reliance on the computer technology for personal identification.

Modern life has become very dependent on the storage and retrieval of personal data. Milton R. Wessel and John L. Lirley may exaggerate a little when they estimate that "over half of our workforce [is] busy producing, storing, using and transferring knowledge."[2] Inventions, once perfected, cannot be made to disappear. They must be controlled to maximize their benefit and to minimize their danger. Administrators therefore must perfect techniques to protect the use of data files by one or more of the following options:

1. Feedback to the individual concerned whenever sensitive personal files are accessed
2. Access tracing
3. Standards for data base matching
4. Bonding and licensing of personnel who operate data banks and of agencies which operate them
5. Data correction and expunging procedures
6. Updating
7. Privacy protection legislation, with due regard for research needs and for freedom of information rights
8. Continued research
9. Appointment of data bank ombudsmen
10. Publicity about alleged or real privacy violations
11. Legal remedies
12. Single versus multiple-function documents
13. Federal, decentralized or private enterprise administration of the system

FEEDBACK TO THE PUBLIC

It is feasible to provide every individual about whom a file is kept with a copy of the information that is added or deleted. Computers can do it automatically and at a reasonable cost. Each person could check the accuracy of the stored information about himself easily and at low cost. His or her tamper-resistant ID card, with a biometric feature, could be used to verify an entitlement to the information. The organization could then be protected from the risk of keeping false information for a long time. Each person would be able to verify the accuracy of his file periodically.

A legal framework for such data verification procedures is found in the Fair Credit Reporting Act, (Public Law 91–508) and the Equal Credit Opportunity Act, (United States Code Title 15). They incorporate a number of significant regulations for consumer protection. For instance, anyone who discovers that he was denied credit, insurance, or employment is entitled to know the name of the reporting agency whose files were accessed. The nature, substance, and sources (except investigative or medical sources) must be shared, free of charge. The individual also is entitled to be informed of which person or organization received a copy of the report during the prior six months to two year period. People can demand a reinvestigation of incomplete or incorrect information. If it cannot be verified, it has to be removed. In a dispute about the accuracy of the information between a data file operator and a consumer, the subject's version of the dispute must be placed in the file and included in subsequent reports furnished to third parties. The law also entitles injured members of the public to sue for damages and—if successful—collect attorney's fees.

Additional protective measures are used by a few private credit reporting agencies. For instance, the code of ethics of the TRW Credit Data organization include the following principles, which go beyond the requirements of the Fair Credit Reporting Act: 1. refrain from recording information on a consumer's general reputation, moral habits or mode of living 2. reject information on race, nationality, religion or other discrimination prone indicators 3. avoid information unrelated to credit standing such as criminal records, traffic violations, and newspaper accounts about a person. Only a few of the business related data organizations limit their collection activities in such a conscientious way. A legally mandated feedback requirement would go a long way toward minimizing privacy threats. An erroneous or malicious entry in such a data bank would not remain secret for long if it had to be shared periodically with the subject or each time someone accesses an unusually sensitive file.

The *Privacy Act of 1974* also gives federal employees the right to view their own personnel files. Pennsylvania and a few other states extend this right to all workers in both public and nongovernmental organizations. If an individual believes that his file contains an erroneous or misleading statement, he is entitled to place a rebuttal in the file. But the laws are generally silent on what kind of information can be kept. Must it be strictly job related? Can employers record details about the personal lives of their workers?

ACCESS TRACING

Employers differ widely in the information they need about their workers. There are no national standards. Anyone accepting employment in a security agency—the FBI, CIA or a police department—needs to acquiesce in his concern with sharing facts about his personal life. Records of comparable personal data would be most inappropriate if kept for sales personnel of a clothing store. It is illegal to discriminate in employment on the basis of race, age or sex, but company records nearly always include these items. The most effective deterrent to inappropriate data collection is the accountability of employers for use made of their files.

Both congress and the fifty states have avoided detailed regulations of the management of data bases. There are technical aspects of privacy protection that could be modified whenever there are changes in the use of integrated circuit technology. As a 1981 study of the Office of Technology Assessment points out, it is possible to fabricate hundreds of thousands of electronic components to fit on a wafer smaller than a paper clip. Satellite and microwave techniques can provide credit card and check authorization service around the world. Privacy must be redefined in terms of feasible electronic safety features.[3]

When a manual file is kept, it is readily available to anyone who can open the filing cabinet. Large organizations which operate central files sometimes make notations every time a file is removed. Such control procedures can be made more precise when data are kept in a computer. Each personal file can then be programmed for limited access, much like safety boxes in a vault. Only a selected roster of persons would be entitled to review the data. A record could be kept of when a file was used, as well of the person who requested the information.

None of these procedures are expensive. In most organizations there is sufficient trust in the record maintenance process that few persons ever worry about who sees their file. Traffic can be monitored with precision, specially if the ID document includes a fingerprint or a machine-readable signature. It will then become difficult for any anonymous snooper to evade the clearance procedure, except if the matter is important enough to invite the attention of a professional computer criminal.

Electronic data cannot be protected absolutely against being accessed by a technically sophisticated, but unauthorized person.[4] However, such efforts can be made prohibitively expensive and risky. The tamper-resistant ID card, far from being a threat to what is left of our privacy, is an important tool to help protect it from potential abuses of electronic data storage and retrieval.

STANDARDS FOR DATA BASE MATCHING

Comparison of different data sets is an important source of knowledge. Scientific researchers examine similarities and differences for clues on how to push back the areas of uncertainty of the world in which we live. Science lives on free exchange of information, including contradictions among knowledge sources. But there are social constraints about full utilization of knowledge. The right to privacy is often accepted in democracies as taking precedence over the methodological advantages of verifying data from different sources. Some files are designated as confidential or secret. Others are being jealously guarded for political, proprietary, or ethical reasons. Many organizations and governments deliberately refrain from investigating conflicting data sources to avoid embarrassment, especially about persons in power.

For centuries, the Japanese have used carved seals called *insho*, *inkan* or *hanko*, to sign contracts. They are short cylinders of wood or buffalo horn, with the family's name carved at one end. Without such a stamp, it is difficult to rent a house, buy a car, or mail a registered letter. It is technically possible for a good carver to copy a seal. But forgeries do not appear to be much of a problem. The same cannot be said, however, about credit cards. Japan has the second largest number in circulation, after the United States. It is estimated that in 1985 they will generate credits of $125 billion dollars. The business firms which issue them do not generally share information, each guarding its blacklist of defaulters as a secret to be kept from competitors. While about one percent of the card holders try to disappear each year when they cannot keep up with their payments, the default rate has not become sufficiently serious to abandon the preference of credit card companies to keep their losses confidential.

Government agencies are mandated by law to take a different position, especially when possible wrongdoings are at issue. High levels of consistency can be expected when facts are supplied to different data files by the average honest person. Discrepancies are usually caused by error. But inconsistency can also be a clue that fraud was committed. Data base matching can lead to self-incrimination, in situations such as the following.

- An employer claiming to have paid expenses to an employee for whom no Social Security taxes were transmitted to the SSA
- Multiple billings by physicians, hospitals, and pharmacists for services rendered under the re-embursement provisions of Medicare and Medicaid
- Default in the repayment on professional education loans that had been made to physicians with a good current income
- Department of Defense retirees who are receiving dual compensation in excess of the pay cap limit for federal retirees

Many states check unemployment compensation payments against simultaneous earnings for a job, or an unreported Social Security Administration pension for disability, black lung benefits, and other income. In Montana, $200,000 to $300,000 in overpayments are found each year. About 500 cases of fraud have been prosecuted.[5]

When two data bases reveal contradictory information, computer experts designate it as a "hit"—a clue to be investigated. Not every such instance is an indication of criminal intent. In the above mentioned unemployment compensation matching program of the state of New York, only 45 percent of the hits turned out to be cases where an actual overpayment was the result of a fraudulent claim. In Pennsylvania 4,570 potential overpayment cases were discovered in 1981. After more careful checking, only 2,046 (45 percent) were found to have cashed the overpayments.

Data base contradictions should never be used to charge anyone of wrongdoing without confirming evidence from other sources. The individual concerned must first be asked to explain or to correct the record. Discrepancies must be regarded as accidental, unless proven otherwise. Without such precautions, roster comparisons can be challenged on constitutional grounds. The American Civil Liberties Union (ACLU) urged a moratorium on all future data base matchings for this reason. It also pointed out that this procedure subjects a large number of persons to hidden search and seizure of their privacy without a warrant. The courts have not, in general, upheld this view. Computer matches are becoming an increasingly significant tool of law enforcement.

The President's Council on Integrity and Efficiency has launched a Long Term Computer Matching Project to facilitae fraud reduction. There are 85 support programs based on need and 51 federal insurance programs, which protect individuals and firms against specified risks. These programs service three out of every ten Americans, with a budget of over $400 billion dollars in 1984. Fraudulent claims have been minimized by publicizing that false claims would be detected by data base matching. Much the same applies to large firms which make unreasonable charges in "cost plus" defense contracts or participating illegally in federal loan programs for businesses and farmers. A newsletter is published to keep federal as well as state public administrators informed of the utility of these programs as a management tool, and of precautions that must be taken to prevent their misuse.

There is little opposition to reducing the victimization of persons by criminals. What remains controversial is the amount of privacy we are willing to sacrifice to optimize law enforcement. In the view of many, the reduction in the victimization of the public through the use of false documents or stolen passports is more than sufficient justification for expanding data base matchings. But this law enforcement procedure also requires that the transactions of the noncriminal majority have to be monitored.

The issue is well illustrated by the rider attached to the Defense Appropriation Act of 1982 to track down youths who failed to register for the draft at age 18. The SSA was authorized to provide the addresses of wage earners who reach their eighteenth birthday. Lists can also be obtained from drivers license bureaus of each state and from high school graduation rosters. When the data base matching technique was first used, 514 young men were located who had not registered for the draft. After a reminder letter, 90 percent complied with the law.

Callers to the Selective Service offices were being warned by a recorded message that such data matching procedures are in use to locate young men who fail to comply with the law. Their names are now being turned over to the Department of Justice for prosecution.

Persons who are ideologically opposed to draft registration are likely to reject any proposal that would give the government additional enforcement power. Opposition to the use of roster comparisons has also been fueled by misuse of information, when contradictions are discovered in two different files. Massachusetts officials automatically cancelled welfare benefit checks of persons found to have a bank account in excess of what is permitted when an individual applies for public assistance. Some of these cancellations had to be rescinded when the affected people protested and were able to prove that they were entitled to their benefits. Contradictory evidence affecting an individual can lead to an investigation, but the outcome should not be prejudged. There often are reasonable explanations when files contain questionable information.

These current experiences with data base matching have led to the formulation of standards for federally managed personal files. Some of the following issues have been addressed by the Office of Management and Budgets (OMB):

1. Enforcement of standards of confidentiality for personal files. Those maintained by the United States census bureau include an absolute prohibition against being subjected to data base matching. Others, like arrest records, are open to the public.
2. Plans for making data base comparisons between different federal files or with those of the business community, must first be published in the Federal Register.
3. Harassment and unreasonable publicity about contradictory information is prohibited, until the facts can be carefully investigated. The individuals or organization involved should first be given a chance to explain or correct the difference, unless this would interfere with the conduct of a court ordered criminal investigation.

These guidelines are not likely to satisfy some constitutional critics of data-base matching. Some object to any use of information collected for a given purpose to investigate a quite different issue—the possibility of wrongdoing. States like New York, Massachusetts, and California are developing extensive programs to minimize welfare, insurance and other frauds through data base matchings. But when personal records are kept manually, detectives often rely on trapping criminals by self-incrimination through inconsistent income tax statements. Computerized data banks have greatly multiplied the use of such self-entrapment techniques.

This capacity will need to be balanced by strictly enforced rules against petty harassment by information specialists, who may wish to embarrass a political enemy or settle a personal grudge. The incredibly intrusive potential of data base matching needs to be balanced by a requirement that a grand jury or judicial order be required before administrators can use discovered data inconsistency to initiate a criminal prosecution. It would also seem reasonable to allow for an appeals process to an independent authority, such as a data protection ombudsman, whenever an individual has reason to complain about being reasonably affected by alleged contradiction of information stored about him in different rosters.

Except in the presence of strong evidence of possible wrongdoing should anyone be burdened with the need to undertake a time consuming and possibly expensive legal defense for data contradictions? A food stamp recipient can have a ten thousand dollar account without necessarily having perjured himself at the time he applied for this benefit program.

Some protective measures are already in force. Agencies which match data files are now required by the OMB to return the original tapes to the organization which compiled them. Congress and the OMB must be notified, if a data base match leads to the creation of a new system of records not previously authorized. But these OMB guidelines apply only to data files of the federal government. State and private files are less explicitly monitored. Those who manage them are nevertheless inclined to be careful to respect the privacy rights of their clients, lest they be taken to court and sued for damage.

There is also precedent in the United States that public assurances of confidentiality be kept. The U.S. census bureau has successfully demonstrated that it can avoid disclosure of information, even if mandated by a court of law. Essex County in New Jersey wanted to have access to the names of all persons who were enumerated in 1980 so that its officials could prove that a significant number of residents had been overlooked. Such data would have enabled Essex County to claim a greater proportion of federal funds that are being apportioned on the basis of an allegedly incomplete census count. The director of the census appealed the case to the Supreme Court. The court upheld the census' mandate to refuse sharing raw data abut any person, even for such a public interest purpose.[6]

No federal agency, including the FBI, the CIA, or the IRS is given access to any individual census file. Care is taken when publishing grouped data about small areas, like a single enumeration district, that no individual respondent can be inadvertently identified. Averages are omitted, if there are just a few cases in the area. This procedure precludes people estimating the income or inferring other details about any of the individual respondents. The U.S. code protects both the census record, as well as the confidentiality of a copy that may be kept in the file of a person who furnished the information.

BONDING, LICENSING, AND CERTIFICATION

Data bank operators need to be screened for trustworthiness and must conform to a code of ethics. This is now rarely done. If accidental or deliberate violations of confidentiality take place, they will be more difficult to detect when files are kept manually than when they are computerized. Technically secured computer files can only be invaded by a programmed process of intrusion, usually with inside help. Those who gain access will be leaving a track when they have to use their ID card.

Manually maintained files are less secure. They can be inspected anonymously or photocopied. This can happen even to carefully guarded records, as were those of a fashionable London medical clinic which were discovered in a village garbage dump by a schoolboy. They included the medical files of such persons as the Duchess of Kent, former prime minister Edward Heath, ballet dancer Rudolf Nureyev, and David Frost. The records were supposed to have been incinerated, but were accidentally deposited in the garbage.

The Society for Worldwide Interbank Financial Telecommunication (SWIFT) codes all information transmitted between banks. The security of the system requires reliable controls of how each member bank selects those entrusted with sending and receiving confidential messages. The system seems to work well. Other safety features could be added, should anyone succeed in breaking the security procedures.

The element of financial and organizational responsibility can be enhanced by licensing and bonding, now almost routine for bank employees and professionals in positions of high trust. Licensing and bonding could also be made mandatory for employees with access to sensitive personal files.

An oath of secrecy has been required of U.S. census employees since 1880. Their suprevisors were exempt from this limitation until 1900. Violation of the secrecy vow would now expose all employees to a penalty up to five years in jail and/or a $5,000 fine. The obligation to maintain confidentiality continues, even after a person terminates employment with the census. Since 1910, the assurance of confidentiality has been reenforced with a presidential proclamation every ten years. President Taft and his successors assured the public that census records would not be used to impose taxes, jury duty, or military service. The promise has been kept faithfully. No individual census employee has ever been convicted of violating his oath of confidentiality.[7] This is quite a record, when one considers the fact that the prohibition against unauthorized revelation is now more than 80 years old.

Even during the West Coast hysteria about Japanese spies after the attack on Pearl Harbor in 1941, the U.S. census refused to furnish information about individual Japanese residents. It upheld the policy of never revealing any alleged security risk by providing the War Relation Authority with an address. The census bureau was, however, criticized by some civil libertarians for assigning one of its statisticians to work with the War Relocation Authority in 1942 to tabulate information about the geographic concentration of Japanese-Americans. These data were used to plan a mandatory evacuation program. At the time, the U.S. Supreme Court upheld this measure as justifiable on national security grounds. Four decades later, it was seen as something quite different—as an unreasonable and unjustified violation of the U.S. Constitution.

Nicholas Caruso suggested an added measure of security to minimize privacy abuses. Organizations could be required to exercise self-restraint and not to entrap their employees.[8] When a computer is used as a surveillance instrument—like a timeclock—both workers and their union would first have to be consulted. No surreptitious surveillance would be permitted. For instance, a Wang Alliance system can match the time commitments of a large group of employees and then schedule a meeting at a mutually convenient time. But to avoid a scheduling error, each employee would have to disclose both his work-related and private appointments to the computer. A top-level company executive would have to be held responsible for guaranteeing that no one would access this information for any other purpose without an employee's permission. As an added precaution, the computer program could be coded so that the data would be revealed only to the designated conference arranger, after recording his or her ID card number.

Congress has repeatedly discussed proposals to police the issuance of false ID documents by imposing added penalties. H.R. 6105 would provide criminal penalties for mailing an ID document bearing a false birthdate. H.R. 352, The False Identification Crime Control Act of 1981, would have made it a federal crime to be in possession of a false ID document.

Both manufacture and possession with the intent to defraud would have become a criminal act. Similar bills are likely to be introduced in future legislative sessions.

DATA CORRECTION AND EXPUNGING PROCEDURES

It is possible to have information deleted from the record. But nothing can undo words spoken before a jury. The possible effect of false data or prejudicial inferences on a listener can be devastating. Computerized data storage makes it technically possible to vastly expand the memory of people and of organizations. This fact has serious implications for privacy rights.

It took nearly half a century before the West German minister of justice ordered the expunging of criminal convictions by the Nazi People's Courts. These were mostly for political actions which are not an offense in the democratic Bundes republic. Few Germans are today likely to feel sensitive about an accusation of Rassenschande: marriage or sex relations between an alleged Aryan and a Jew or a non-Caucasian person. Such events were kept in the records of the German criminal police for decades after the Hitler period. Deletion of such information would not be politically controversial now. Administrators tend to be conservative about destroying information, if only for legal or historical reasons.

Few people would question a prohibition against keeping a criminal file about anyone who was found to be not guilty of an offense with which he or she had been charged. But would this presumption of innocence be accepted by the law enforcement community in the case of an accused rapist, whose alleged victim refused to press charges? There also is the question about the length of time after arrest and conviction records of criminals should be kept. Is it necessary for an adult, when applying for a security sensitive post, to admit that he had been treated for a psychiatric illness at the age of 12? Is it reasonable for parents to know if a Boy Scout leader is a chronic alcoholic? Should shoplifting of a pair of gloves at the age 14 affect the appointment to a teaching or police job at the age of 30?

Expunging a court record is a controversial administrative issue. It rarely occurs when the accused was found to be "not guilty," or when charges were dismissed on a technicality—such as the nonappearance of the plaintiff. Local and state courts do not routinely inform the FBI of the outcome of a criminal trial. Courts will pay for the services of a public defender in a criminal case, but fees are rarely authorized to have the record expunged even when the court chooses to dismiss the charges. Poor people rarely have the $250 or more needed to obtain legal counsel to make sure that is done. A simplified procedure would be helpful, if the power of individuals to monitor the quality of information is to be matched with the speed and simplicity of storing negative personal information.

When expunging is ordered by the court, should the data be totally removed, or a residue be maintained somewhere? This would allow the tracing of suspects, who continue to live under suspicious circumstances, in efforts to help law enforcement agencies to reduce the incidence of sex crimes, drug pushing, and other law violations. Dismissal of a case does not *prove* a person's innocence. But such "hit" lists of possible offenders exposes them to a great deal of surveillance and would violate their civil rights, unless authorized by legislation that meets constitutional tests.

In cases of criminal conviction, after a sentence was served, should the file be closed and expunged? Under plea bargaining practices, some serious offenders are offered immunity or given short sentences for having cooperated with law enforcement officials. Procedures for expunging negative data therefore need to balance the public's right to have information that is important and the right of people to get a new start in life. Should these rules be the same for a drunk-driving charge as for a person who committed arson or raped a child?

Or should the public forego the correction of such errors? This can be costly to the taxpayer. The SSA in 1982 checked the death records of eleven states, New York City, and of the Veterans Administration (VA). The computerized payment program had been sending pension checks to thousands of dead people. The total leakage might add up to several hundred millions of dollars, once this verification program will be extended to the entire country. In a pilot study of 1,525 cases listed as *dead* in one file but as living in the files of the SSA Administrations, a total of $6 million had been paid out to deceased beneficiaries. Some of their relatives had notified the SSA, but its complex record system failed to register the fact and continued the payments.

Dead people cannot claim civil rights violations. Some of their relatives after being targeted by a data bank matching process were accused of fraud because they cashed Social Security checks issued to their dear departed. The ACLU takes the position that this is a legally questionable procedure. It is being done without a search warrant. The inspector general of the Department of Health and Human Services points out that such procedures are a logical way to implement the Deficit Reduction Act (PL 98–369).[9] Both would agree, however, that no one should be prosecuted merely because of evidence that checks were cashed that by law should have been returned. Enforcement standards need to differentiate between relatives who carelessly or in ignorance cashed a few checks and those who knowingly violated the law. A seemingly illegal act, discovered by matching data bases, sometimes turns out to be quite legitimate.

Robert Ellis Smith reports the case of a mother who knew herself to be near death.[10] She added her daughter's name to her bank account. She was to get the money at once upon her death, without going through probate procedures because the daughter was short of funds, subsisting on welfare payments. A computer match of Massachusetts welfare rolls with a roster of bank deposit holders identified the daughter as the owner of assets, which she had failed to report when applying for public assistance. It would be unreasonable to infer criminal intent into such circumstances.

The public's right to be well informed often conflicts with personal privacy preferences. Every individual or agency would prefer to have unfavorable information deleted. But this preference runs counter to constitutional rights of "freedom of the press." There are no easy answers here.

No user of computerized information is immune to having incorrect information recorded about him. The evening this author wanted to have a final copy of this book printed by the university's computer, he was refused access: a clerical error had led to the automatic cancellation of his ID code number. It can take days, weeks or months, to clear up such errors.

Accurate ID documents are useful support instruments rather than a detraction from such a safety feature. While some of these horrors result from deliberate fraud and misrepresentation, many reflect random error or administrative carelessness. One solution, however, is impractical: stop keeping personal records. It would be difficult to do without them, without our bank account, without an educational transcript or without our credit cards.

There are too many people now living on this globe to make retreat to a pre-modern level of privacy a feasible option. Privacy can only be protected by limiting access to available information to authorized persons on a "need-to-know" basis, normally after prior consent of the individual whose file is being checked. Exceptions to this rule, for public and security purposes, need to be legally circumscribed. The technology to monitoring that these regulations are adhered to is well advanced for files that are computerized.

FBI regulations now require that data collected in pursuit of a White House ordered investigation shall be destroyed, subject to two conditions: 1. The data are of no historical interest and therefore would not be desired by National Archives, 2. Information can continue to be held if it relates to persons who have recently been reinvestigated.

When investigations are made regarding civil disorders, they may not be indexed to permit retrieval about a specific individual, unless this person is also the subject of an authorized law enforcement investigation.

Many of the same ethical issues arise in the management of private and business files. Is it fair to preserve a lapse of propriety forever? But is it fair to withhold from a creditor evidence that a loan applicant went bankrupt five years ago, defaulting on all his debts? The Fair Credit Reporting Act of 1971 prohibits the use of adverse consumer information after seven years. Bankruptcies can be reported for 14 years. But under what circumstance would it be proper for a company to share the fact that they dismissed a person on suspicion of sexual harassment of a fellow employee or for incompetence?

West Germany has a privately owned credit security protection agency, used by more than 30,000 companies, landlords and retail stores. This Schutzgemeinschaft fuer Allgemeine Kreditsicherung (Schufa) receives data free of charge from its members plus other sources, including police informants. Each day, Schufa makes 80,000 credit reports, one-third of them over the telephone.

Errors are inevitable in such an operation. For instance, a perjury charge against a certain Paul S. was erroneously filed in the record of another person with the same name. Four banks promptly stopped doing business with the unfortunate victim. Checks he had already written were refused. No cross references had been made of the respective birthdays of the two like named individuals, which would have prevented the confusion.[11]

Private and public data banks will generally correct errors that are brought to their attention. There are no standards on when and how quickly this must be done. In the United States the risk of a costly lawsuit makes most data collection agencies inclined to act promptly. But as more and more computerized data banks are being used, the average individual cannot monitor all of them. He cannot check periodically if his qualifications are portrayed properly. Existing laws need to be reviewed to update their capacity to protect the public against accidental or intended (dirty trick) revelations of false or needlessly damaging information.

UPDATING

Once born, a person retains his identity until death. There can be a court approved name change, one or more marriages, or the loss of a limb. But each person's brain and sensory system remains unique. The health and the performance of these interactive organs will vary over a lifetime. The core remains, as a continuous biological identity, including memory. This is what is symbolized by an identity card, the social-psychological basis of continuity of each living person.

Personal data files need to be updated, since changes in status occur continuously. An infant matures into an adult. An occasional person has a sex change operation. There is no law requiring him or her to advertise this fact, but when a new driver's license is applied for, the individual would have to alter their previous sex designation. Such corrections would also be legally required when changes occur in the dependency status of children, a name change, or a new address.

Organizations tend to be more thorough in recording information they regard as important for their work, than to remove it, when it is no longer needed or when it turns out to be false. A negative credit report will be transmitted without delay. Its removal, if found to be without substance, is quite likely to be overlooked. In the Terry Dean Rogan case, the Los Angeles police failed to request the removal of a false arrest warrant against an innocent man, whose identity cards had been used by a robber and murderer. Only after Rogan had been arrested five times because of an erroneous entry in the National Crime Information Center and after the ACLU took the Los Angeles Police to court was this victim of false identification relieved of the mark of Cain. It would have continued to expose him to false arrest in any of the roughly fifty-eight thousand law enforcement jurisdictions which have access to the FBI system of criminal suspects.[12]

Sweden has provided its residents with a right to access and to correct unclassified data about them since the 1930s. In Denmark, the process of updating is being done well enough so that the government could use its population register to make its 1981 population census. All that was needed to let the computer analyze the data on file, avoiding the need to conduct a costly house to house enumeration.

There is no central source in the United States where similar status change corrections are being recorded. The U.S. census enumerates every person once in ten years. But there is no collation with data furnished on prior census surveys.

Personal data files in most organizations are corrected only when there is a compelling reason for the individual to request it or when an organization requires updating in connection with some specified purpose. Certification for graduation is preceded by a new application to make sure that diplomas are sent to the current address. At present the University of Pittsburgh keeps in excess of half a dozen files for each employee. If payroll is notified of a new address, this will not affect the address file kept by the retirement benefits office or the mailing list of the Alumni Bulletin.

The adoption of a Valid Identification Procedure (VIP), either on a voluntary or mandatory basis, would require the implementation of an updating policy, with sanctions against the storage of unverified gossip or allegations. They are sometimes found in employee files, FBI, police or other records. No population register will remain useful without a system for making corrections. A current address reporting equipment is something that has not generated much opposition in Western Europe. It has been commonplace there for more than a century. Not so in the United States, where no national ID system exists.

The goal of having updated files could be achieved by relying on positive rather than negative incentives. On occasions, when proof of identity is to the advantage of the individual, he will be required to verify the last address and other information. Data files are thus likely to be updated every time an individual registers to vote, gets married, starts a new job or notifies the post office of a new address. Precautions would have to be taken that no one could fraudulently change the identity file of another person. Digitally matching biometric indicators would practically eliminate such risks.

Each public agency now needs its own staff to update its records. The task would become simpler if a person could check a basic file periodically to verify its accuracy. This basic file could then be programmed to update a large number of cross-filed records. In Canada, each post office is able to furnish a list of federal agencies which keep files about a given individual. A postcard sent to any of these agencies will provide the individual with a chance to inspect the accuracy of any one of them.

A national ID system is most likely to gain acceptance, if it is focused on its utility for each individual. Updating could occur without any negative sanctions. Fines would be both expensive to collect and politically counterproductive, except in situations of excessive negligence. Positive incentives are much easier and cheaper to enforce than a punitive approach.

PRIVACY VERSUS FREEDOM OF INFORMATION

The U.S. Constitution supports two legal principles, often at variance with each other: Individual *Privacy* rights and *Freedom of Information* rights. Privacy, or "autonomy of control over the intimacies of personal identity"[13] can never be absolute. Most states insist that partners in a marriage have a right to know much about each other before the wedding. This might include data about any still valid prior marriage, or one of the partners having social disease. No one can receive optimum educational or medical services without revealing many facts about their private life. Neither newspapers nor law enforcement agencies could operate without access to information that people might prefer to keep to themselves.

Sensitive information about personal and business affairs enjoy no immunity from either news media or law enforcement agencies. Tom Gerety cites such cases as *United States* versus *Miller*[14] and *Fisher* versus

United States.[15] Miller was convicted for trafficking in "moonshine" liquor, sold without payment of federal excise taxes. Part of the evidence against him came from signed checks and deposit slips, maintained by a local bank pursuant to the Bank Secrecy Act, 12 U.S.C. 829 b(d) (1970). The Supreme Court affirmed Miller's conviction, ruling that checks were not confidential. They had been issued by Mr. Miller as a negotiable instrument in a commercial transaction.

"All the documents obtained," the Federal judges ruled, "contain only information voluntarily conveyed to the banks and exposed to their employees in the ordinary course of business." A similar ruling was made in the Fisher case, involving client tax records in their attorney's office.

To what extent should the news media be entitled to reveal the details of a person's private life? The U.S. government accumulates detailed inventories on almost every resident in the United States and many foreigners through the confidential U.S. census and the annual tax returns. Access to them is subject to legislative restrictions which are generally well enforced. Twenty nine lawsuits have been filed as of February 1982 alleging improper disclosure of confidential information by IRS employees while investigating a case of alleged tax fraud. Only one was successful as of February 1982 and it is being appealed by the government.[16]

Laws are less explicit in regulating access to personal details accumulated by private bodies, including banks, educational institutions, medical facilities and other private services. Determined investigative reporters, divorce lawyers, business rivals and private detectives often succeed on collating much of this information. Dossier collecting is even easier when there are industry-wide data clearance centers, as in the credit, insurance, and the mailing list business. Concerns of this nature led to the enactment of the Federal Privacy Act of 1974.

A three year effort to legislate comprehensive state protection of privacy was stalled by objections from representatives of the news media. A National Information Practices Code proposed for adoption by all state legislatures by the National Conference of Commissioners on Uniform State Laws was opposed by the National Newspaper Association, the National Association of Broadcasters and the Society of Professional Journalists. All regard the Code as ill-conceived. It would prohibit public agencies from releasing medical information, criminal investigation data, welfare records, tax returns and others, unless there is a court order indicating that public interest in the data would outweigh individual privacy concerns.[17]

The proposed code aims to balance public interest. It includes provisions to maximize access to information about the operations of government, including corrupt practices, malfeasance, ineptitude and injustices to and by individuals. On the other hand, it includes measures to protect individuals against unreasonable injury, embarrassment and violations of their privacy. The latter can be damaging, when innocuous information is allowed to fall into strange hands inclined to misuse it.

Freedom can be seen as particularly endangered when there are no limits on linkages between different repositories about people's private lives. In the advertising business there is an active trade in mailing lists. Personal preference data are either stolen or are sold by organizations which compile them. This junk mail industry is currently subject to only a haphazard set of legal restraints. One can purchase lists of persons inclined to make donations to Christian missions, or who are interested in stamp collecting, sexually explicit books or who have shown an interest in conservative political causes. In Germany such lists were sold by the post office, which keeps up-to-date address files about the entire population.[18]

One model of protection is the Privacy Protection law passed in Israel.[19] It tried to balance privacy rights with public interest in disclosure of personal information about leading persons and situations excepting "such linkages and disclosures would be of no special public interest and would tend to exploit or degrade people." Such legislation can do little to help political personalities or other prominent people who are often subjected to public review of their real or alleged personal circumstances. No information is yet available on how this law is enforced.

In Holland a commission is being proposed which would be empowered to award damages to citizens who can claim to have been injured by unwarranted disclosure of their personal affairs. The commission would not require that an individual undertake formal legal proceedings or engage the services of a lawyer. It would have the power to investigate (like an ombudsman) plus the power to make a judicial ruling (like a judge).

Current legal practices, in spite of the unresolved issue about where the right to privacy ends and where freedom of information begins, offers considerable protection to wealthy taxpayers and to major corporations. They can afford to expend sizeable resources to take legal action and thus require those who may have injured them to do the same. Lawsuits involving hundreds of millions of dollars have been brought against U.S. publishers for misuse of their right to disseminate information about the private life of prominent persons. While such legal remedies are rarely available to poor persons, they provide a strong disincentive against unreasonable disclosure of personal information.

Professor Alan Westin, the pioneer of privacy studies, would prefer to spell out the balance in a constitutional amendment.[20] He believes extensive public discussion should precede the adoption of a national and more secure ID program. The consensus should be enshrined in rigid rules, changeable only by consent of two-thirds of the state legislatures or other constitutional processes. He justifies this "poured in cement" approach by the observation that the privacy of minorities are all too readily violated by the majority. Westin's viewpoint will be countered by those who question that legislation in any rapidly changing technological area —like information storage and retrieval—should be subject to the inflexibility of a constitutional amendment. This proposal does, however, document a depth of concern that privacy is a precious commodity.

Few would question the general policy that privacy needs special protection, as it is being redefined technologically. At present it is up to each agency to develop administratively sound procedures, without violating reasonable standards of openness in conformity to freedom of the press and free speech considerations.

RESEARCH ENCOURAGEMENT

A special case of the Freedom of Information issue is the use of personal data files for research purposes. The collection of social, psychological, economic and medical research has become legally complicated. Computers collect data and analyze them, precluding the necessity of any person having to read individual case records. Prior permission must be obtained from most human subjects before information about them can be used for research purposes. Often this is difficult or impossible. People have moved and cannot be located or they are unwilling to cooperate, in spite of assurances of confidentiality.

In the battle against disease, epidemiological researchers need access to relevant samples of persons whose health experience could provide clues that will advance medical knowledge. Prior permission would have to be obtained from the family before the hospital can release such information. Most families would cooperate, if requested to be of help, to advance human knowledge. It might be more difficult to get a high rate of voluntary response in a study of stigma prone experiences, like unemployment. But no modern society can operate without an optimum flow of information for research, when there is little or no risk of anyone being harmed.

In most social surveys researchers have no need to know the identity of any particular case. The U.S. census will sell grouped data to any person who requests it, provided it covers an area large enough so that there is no risk that information can be deduced about any single person, business, or small area.

When personal files are stored in computer data banks, school officials can monitor how eighth graders performed on a mathematics test in comparison from a year ago, when instructions were interrupted by a month-long teachers strike. Did this interruption affect learning? No one needs to see the score of any particular child or of a particular eighth grade class. Nor would information be made available on the performance of the pupils of any particular teacher. Yet the Board of Education would have access to valuable data for future planning.

OMBUDSPERSON

The high cost of enforcing one's legal rights to privacy in court could be reduced by appointing data protection ombudspersons. Such officials have functioned for several years in West Germany (Federal Republic of Germany), at both the federal level and in each *land* (state). These Datenschutzombudsmaenner (they include at least one woman) have the staff and the legal powers to review complaints about the misuse of data in both private and public data banks. They and their staff also can investigate how data banks exchange information with one another.

They are empowered to become involved in approving both social and medical research studies which involve access to public records. The police, secret services, national security authorities, the public prosecutor's office and some fiscal authorities have the power to provide information only to the ombudsman himself or to someone he specifically designates in writing to represent him. Only two such restrictive cases, involving the intelligence services, occurred during the first three years of operation of the new office.

Professor Hans Peter Bull, the first federal ombudsman of West Germany, was supported by a staff of about 30 persons, most of them lawyers. Also included were data processing experts, a mathematician, and an electrical engineer. They monitor all new laws that involve record maintenance and the administration of existing public and private programs. In the first year, over 1,000 requests for information and petitions for redress were received, many from accused or convicted criminals. During the second year in office, the number of inquiries exceeded 2,500, including the following:[21]

- Unemployed persons registered by the labor administration claimed that unfair and false information and obsolete medical and psychological statements were kept in the records.
- Criminal offenders complained that, although their criminal history records had been erased by the Federal Central Registrar, the police continued to disseminate such information even to other countries.
- Persons protested that they were subject to inquiries infringing on their privacy.
- Protests were recorded about the activities of internal intelligence

services which were not obliged to reveal what information they had or how they came by it. Other protests concerned gathering personal data for use in criminal prosecution and safeguarding public security against terrorism.

Charges have been made that the ombudsman offices are excessive in their zeal to inhibit information sharing. Significant scientific studies could not proceed because of excessive rigidity in the enforcement of data protection procedures.[22]

On the other hand, Professor Bull prevailed on the telephone company to refrain from registering subscriber numbers on calls made. The Bell Telephone Company, Sprint, Allnet and other phone services routinely furnish this information to allow their customers to verify calls as having been authorized.

Conversely, U.S. phone companies collect an extra fee from customers who want to have an unlisted number. Not so in Germany. Each West German telephone subscriber must justify such a request on grounds that he is a public figure or otherwise subject to harassment. The assumption is made that it is in the public interest that as many people as possible can be located in a telephone book. The public's right to know anyone's phone number has precedence in this instance.

While the German Ombudsman can take up individual cases, there appear to be few serious violations of the law. Much of the time of the Ombudsman and his staff is devoted to negotiating procedural solutions of data storage and retrieval problems with the view of upgrading people's rights to reasonable privacy. For over three years, a single illustration cropped up repeatedly in official reports, leading to the question: Should there not be others? A citizen had refused to pay a traffic ticket. After a court conviction, his name was added to a bad credit list. For this reason a bank refused to open an account for him, although in the meanwhile, he had paid the fine. His name had not yet been removed from the blacklist. Peter Mertens therefore makes a case that the West German government may have appointed too many ombudsmen. Also too much of their budget is allegedly expended on conferences and the writing of annual reports.

If tamper-resistant ID programs are to be introduced in the United States, an ombudsman office could provide the public with reassurance against the widely feared misuses of the system. Those who manage personal data files will be put on notice to deal with complaints quickly and responsibly. Judges could be required to consult with the Ombudsman before authorizing release of normally prohibited data to public officials in cases where the security of the country is at stake or where there are grounds for suspecting a particular person of a heinous crime. The ombudsman would be both an administrative watchdog and someone with quasi-judicial powers. The office would be expected to deal with complaints promptly, with a judicial appeals process similar to the relationship between the Internal Revenue Service and the U.S. tax court system.

Canada has appointed a Privacy Commissioner, with a double task. He is authorized to investigate complaints about difficulties of gaining access to personal information stored in government data banks. The office can also act on petitions to protect such data from being publicly disclosed.

During the first year of operation of the new law, many complaints were solved quickly, half of them from penitentiary inmates. Most often they involved a clerical error or failure in prompt answering by the responsible administrator. Agency officials had to learn that they could no longer rely only on their own judgment in making information release decisions. The ombudsman has extensive powers to investigate. But if there is a dispute between his finding and the administration concerned, the issue has to be reviewed by the courts. There is no absolute right to Freedom of Information if the public interest or safety are deemed to be involved to protect informants or the privacy of others. The ombudsman's report concludes:[23]

> New rights means new problems. It is obvious that many new challenges for ombudsmen, for lawyers, managers and employees, businesses and their customers will have to be faced as a result of legislation of information rights. I think there is no turning back. I am in favor of as much disclosure of information as possible. But I also believe in balancing disclosure with protection of the privacy of others and with the general public interest and the safety of society as a whole.

Technically well-staffed administrative offices are handling privacy complaints from citizens in other democratic nations, without the need for expensive and time-consuming litigation. What needs to be watched, however, is that this new public service does not turn into a "don't do anything without us" tyranny. Excessive ombudsmanship can hamper efficient operations by excessive caution in authorizing administrative changes in the way data files are kept. Improvements in technology necessitate frequent alteration of procedures, most of which do not affect the confidentiality of stored data.

Administrative standards must therefore be developed and enforced to balance the somewhat conflicting concerns of those involved in the information utilization industry. They include privacy rights, the right of access to developments of public interest, the proprietary right to data banks and the need of access to information in criminal cases, where a warrant has been issued.

PUBLICITY

Every U.S. census form in 1980 included the following statement by its Director:

> The essential need for a population census was recognized almost 200 years ago when our constitution was written. As provided by Article 1, the first census was taken in 1790 and one has been taken every 10 years since.
>
> The law under which the census is taken protects the confidentiality of our answers. For the next 72 years—or until April 1, 2052—only sworn census workers have access to the individual records, and no one else may see them.

Public knowledge of how data will be used which people furnish in order to get an ID, drivers license, or bank credit would go a long way toward providing a similar degree of protection against their unauthorized use. Employees would know when they are being asked to violate the privacy assurances, under which the data were furnished. Nothing short of complicated—and therefore risky—collusionary arrangements could then lead to unauthorized data exchanges.

Few private and/or public agencies now issue periodic reports on how the data are stored, used and under which circumstances they can be shared with others. A requirement that such statements be furnished could be made mandatory. Individuals and organizations would then incur legal liabilities for violating such assurances.

None of these sanctions would be considered in authoritarian countries. Their citizens have little or no control over how data are being used, which deal with their private lives. They never know how much "Big Brother" knows about them.

In contrast, democratic nations continue to look for ways to enhance privacy rights. A protective body has been proposed for the United States, possibly to be named the Temporary National Information Committee, to be funded either by the private sector, the government or both. It would not have any administrative or policy making power. But it could make recommendations on the basis of the information collected by its staff on how the computer and communication revolution is affecting our lives. The proponents explain:[24]

> Nowhere is it written that science and technology must proceed unchecked. Nowhere is it guaranteed that technological innovations will solve the problems that technology has created and that information policy should take a back seat to frantic razzle-dazzle of high-tech competition. The more our systems become encompassing, the more we need to systematically confront and understand them.

Publicity and understanding by themselves will not suffice to counter-act the potential for misuse of personal data banks. But they can do much to generate public interest in privacy protection through the previously mentioned control devices, especially through law enforcement and prosecution of those who violate their public trust. Those found guilty or negligent would face the risk of being fined, having their bond cancelled and losing their job.

LEGAL REMEDIES

Violations of privacy in the management of data files in America are actu-ally quite rare, as are breaches of confidentiality by those who operate them. There is a good deal of self-policing and common sense decision-making in most government and private agencies which manage per-sonal information. A breakdown could turn out to be expensive, if an individual were to be harmed and proceed to litigate for damages. The ex-istence of legal right for redress always serves as an ultimate corrective mechanism to police data file management, even in the absence of well worked out privacy protection procedures.

Dutch legislation, now under review, would provide for a Citizens Su-pervisory Board empowered to award damages to an injured party with-out requiring them to go to the expense of hiring a lawyer.

While the rights of each individual warrant protection, there also is a need to protect the system from nuisance lawsuits. As American law schools turn out more lawyers, some observers fear that the country will explode into a "litigation society." Multimillion dollar legal fees and even larger awards are becoming commonplace. More and more service pro-viders find it necessary to purchase malpractice and liability insurance. In the management of multi-billions of items of information, clerical errors can never be fully avoided. A distinction will have to be drawn between evidence of being subjected to substantial embarrassment or harm and the inconvenience of having a check returned by a bank marked "insuffi-cient funds" when more than enough money to cover it had been on de-posit. The cost of information systems could mushroom unless some limits are imposed on liability for accidental and minor errors. Distinc-tions will have to be worked out for the times when legal actions are an appropriate way to give an injured party his day in court. Routine break-downs are a normal risk of operating any complex program.

In more general terms, a reasonable balance needs to be struck between extending the Bill of Rights to fit the computer age and the importance of providing data services to the public at minimal cost. A high level of secu-rity and privacy protection may be appropriate for medical or psychiatric data. Much less is needed for the basic personal ID file, which can be operated well with data routinely shared by an individual in the ordinary conduct of his life.

SINGLE VERSUS MULTIPLE-FUNCTION DOCUMENTS

The 1982 Simpson-Mazzoli Immigration Reform and Control Act advocated a single purpose approach. Its sponsors feared that calling for a multi-purpose ID document would generate too much controversy. The bill therefore included explicit prohibition that its ID certification procedure be used for anything but the verification of entitlement to work for a U.S. employer.

Specialized ID systems are now in use by many organizations. The Defense Department is experimenting with several technologies to upgrade the security of its documents. The Department of Agriculture is issuing its own photo ID cards for food stamp recipients with the possibility that each of the fifty states adopts its own standards. When moving across state lines in search of a new job, citizens would have to get a new food stamp entitlement card. The Department of State has begun to produce a machine-readable passport. Each document includes two types of information: 1. identity data, such as the holder's name, a number, birthday, and sex, 2. entitlement data, such as the administrative category for food stamp entitlement, legal basis for using Defense Department Post Ex change facilities, or in the case of passports, date and place of birth or naturalization. None of these ID documents have biometric features.

Much utility would be added if all of these different ID cards were to be produced according to a common standard for machine readability. If one digital reader could handle all of them, much money would be saved. Standardization would also facilitate the growing volume of international travel. Passports, for instance, need not be of the same color but they would need to include comparable and digitally readable information. As previously noted, uniform technical specifications for a machine readable passport have already been adopted by 120 nations.

Standards will have to be modernized periodically to function more efficiently. Technology will not stand still, even if a worldwide digital reader is adopted. But without standardization, the public has to use too many different documents. More than one digital reader will have to be available at many of the public offices. It will also be difficult to monitor compliance of privacy protection procedures.

When nations entered the industrial age, each manufacturer made his own screws. Garages and machine shops still suffer from the fact that they must stock many extra tools, even though there has been standardization of screw sizes in Europe and in the United States. One acquaintance reported that her European car was out of commission for a week and a half for lack of the proper tool to dismount a generator. An agreement was made to adopt the metric system for screw sizes on a worldwide basis, but its full implementation is still several years away.

There is no need to repeat the error of non-standardization with the ID security technology. Fraud prevention, crime discouragement and immigration control are worldwide in scope. It will take years to implement an agreement, even after it is ratified, but steps can be taken now within America and in coordination with the European Economic Union to proceed on a common technical basis. If this is done soon, before heavy investments in different machine readers are made, a worldwide standard can be negotiated. In the words of Frank Kubic, Technical Director of the Systems Application Staff of the U.S. Department of State: "We live in one world and our technology must reflect this."

POWER TO THE PEOPLE

Storage and retrieval of a central personal file for two hundred and thirty million Americans and the millions who come to our shores as temporary residents will not be difficult when a tiny silicon chip can store over half a million items. But a computer ID Bill of Rights will require a lot of imaginative administration. The central feature proposed in this book is a process of shared responsibility for the accuracy of the data between the operators of each information system and individuals whose information is being stored for future use. The latter have a right to find out how it is used, when it is sold to others, and when agreed upon changes or corrections have been made.

Collecting information about all newborns and newcomers, as well as extending the file retroactively to all other Americans will be a one-time administrative overload. Security features will need to be designed based on a reasonable check of breeder documents. The small proportion of persons who cannot obtain a birth certificate or some other life history document, can be absorbed into the system, with a notation to this effect in their file. The security services would be alerted if evidence were to surface that the document was generated without the normal verification precautions. Not only the government, but the individual will be responsible for what is stored, once the identity of each person has been certified on the basis of biometric indices, like fingerprint and/or signature verification.

No one will need to be prosecuted for failing to notify one of his files of a new address. But they may be unable to get a bank loan without an updated address, since banks tend to verify the borrower's background before the loan is approved. The post office could be instructed to stop forwarding mail after two months, unless the person's ID card has been corrected to show the new address. Updating can also be required when people get married or experience other major status changes, like the birth of a child, a divorce or a death in the family. The updating process is most likely to work well if it is made easy for the public to make corrections by being able to access their central file on a twenty-four hour, seven day a week basis through conveniently located automated information machines.

A computerized VIP document will end the existing differences between the wealthy and the privileged and the people at the periphery of our social system, the poor and recent immigrants. All will become equal in their capacity to prove their identity.

OPTIONS FOR ADMINISTERING THE ID SYSTEM

There are several organizations in the federal government with experience in handling large scale data banks. Foremost among them are the U.S. census bureau and the IRS. Their files are already quite comprehensive. They could be used to locate addresses and to mail application forms for the new ID card. Their constitutional status would be affected if their already extensive research responsibilities were supplemented by the mission of collecting and operating a basic ID file for everybody.

The FBI has a civilian noncriminal fingerprint file, kept separately from its Criminal Identification Division. But there would be much utility in distancing a national ID program from symbolic association with law enforcement. The primary purpose of the VIP is to serve the convenience of the individual. It can also protect each person's unique VIP identity from being appropriated by someone else. It is offering people protection from easy victimization by fraudulent claims to a phony identity.

A strong case can be made for establishing a separate Federal Identity Coordinating Agency FIDCA, working through the eight thousand state and local vital statistics offices throughout the country. The latter already have responsibility for issuing birth, tax, and death certificates. They could be given a federal contract to manage this new function. The innovation would add rather than detract from their previous responsibilities. In due time, most states would probably voluntarily abolish separate birth and death registration.

A significant component of any such program will be the element of public trust. The basic file could be made available for preparing the front sheet of each year's tax returns, which are sent out to the public. Or the data could be used by the Bureau of the Census, to make a population study in a district planning a new school. The file would also be available to provide the information to reissue a passport. None of these uses would be secret. The information would always be subject to being checked and corrected by the individual concerned. The FIDCA could be entrusted with monitoring the program guided by a board of directors representing many segments of the public, including civil liberty specialists, minority group members, and representatives of private users of personal files.

Sweden was the first country in the world to enact a comprehensive Data Act in 1973. It regulates both public and private data banks. It is designed to protect individuals from unreasonable misuse of the information they provide for different administrative data files. The law requires that all responsible keepers of data files be licensed. A fee is charged for this privilege, which is applied to operate the Data Inspection Board. This autonomous agency administers the data Act. It is chaired by a director general, with prior judicial experience. He is supervised by a citizens board of directors, many of them members of Parliament from different parties.

Sweden prides itself on being an information society. A private car dealer can be linked, via his terminal, to the Motor Registration office. State bureaus can have equally direct access to the files of private credit investigation bureaus. The Data Inspection Board makes sure that such sharing of information proceeds with due regard to individual privacy rights, such as the following:

1. Each personal data file should be kept for a specific purpose.
2. No other data may be filed than that which corresponds to this purpose.
3. The data may not be compiled, released or used except in accordance with this stated purpose or with the law or other statutes, or the consent of the registered party.
4. The data should be protected from unintentional or illicit destruction or against illicit alteration or distribution.[25]

There have been few enforcement problems. Among 37,500 actions taken by the board, to grant licenses and to hear complaints, only 70 or less than 2 per 1,000 were appealed. Convictions for violations were rare and punishments were in the form of fines against the offending individual or organization.

The work load of any central personal data file might expand quickly, as more and more businesses, banks and other organizations might want to use it to verify the credentials of an individual. This function would also be a source of income, probably more than enough to pay for the expenses of administering the data protection law. A fee could be charged for each verification so that the central data bank could derive its income from user fees rather than from the federal treasury.

Commercial organizations would first have to get each person's permission to access his file in order to construct a mailing list. In return for such agreement, people would be paid a royalty.

Most Americans have a checking or savings account. They no longer represent a stack of bills in a vault or a portion of a gold bar. Our bank accounts consist of a set of digitally recorded indicators. But these blips on a silicon chip are insured by the federal government against bankruptcy and other hazards.

It is no longer possible to reverse the information revolution. Our economy, the human services, medical care, and the media demand more and more speedy and detailed data exchanges. Untrustworthy ID records, which are now so commonplace, invite continued fraud and misrepresentation. They can be curbed significantly by relying on a growing technology to encourage public awareness of shortfalls in protective procedures.

Protective regulations will need to be updated to fully guard these data banks against improper use within a reasonable margin of minor errors. One of the most significant protective features might be the fact that personal files can be monitored by each person against unauthorized access. Before anyone can check a file, a tattle tale record would be generated of "who, when and why." This "Leave your Access Code" requirement would be the key for maximizing privacy in the computer age.

REFERENCES

1. *Collins* vs. *Retail Credit Company*, 410F, Supp. 924 E.D. Michigan 1976.

2. Wessel, Milton R. and John L. Kirkley. "For a National Information Committee." *Datamation*. 234–246.

3. Office of Technology Assessment, *Computer Based National Information Systems: Technology and Public Policy Issues*, U.S. Government Printing Office, Washington, D.C., September 1981:ix.

4. Kolata, Gina, "Students Discover Computer Threat," *Science*, vol. 215, March 5, 1982:1216–1217.

5. President's Council on Integrity and Efficiency, Washington, D.C., 1982.

6. *Washington Post*. June 2, 1982.

7. Kaplan, Charles P. and Van Valey, Thomas L., *Census 80, Continuing the Pathfinder Tradition*. Washington, D.C., United States Department of Commerce, January 1980.

8. Caruso, Nicholas, University of Pittsburgh, Personal Communication, 1982.

9. Shattuck, John, and Kusserow, Richard P., "Point Counter Point" *Computer Matching*, volume 4, no. 1, January 1985:3–4.

10. Smith, Robert Ellis, "Statement at Hearings on Computer Matching," Washington, D.C., Senate Committee on Governmental Affairs, Subcommittee on Oversight and Management, December 16, 1982:4.

11. Cobler, Sebastian, "Buerger in Wuergegriff der Computer" *Stern*, February 12, 1981: Heft Nummer 8.

12. Burnham, David, *New York Times*, January 12, 1985.

13. Gerety, Tom. "Redefining Privacy." *Harvard Civil Rights Civil Liberty Review*, vol. 12, no. 2, Spring 1977:234.

14. *United States* vs. *Miller*, 425 U.S. 435, 1976.

15. *Fisher* vs. *United States*, 425 U.S. 391, 1976.

16. Department of the Treasury, 1982, personal communication.

17. National Conference of Commissioners of Uniform State Laws, *Uniform Information Practices Code*, Chicago, Illinois, Approved for Enactment in all States at its Annual Conference, July 26–August 1, 1980.

18. Goetz, Rainald. "Addressengeschaefte." (Mailing Address List Businesses) *Kursbuch*. 66, Berlin: Kursbuch/Rotbuch Verlag:1–5.

19. Rubinstein, Aryeh, *Jerusalem Post* 1981.

20. Westin, Alan. Personal Communication, 1983.

21. Bull, Hans Peter "The Federal Commissioner for Data Protection," Caiden, Gerald, ed., *International Handbook of the Ombudsman*. 1982: 86–87.

22. Mertens, Peter. "Gefahren eines ubertriebenen Datenschutzes." *Datenschutz und Datensicherung*. Datenschutz und Datensicherung, January, 1982.

23. Hansen, Inger. "The Ombudsman and the Freedom of Information in Canada," Caiden, Gerald, Editor, *International Handbook of the Ombudsman*, 1982: 111–119.

24. Wessel, Milton R. and John Kirkley. "For a National Information Committee." *Datamation*: 234–246.

25. Freese, Data Inspection Board Report, Stockholm, Sweden, January 1983. Data Act as amended July 1, 1982.

CHAPTER TEN

SUMMING UP

TAMING TECHNOLOGY

More inventions are alleged to have been generated in our lifetime than during the entire prior span of human history. Certainly Americans who subsist below the poverty line enjoy comforts unknown to George Washington. The life expectancy has been lengthened, many illnesses can be cured and others made easier to live with. But the state of freedom, privacy and security leaves much to be desired. Just over a third of the human race lives under a democratic government.

It is reasonable, under such circumstances, that vigilance be exercised against any perceived threat to these cherished values. Many civil libertarians are concerned that a nationally monitored and tamper-resistant ID card would constitute a threat. What they often overlook is the fact that Americans are already enmeshed in a web of identification systems. Many of them are mandatory, unless people avoid driving a car or can do without an income on which taxes must be paid. Public officials can already access nearly all personal data banks.

Will this lead to an erosion of constitutional rights? In a congressionally sponsored study of the social-political impact of the computer technology these rights were summarized as follows:[1]

1. Freedom of speech and press (First Amendment)
2. Protection against unreasonable search and seizure (Fourth Amendment)
3. Protection against self-incrimination and guarantees of due process of law (Fifth Amendment)
4. Right to a trial by an impartial jury (Sixth Amendment)
5. State guarantees of due process and equal protection of the law (Fourteenth Amendment)

Technology is neutral regarding how its products impact on the enforcement of civil rights. There is a rapidly growing variety of electronic surveillance devices, but they can be used both to improve the quality of life or to diminish it. Criminals and unscrupulous business people use automobiles, but the very same vehicle is a luxury product few Americans would want to be without. George Warfel sums up the comparable ID technology developments, noting that identification is rapidly moving from "an art, practiced by everyone, to a science, performed by computers. Proof of identity will soon be the task of electronics, optics and chemistry".[2]

Violations of privacy through the use of this technology do occur but they are exceptional. Federal protective legislation plus privacy protection laws in most of the states have worked quite well. In spite of a growing multitude of files about almost every American, serious privacy abuses by file keepers are rare. Few Americans are losing much sleep about the risk that either the government or their bank will abuse the personal information with which they have been entrusted.

There is much more worry about criminal abuses. For every case of unwarranted use of a tax, health or police record, there are probably hundreds of invasive violations of people's privacy and security by the criminal underworld.

Only one of the experts who in 1975 served on the Federal Advisory Committee on False Identification (FACFI) reported that the advantages of adopting tamper-resistant identity documents by far outweigh their risks.[3] A strong contrary conviction was expressed by most other members of the Commission. They dismissed the proposal for a nationally controlled ID document out of hand, asserting that it was contrary to America's tradition. Fear was expressed that data required for a basic ID file, administered under nationally set security standards, would be abused by government and private interests. This theory was never tested against the actual evidence, unlike most of the other conclusions of the FACFI study. It seemed to be accepted on an a priori basis that even a voluntary national ID card would endanger constitutionally guaranteed freedoms. Some of the contrary data presented in this book were already available in 1975.

Any new system for issuing and verifying ID cards for a nation of more than two hundred and thirty million people will have growing pains. But if the airlines and credit card companies can operate a worldwide data system, there is no reason why the federal government or a federally licensed public utility could not do as well. To initiate the service, a new budget item will be added to our already overburdened national accounts. But the decision to do nothing — to stay with the status quo — will be much more costly, in money, in safety and in privacy.

A national ID system can also be used to generate revenue. Banks, credit card agencies and others that wish to verify the accuracy of someone's identity can, with the person's permission, compare their information with what is contained in the national roster. There is a big market waiting to be serviced, considering the fact that within a few years, there probably will be in excess of a billion commercial credit cards in circulation just in America.There also are many other occasions where it would be worth paying a fee to obtain a verification service more trustworthy than those now available. Consumers could control each such request, since they would have to authorize each verifcation action with their own ID card. At present, credit agencies and others will release sensitive information with a signed authorization on ordinary paper that can be forged easily.

THE VOLUNTARISTIC OPTION

No legislation is likely to be passed in the United States mandating that ID cards be carried at all times. Most adults now do this voluntarily, as a matter of personal convenience. The vast majority would rush to obtain a widely trusted tamper-resistant ID document, especially if it could be obtained free of charge. It would provide the holders with evidence of their exclusive and unique identity in return for a few innocuous facts, like their name, a number and a digitalized biometric measure. The central file would not need to include information most Americans regard as highly personal—our income, education, marital status, religion, and other life history items. Such data would remain in hospital, school and commercial files, which could be protected against misuse by giving each card holder ready access, so that inaccuracies that might have been recorded can be promptly identified. The subject of such questionable files could then submit evidence, if needed, to get the information corrected or expunged.

The privileged, the well-to-do, and persons employed in security sensitive jobs now enjoy an advantage over the average American. The former already possess several ID documents, computerized credit and other privileges. Not so the poor. They along with immigrants and the homeless would have a strong incentive to apply for a *Valid Identification Program* (VIP) document. They will be able to use it to qualify for various governmental entitlement programs and to prevent others from impersonating them. Under a voluntary system, very few people would be without an ID card. It would be very inconvenient.

A national ID system also will improve the equity of tax payments. Criminals will find it more difficult to avoid paying their fair share. Divorced fathers will become more conscientious in making child support payments. The courts would find it easier than at present to locate those who moved to another part of the country, in the hope of evading their financial commitments.

Most immigrants will apply through legal channels, if legislation were enacted that employment in United States will become nearly impossible without a proper entry visa. Yet, our doors need not be sealed to refugees who can be admitted under already existing legislation.

A central data bank could produce national, regional or local population statistics more up-to-date than the decennial Census. Public services can be planned on the basis of relatively complete demographic data, even in areas where the population is quite mobile. Federal grants based on the proportion of low-income people in an area would then be distributed more equitably. The 1990 U.S. Census may well be the last one to require an expensive household enumeration in order to obtain basic population data. More specialized field surveys would still be needed to obtain information about the use of household items, business and agricultural data.

GOVERNMENT COLLUSION IN CRIME

It is people who violate laws. Their greed, their anger, and sick emotions are often translated into criminal actions. Provisions are sometimes inserted into a law to legitimize questionable privileges for an influential pressure group. The FACFI cited evidence that some governmental policies systematically facilitate criminal acts. A few so-called tax loopholes actually invite unreasonable exemption claims of tens of billion dollars of income. Another is the "Texas Proviso," exempting employers from liability for knowingly employing illegal aliens. The loopholes primarily benefit the well-to-do and corporations.

Many jobs are restricted to persons with proper qualifications and training. But it is technically easy to steal someone else's professional identity. Dr. Ann Stace Wood recently discovered that an imposter was claiming her credentials, including her Ph.D. degree in Speech Therapy.[4] Her bogus double never finished college, but she had been in a class with Dr. Wood at the University of Cincinnati. There she managed to copy Dr. Wood's Social Security number (SSN). She also was able to estimate just when Dr. Wood had attended the university. With these items of information, the forger was able to secure certified copies of Dr. Wood's academic transcript from the university registrar. These documents enabled her to secure professional credentials in five states. Due to a complex personal and marital life, her imposter moved a good deal, under different married names. But she aways claimed Dr. Wood's name as her maiden name, to qualify for employment as a speech therapist.

Over twelve years, many children received substandard therapy without knowing it. Comparable frauds occur in the practice of medicine, even in surgery, among nurses, and others who need a license in order to practice a skilled trade or a profession. No one is in favor of such misrepresentation, but there are public figures who regard such an occasional incident as a lesser evil to adopting a national ID system.

Among them are senators and members of the House of Representatives. They fear being tagged as insensitive by the American Civil Liberties Union (ACLU) to privacy threats or as racist by spokespersons for American-Mexican lobby groups. Nor do they wish to be criticized by substantial business interests which prefer to hold on to an available option to hire illegal aliens without risk of prosecution for aiding them. There also are delinquent taxpayers who prefer to be left alone, free of the risk of being discovered as law violator by data base matching procedures. Any significant enhancement of document security and validity would reduce the ease of committing such violations.

Traffic in commonly stolen goods, such as precious metals, used cars, and used electronic equipment is essentially unregulated. Much could be done to make it difficult for such loot to be recycled into legitimate marketing channels. Professional burglars often do their business under several counterfeit identities. False documents are also important in the commission of many white collar and computer crimes. Sensitive medical and national security files continue to be invaded by amateurs playing computer games. For lack of a central ID document, it is easier in the United States to be a fugitive from justice than perhaps in any other modern nation.

In prior centuries, governments placed little emphasis on crime prevention. The full force of state power was reserved to apprehend and punish those who violated laws and morals. Punishments were generally cruel, including confinement in a dungeon, torture, starvation, and deliberate degradation. The adoption of the American constitution precipitated the penal reform movement by prohibiting such cruel and unusual punishment. But those who prefer to retain stiff penalties in the hope that this would deter crime offers little to the victim. He would benefit more if a significant proportion of law violations could be prevented by well-planned public policies. Tamper-resistant ID cards would make it easier to implement as yet underutilized crime prevention tactics, to reduce the incidence of burglary, fraud, misrepresentation, computer crime and terrorism.

THE LESSER EVIL ISSUE

There is no free lunch in administrative reform. There are only trade-offs between one troublesome policy preference and another, viewed as a lesser evil. Living often involves hard choices among alternatives, none of which are an occasion for rapture. Smokers know this well, every time they light a cigarette. They are reminded of lung cancer but they prefer the enjoyment of the moment to an improved chance at longevity. Most public problems have a similar cost-benefit equation.

Toleration of easily counterfeited identity documents is another of these "friendly" problems many prefer to live with rather than to resolve by resorting to the available technology. Few administrators and elected officials have had time to catch up with developments in the secure ID card industry. They are not aware of the fact that it has the potential to enhance personal as well as national security, while improving privacy protection.

At the same time, the status quo of how identity documents are issued and administered has few defenders. Congress has taken the first step to look at this important policy issue. The federal executive is now mandated by law to investigate the technical as well as the policy options for providing Americans with more trustworthy means of identifying themselves.

PRIVACY REDEFINED

Noncriminal personal data files could be defined by law as the joint property of the organization, which maintains a dossier and the individual, who provides the information. When inaccuracies turn up, they need to be corrected. Under the present system, the average person would find it quite difficult to access all of his files and to get them corrected speedily. Only a few organizations use the precautions to maximize accuracy of their data files as does *Who's Who*. Its editors annually ask their listees to update their biographies.

Local credit bureaus and the FBI are more casual about updating their stored information. An arrested person, who was found not guilty in a court of law, may be carried in the National Crime Index of the FBI for the rest of his life and beyond. The service of an attorney is required to insure removal of the false arrest record. Few poor people have access to such help. Privacy for the poor, the busy and the timid could be strengthened by means such as the following:

1. Regulations to require that individuals be notified when certain of their files are accessed, such as their birth or school records. They should be informed of who made the request, when it was furnished and on the basis of what specific regulations. They could also be told where the equipment was located through which the request was processed. After a file is opened, and every five years thereafter,

they might be sent a copy of their file, with a request that it be updated, if needed.

2. The adoption of standards to govern the matching of different data bases within or between organizations which maintain them, beyond those which are now in force for data matching programs in the federal government.

3. Bonding of personnel handling sensitive data files. Organizations which maintain files might be licensed, on condition that they adopt a set of privacy protection standards.

4. Establishment of an office to enforce these standards, such as the ombudsman programs in Europe. They would also have the authority to hear grievances and administer penalties up to a certain level. More flagrant violations would be presented to a court.

5. Public support for privacy protection could be enhanced by publicity on the state of balance between self-policing of privacy standards for file keepers and evidence of complaints and of violations.

There is a need to balance the power of police when they can stop people or enter their homes to make random and intrusive searches.[5] But there are no legal grounds for insisting that when such searches are authorized, that the criminal subset of society be immune from having evidence disclosed that will reveal their law violations. It is not necessary that in the name of privacy the Mafia be enabled to operate under multiple false identities. The "right to be let alone," to repeat Justice Brandeis definition of privacy, need not be expanded into an unlimited right to deceive and defraud.

Vital human rights are most likely to be sacrificed by a public and by the legislators, frightened by a lack of security. Under panic on the West Coast, after Japan declared war on the United States in 1941, the U.S. government, including the Supreme Court, violated the constitutional rights of American citizens of Japanese ancestry. They were interned and lost much of their property, without due process of law. Legalized vigilantism is most likely to reappear if too many of our streets and parks continue to be more under the control of the underworld than the guardians of law and order.

The technology for protecting personal files against unauthorized or Comprehensive Information Analysis (CIA) is well developed. It is improving almost monthly. There also is a good deal of protective legislation on the books to prevent unauthorized dossier maintenance. Added precautions will need to be enacted since outside the federal government there is little supervision over the matching of state, local government, and private business files. But no element of safety is added by the mere opposition to overdue reforms of the irresponsible procedures used to generate most American identity documents.

BIAS PROOF INDICATORS

A significant degree of privacy can be added by shifting from name to number coding, when personal files are managed. It is only human that a file clerk will pay special attention if he runs into the credit file of his U.S. senator or a movie star. If the file is only numerically coded, with names being kept separately, a much higher degree of confidentiality can be maintained. Far from making people into just numbers, number-coding provides them with an added element of privacy protection.

As a further protection, very sensitive files can be scrambled electronically. They can be retrieved only by carefully screened personnel. Such safety devices cannot be applied to non-computerized rosters.

Data file confusion among persons with the same name can be avoided by relying on a biometric indicator and a neutral index number. They do not change when people accept new employment, adopt a different name by marriage, or move to a new address. But under present circumstances, it is easy for persons to acquire several personal numbers. In 1975 more than 4.2 million Americans were estimated to have had two or more Social Security numbers. Among them are an unknown but sizable proportion who use their multiple cards to defraud the tax system of business and welfare entitlements. Unpaid taxes and false benefit claims have to be made up by higher taxes from those who obey the law.

A single index number would relieve people from having to memorize the many different eight plus digit numbers used routinely on credit cards and gas and electric bills. A serial number reveals nothing about the holder. Nevertheless, a uniform numerical identifier was opposed by a citizens committee appointed by the Department of Health, Education and Welfare in 1973.

> We recommend against the adoption of any nationwide, standards, personal identification format, with or without the SSN (Social Security Number) that would enhance the likelihood of arbitrary or uncontrolled linkage of records about people . . . What is needed is a halt to the drift toward an SUI (Standard Universal Identifier) and prompt action to establish safeguards providing legal sanctions against abuses of automated personal-data systems.

Technology has outdated these well-motivated sentiments. If reasserted now, they would reflect an uninformed view of how data files already are being matched. Telephone subscribers around the world can be located by dialing their number or by checking with "Information". In more and more states, the police can check details about drivers and automobiles from their squad cars, by telephoning a computer in their headquarters. Data base matching techniques with or without a Personal

Identification number (PIN) are being taught in tens of thousands of computer classes all over the world.

OUR FAUSTIAN CONTRACT

Entry into the twentieth century has forced all of us into a number of Faustian contracts with the devil. We have surrendered a lot of our privacy in return for the good life that was beyond the dream of our forefathers.

The battle for privacy starts with a retreat from it. Our children are born in hospitals, where infant mortality is low, in part because professional care is based on the availability of medical indicators to conditions that could be life-threatening.

When we get a job, the degree to which we disclose intimate details about ourselves varies somewhat with the responsibility of the position. Purchase of insurance is predicated on revelation of some quite sensitive information, about personal belongings, health problems and our automobile driving record. People who enter politics must be prepared to publicize their tax returns and tell all about their divorce settlement or prior hospitalization for a mental illness.

Who is responsible for these intrusions against privacy? We must look in the mirror to find him. Those who speak out against tamper-resistant ID cards should first look into their own wallet. They need to consider the fact that the right to much of our privacy was lost with the income tax, the investment counselor, and good medical care.

A United States Census report dated June 10, 1985 indicated that the average American household gets 10 percent of its income from federal government programs. Those earning $7200 a year or less obtain 50 percent of their income from Federal entitlement programs. Inaccurate eligibility procedures represent a burdensome loss of tax revenues. Should privacy rights prevent investigation of discrepancies that data base matching procedures would disclose? The IRS does not publish the names of persons who make arithmetic errors on their tax returns. But it will proceed against persons whose returns suggest that they may knowingly have tried to defraud the government.

The near tamper-proof ID document is also an essential part of our defense against misuse of data furnished for expressly limited purposes. Should an employer be allowed to access the medical files of his workers, even though his firm pays for their medical insurance? Falsely identified people could steal such information in milliseconds. Computers could do much to protect people's files from such victimization.

A VIP system also could contribute considerably to enhancing our national security. There were 4.3 million civilians and military personnel with security clearances in March 1985, according to statistics compiled by the General Accounting Office. Existing procedures are too cumbersome to maximize precautions against security leaks. VIP cards, with a biometric indicator, would make it relatively simple and cheap to connect each use of a secret file to the person who had a "need to know" clearance. Access could also be restricted to designated terminals, which are carefully guarded.

American military bases around the world can be entered during rush hours with only a perfunctory clearance. Guards are too busy to do more than glance at a decal attached to the windshield of cars of authorized base personnel. By stealing such a car, terrorists can often gain entry. Security gaps of this nature could be reduced by requiring each person to use his ID card to gain entry to the installation. Air safety against terrorism could also be enhanced by checking tamper resistant and machine-readable ID documents before each flight. Those without them could then be checked more carefully. In the event a hijacking takes place, those who perpetrate it will often have been identifiable by their unique biometric characteristics. They will not be able to travel freely in the future, without great risk of being caught.

In 1972 the Project on Computer Databanks published conclusions that appear to be still valid, although more than a decade has passed.[6]

> Computers are here to stay. So are large organizations and the need for data. So is the American commitment to civil liberties. Equally real are the social cleavages and cultural re-assessments that mark our era. Our task is to see that appropriate safeguards for the individual's rights to privacy, confidentiality, and due process are embedded in every major record system in the nation, particularly the computerizing systems that promise to be in the setting for the most important organizational uses of information affecting individuals in the coming decades.

The project was sponsored by the Computer Science and Engineering Board of the National Academy of Sciences and supported by a grant from the Russell Sage Foundation. Its staff visited fifty-five major leading organizations maintaining personal data banks and interviewed its staff regarding their technical procedures, the management of information storage, retrieval, and the concern with civil liberty and privacy issues. They concluded that privacy protection could be improved. But they reported few glaring violations.

THE NEW ESPERANTO

The computer is about to achieve much of what Esperanto tried and failed to accomplish: acceptance of an international language.

It is easy to transmit data electronically. Much of the information stored in one language can be retrieved in another. The binary system through which such storage and retrieval are accomplished is the same everywhere. American and Russian computers can be programmed to talk to each other without translators or trust in each other.

ID documents are being internationalized – especially drivers licenses, passports and credit cards. There were in excess of 68 million Visa and Mastercards outstanding in the world, in addition to over 127 million held by Americans. More and more U.S. travelers acquire an overseas Eurocard to facilitate their money transactions. To the extent such documents can be forged, stolen and otherwise abused, local cases of fraud and misrepresentation are assuming nationwide and international ramifications. Data banks, which store information used to validate such ID documents need to develop minimal standards of creditability. A transnational policy needs to be evolved.

Negotiations to bring this about are proceeding on several fronts. The Council of European Communities is working on a common set of privacy standards in preparation for a projected passport union. The International Civil Aviation Organization (ICAO) has adopted standards for a uniform machine readable passport. The International Police Organization (INTERPOL) has a Computer Control Commission to prepare for a more comprehensive use of computerized identity information in pursuit of its mission to minimize international crime conspiracies. The Society for World Wide Interbank Financial Telecommunication (SWIFT) is already functioning well on the basis of standards for protecting the multibillion dollar transactions which are processed daily through its channels.

Credit cards issued in one country are generally honored in others. They are an international currency, more flexible than travelers checks. Individuals are given power to do something previously reserved to national banks: the power to issue "currency" not just at home but in a foreign land within the limit of their credit rating. This extraordinary convenience depends on transnational cooperation to provide each card holder with evidence of his unique identity.

The liberal commitment to maximum enjoyment of privacy is being undermined by conservative rigidity in the assessment of the impact of the ID card technology. Sophisticated techniques of counterfeiting can only be defeated by even greater technical sophistication in protecting the privacy and inviolability of a person's unique identity, along with appropriate protective legislation and its vigilant enforcement.

Without a trustworthy ID card, none of us can monitor the multitude of files kept about us. The campaign to contain terrorism, especially in the skies, will gain momentum once it becomes possible for people to acquire an ID card with unique biometric indicators, which can protect us from being readily impersonated.

No system of identification can be absolutely error proof, but much can be done to *increase* our privacy and freedom. Americans deserve the right to make a choice between the chaotic status quo and the acquisition of a trustworthy document that warrants trust.

The prevailing ID procedures have little to recommend them. They are readily abused. The adoption of a voluntary and better coordinated system, operated under federally enforced standards, would be no threat to anyone or anything, except the underworld.

REFERENCES

1. Office of Technology Assessment, *Computer-Based National Information Systems: Technology and Public Policy Issues*, Washington, D.C., September 1981: 105–112.

2. Warfel, George H., *Identification Technologies*, Springfield Illinois, Charles C. Thomas, Publisher, 1979.

3. Federal Advisory Committee on False Identification, (FACFI) *The Criminal Use of False Identification*, United States Department of Justice, Washington, D.C., U.S. Government Printing Office, Stock Number 052-003-00226-4, November 1976: Page F–5.

4. American Speech-Language-Hearing Association, *ASHA*, Volume 27, Number 5, May 1985:7–8.

5. McClellan, Grant S. *The Right to Privacy*. New York: H. W. Wilson Company, 1976.

6. Westin, Alan F. and Baker, Michael A., *Databanks in a Free Society: Computers, Record Keeping and Privacy* New York, Quadrangle Books, 1970:405.

STATEMENT OF NEWTON VAN DRUNEN FOR THE HEARINGS ON FEDERAL IDENTIFICATION FRAUD*

Mr. Chairman and Members of the Subcommittee: my name is Newton Van Drunen. I am 54 years old. I was born in Canada and I am a citizen of the United States. I am presently incarcerated in a federal prison in Chicago, Illinois, and I am serving a ten-year sentence for counterfeiting and conspiracy offenses.

Throughout my youth, I spent a great deal of time working with members of the Mexican community. As the years went by, I began to identify more and more with their plight in this country. I speak Spanish fluently, and today I consider myself a part of the Mexican community.

I began my career smuggling aliens in 1956 or 1957. I can't recall how I got started, but during that time I also worked as an industrial arts teacher. On the side, I exported cars from the U.S. to Mexico. I started dealing in documents, as a middleman, not a counterfeiter, in the late 1960s. I provided documents for illegal Mexicans and arranged work for them in factories around Chicago. In order to get jobs for Mexicans, I first had to get them a social security number. I did this by simply completing the application forms as there were no specific requirements at that time to get a number. When employers became concerned about hiring illegal aliens and began requiring more documentation, I furnished aliens with baptismal certificates in addition to the social security cards. I purchased these at church supply stores and just filled them out for each of my clients.

---

*Oversight Hearing on Fraudulent Identification Documents and Penetration of Benefit Programs, U.S. Senate, Committee on Governmental Affairs, Permanent Subcommittee on Investigations, June 16, 1982.

I was arrested and convicted in 1973 for illegally smuggling aliens from Mexico. In 1975, I was sent to Sandstone Federal Prison in Minnesota.

It was at Sandstone that I had my first experience with printing. I had not counterfeited any documents before going to jail, although I was very interested and eager to learn. Unbelievably, I was placed in the prison print shop to work and learn the trade. This shop did a lot of work for the Immigration Service.

Various INS internal documents crossed my hands in the print shop. Most important to me later on would be the information about the new INS alien registration card and the fact that INS had contracted with Polaroid to manufacture the card.

I couldn't believe this information was actually coming through my hands while in prison. I thought at first the government was setting me up because my wife continued running my business by furnishing vendors from the stock of documents I had accumulated. After I got over my fears, though, I learned various tricks of the trade from other inmates who were professional printers and counterfeiters.

When I got out of prison in 1976 I continued to sell documents as a middleman. It was at this point that I set up a print shop by purchasing commonly available equipment. I did not try to counterfeit the INS card in use at that time, as I did not choose to create an inferior document. All of the information I had learned in jail about the new INS alien registration card was stored in the back of my mind until such time as the card would be issued in 1977. However, I did some experimenting to create my version of the new card. I assumed the government would use a sophisticated magnetic strip with coded information which would be placed inside the card. I later learned I was wrong—INS did not use as sophisticated a process as I had envisioned.

Meanwhile, I began producing my own Texas birth records, Selective Service cards, and social security cards. All of the Mexicans I sold to, through a network of vendors, knew the documents and the social security numbers were phony. I was selling identification packets consisting of the social security card, Texas birth certificate, baptismal certificate, and the Selective Service card for $75.00 per package. This price was usually doubled by the vendors when they delivered the documents to Mexicans.

A few months after my release from Sandstone, I was arrested again by INS in 1977 but fled after I was released on bail. As a fugitive, I continued to operate my business in the Chicago area. To avoid capture, I used several fake identities which I created, and I manufactured the documents to support these identities.

One of the most successful documents I counterfeited during this fugitive period was a reproduction of the photocopied letter issued by U.S.

District Court Judge Grady as a result of his decision in an important immigration case. One hundred and forty-five thousand copies of this "Silva-Levi" letter were issued to aliens who, by possession of the letter, could remain legally in the U.S. and work. I simply reproduced hundreds of copies of this letter and sold it to vendors for $15 each. The letter was a cinch to counterfeit, it did not have a serial number which could be traced, and it did not identify the person to whom it was issued. For false identification purposes, it was an ideal identity document.

I also counterfeited the INS form I-94 and issued it with the "Silva-Levi" letter. This is another dream document to reproduce. With an unsophisticated stamp noting "work authorized," a Mexican illegal can work almost without trouble in the U.S.

For a brief period, I made out income tax forms for Mexicans if they wanted me to. Some used the phony social security numbers I gave them to file for refunds. I don't think there is much coordination between IRS and the Social Security Administration. I figured it would take a while for these agencies to find out if any of the Mexicans were sharing social security numbers or using phony ones.

On a scale of "one to ten," the social security card is a "one"; it's just extremely simple to reproduce. Also, from various sources including social security office workers, I learned generalities about the social security numbering code. As far as I was concerned, phony social security numbers were undetectable by employers. The danger, if any, was in using a number issued to another person. Anyone could use my card for at least one to three years before detection, if at all. That was sufficient for my client's needs. By 1980, I had learned enough about "unissued" social security numbers—those to be used by a state in fifteen or twenty years—and then only gave "unissued" numbers to my clients.

By the time INS first issued its new alien registration card in July 1980, I had already developed a loyal following. At one time I had a large number of vendors working throughout the Chicago area. Some of my vendors migrated to California, Arizona, New Mexico, Texas, Florida, Georgia, Indiana, Illinois, Michigan, Minnesota and Nebraska, and continued selling my documents in these states. I set the prices for the vendor and told them how much to charge the customers. For example, social security cards, birth certificates, and drivers' licenses cost the vendor $15 and the customer $30. Harder-to-produce Texas birth certificates and birth registration cards together cost the vendor $45 and the customer $90. I took special request orders, and even counterfeited government agency envelopes. Since I did not deal directly with customers, I can't say exactly how many people purchased from my vendors the tens of thousands of documents I counterfeited.

I was finally able to get my hands on a just-issued INS alien registration card in the summer of 1980. Over several days, I worked out a theory of just how the card could be fabricated. I could not destroy the card I was studying, because it was someone's valid card, so I took measurements and made a few test cards. About two weeks after I first saw the new card I created my first acceptable copy of it.

I knew that optical readers for the coded information on the back of cards would not be available to immigration inspectors at the same time the cards were to be issued. So, I didn't worry about breaking the code but used alien registration numbers that I made up. I knew that one number stood for the country of birth, therefore I used the correct number for Mexico. I also knew that another number on the back stood for the alien's date of entry or date of legalizing status.

I gambled that the government would use phosphorescent ink on the new card. I lost. INS used florescent ink, which is of a lesser quality ink and requires ultra-violet light for detection. I stopped using the more difficult phosphorescent ink quickly, but I never bothered to change to florescent ink.

I also erred in the type of film used to photograph one layer of the card. It turns out the government uses a different type of film, which is readily available on the commercial market.

The biggest problem with the new INS card is that every part of it can be completely reconstructed once the materials are discovered. The type, style, ink, paper, and even the overlays are commercially available.

I was able to counterfeit only 300 of the new alien identification cards before my arrest in 1981. After I made a new card, I maintained a filing system for everyone who bought a card from me. I guaranteed each person that the card would be corrected, within a 30-day period, if there were any errors. As I perfected the new card, I planned to have each customer receive a new and better one. Since I did not keep in touch with my customers, I put a series of identifying numbers alongside the file card, which also had a picture of the customer. If I gave the person a social security number, I would write that down on the file card. I also had a code on the file card for the vendor who sold the document.

I sold this INS card for $60 to the vendor, and told vendors to charge customers $120 each. I was adamant about making sure my vendors told illegal customers these identity card were phony. I even quizzed customers, through vendors, and had the vendor give me the customer's response so I could be certain the customer wasn't fooled into thinking the purchased documents were official.

My purpose in testifying today, Mr. Chairman, is to offer some positive suggestions about the reliability of identification documents currently in use. In general, I think the INS alien registration card (I-551) has some very attractive features to withstand tampering. The document, however, is not counterfeit proof. To improve on it, INS should consider:

- using decoders which can be carried around easily by the Border Patrol and other Immigration inspectors;
- adding original art work to the border of the card;
- using phosphorescent ink so the card can be checked with a flashlight during inspection, and would be more difficult to photograph;
- using a serrated edge on the insert;
- using a two-color plastic to make photographing more difficult; and
- imprinting "U.S.I.N.S." on the plastic laminate itself.

I want to thank you for this opportunity to testify. I am available to answer any of your questions.

INDEX